TIMOTHY EATON

and the rise of his department store

Timothy Eaton, 1906

TIMOTHY EATON
and the rise of
his department store

Joy L. Santink

UNIVERSITY OF TORONTO PRESS

Toronto Buffalo London

© University of Toronto Press 1990
Toronto Buffalo London
Printed in Canada
ISBN 0-8020-2720-2

Printed on acid-free paper

All pictures courtesy of the T. Eaton Collection,
Archives of Ontario

This book has been published with the help of a grant
from the Social Science Federation of Canada,
using funds provided by the Social Sciences and Humanities
Research Council of Canada.

FOR NICO

Contents

Foreword

When Michael Bliss phoned seeking permission for a graduate student to have access to our archives, I asked only for the assurance that she was a serious student, a historian who would approach her job with respect and honesty.

The Eaton Archives, now part of the Archives of Ontario, has been maintained by the company for some years under the leadership of the chief archivist, Judith McErvel. They had always been private, in keeping with an unwritten policy of privacy practised fervently by my family. While many people have used our catalogues to establish authority about what was in vogue in a particular period, no one had ever before delved into the archives so closely as Joy Santink now proposed to do.

Over the years while she laboured on her thesis her endeavours lost their 'top of mind' awareness for me, and so it was with some trepidation that I turned to the large red manuscript that appeared on my desk in May 1988. The reader must understand that a fourth-generation descendant of Timothy Eaton is imbued with a sense of history in which an illustrious great-grandfather shines forth with the strength of legend; the myths that surround him have heightened his stature for me and indeed for everyone who has been touched by this great entrepreneur. Having set Joy Santink the task of finding the truth, I was now faced with the reality before me.

That Timothy Eaton was a merchandising genius cannot be questioned; nor can the fact that he was a mere mortal. This book establishes the man in the times in which he lived and judges him by the standards of his day. From our perspective we see a society apparently more primitive than our own, but we can perceive also the roots of our modern world.

Everybody at some time or another goes shopping, and it is fitting that the vast changes in buying and selling, which rivalled the innovations in mass production and transportation that so affected the growth of Canada, should also be examined in depth for the first time. This is the story of the development of shopping from the barter system in small retail units in which Timothy apprenticed to the flowering of the department store with its mass marketing techniques so prevalent today. The book examines Timothy's struggles and his successes and shows us a determined man who originated or assimilated new systems and methods and constantly explored new ways of merchandising. It tells us how the department store was created in Canada in one man's lifetime. It is a fascinating story, even if your name is not Eaton.

I believe Joy Santink has made a significant contribution to the history of retailing in one of its golden moments and she shows how these developments profoundly influenced so many facets of Canadian life.

Fredrik S. Eaton
Chairman
T. Eaton Co. Limited
7 July 1989

Preface

This book is an attempt to investigate one aspect of an industry that has received little attention in Canada. Aside from Douglas McCalla's excellent book on the Buchanans, some sections of Michael Bliss's book on Joseph Flavelle, and a few general books on major retailers,[1] little of really academic value has been produced. Although the general lack of primary resource material has made the retail field difficult to investigate, British historian Asa Briggs proved with *Friends of the People*, his history of the Liverpool department store Lewis's, that a solid piece of work could be produced by making use of material widely available in the public realm.[2]

Over the past sixty years several books have been written on Timothy Eaton and his store, but in the main these have focused on the Eaton family and have dealt only briefly with the financial growth and geographical spread of the T. Eaton Company across Canada.[3] To date no serious study has been undertaken of the actual rise and development of this department store or of the transformation of the Canadian retail industry.[4] Although much interest has been demonstrated in the spread of urbanization in North America, a phenomenon concomitant with the spread of industrialization and manufacturing, little attention has been given to the changes in the field of retailing during the last decades of the nineteenth century and the early years of the twentieth.

For this reason an in-depth study of a large department store familiar to all Canadians should prove useful from several aspects.

A store that has grown almost with the country itself and whose geographic spread has paralleled that of the nation cannot fail to have had a major impact on the life of that country. This, then, is the story of Timothy Eaton and of the store that he built.

My research was assisted by a doctoral fellowship from the Social Sciences and Humanities Research Council of Canada and by two fellowships from the University of Toronto. I have also received the assistance of numerous individuals and organizations. My greatest debt is to Fredrik S. Eaton for granting me access to the company archives and more directly to the Eaton archivists, Judith McErvel and Fay Wood. The infinite patience and unstinting interest with which they dealt with my constant visits and endless requests and questions were of immeasurable assistance. Sincere thanks are also due to Michael Bliss, who provided guidance, advice, support, and direction throughout the preparation of my doctoral dissertation and was kind enough to read the revised manuscript. The constructive suggestions made by Robert Bothwell, Jim Lemon, Douglas McCalla, and Laurel Sefton McDowell (all of whom subjected the earlier draft to close and careful consideration) and by the anonymous appraisers at the University of Toronto Press and the Social Science Federation led to changes which, it is hoped, can only be for the better. The faults that remain are my own. I would like to express my appreciation to Gerry Hallowell at the University of Toronto Press who provided advice and assistance during publication, and to Margaret Allen, who subjected the whole manuscript to meticulous scrutiny. My deepest gratitude is to my husband, Nico, for his constant encouragement, patient understanding, and support over the whole period that it took this study to reach completion.

TIMOTHY EATON

and the rise of his department store

Introduction

The small dry goods shop with which Timothy Eaton began his commercial career in an unfashionable area of Toronto in 1869 had by 1907 been transformed into not just one but two of the largest department stores in Canada. In 1869 the term 'department store' was hardly known, for most stores operated in small quarters with a limited stock of merchandise. By the 1890s, however, the term attained wide circulation and was used either to disparage or extol a phenomenon recognized on both sides of the Atlantic. For the Eaton store in Toronto, as for William Whiteley's emporium in London, Aristide Boucicault's Bon Marché in Paris, and Rowland Macy's great store in New York, the transformation from tiny retail outlet to one of mammoth proportions had occurred in roughly the same manner and at approximately the same period in history.

The question of which store was the first to achieve department store status continues to exercise the investigative skills of historians. Ralph Hower argues that the Macy store was unique and followed no European example. In his opinion, moreover, department stores arose not in response to demand but because certain business administrators sought a new means of making a profit. Dorothy Davis, in a wide-ranging study, points to the development from a common tradition, while Michael B. Miller seeks rather to discover the external influences common to all that gave rise to similar growth.[1] The most obvious of these – urbanization, industrialization, population growth, mass transportation, mass production, a general rise in the standard of living, and the materialistic expectations of the industrialized masses – allow one to arrive quickly at the answer as to why such stores developed. This topic has been the subject of numerous studies. Few, however, have dealt satisfactorily with the question of how these stores were transformed and the various ways in which their development took place.

It is my hope that the following chapters will not only answer the question of how the Eaton store became a department store, but also perhaps pinpoint the reason why Timothy Eaton succeeded when so many others failed. Particular attention will be given to the actual business aspect of this institution and also to the social, institutional, and metropolitan implications of its activities both within the retail industry and within the larger social community.

Retailing, as Peter Samson points out, is very sensitive to its social and economic surroundings and cannot be considered apart from them. For this reason I have tried to set the Eaton store in a firm economic and social context and in the process to lift this study above the level of institutional history.[2] Since retail stores in a sense serve as mirrors of society, they cannot be examined in isolation, for no other industry so closely touches the common life of the people. Shopping, as opposed to marketing, is an occupation enjoyed by most of the world's population.

The topic has been dealt with chronologically to allow for the gradual development of themes as these occur. The most important theme, which surfaces again and again throughout the whole period of Timothy Eaton's business life, is that of competition. How he handled it, therefore, is a continuing subject for discussion. Indeed it might almost be said to have formed an integral part in his expansion.

Change and evolution are also constant themes, for the retail industry during the nineteenth century was in a continual state of flux. Douglas McCalla's conclusions about the 1850s can thus be carried to beyond the turn of the century, for both wholesalers and retailers continued to demonstrate the same 'high rates of mobility and transiency that the quantitative historians' have revealed.[3]

Although the major topic of investigation is the rise of the department store, several important subsidiary topics demand inclusion. Of these the entrance of women into the retail work force is of special interest, largely because this field has attracted little attention. The period also sees the emergence of white-collar workers and the advent of the professional manager, as companies exceeded the earlier sure grasp and limitations of the owner-operator. A study of the relationship between Timothy Eaton, a typical nineteenth-century businessman, and his employees casts light on the attitudes and mores of management and labour during this period. The gradual influence of external factors in effecting change in the internal workings of a private organization is another aspect of this relationship.

The move by Timothy Eaton towards greater vertical integration through his involvement in wholesale purchasing and manufacturing was responsible for much of the store's success. The fabrication, production, and promotion of new lines of merchandise allowed for the development of an aggressive competitor in an industry that was still being run very largely on nineteenth-century lines.

Timothy Eaton, like many other famous Canadians, was not born in Canada, but immigrated to this country as a young man. His background, early education, and commercial training in Ireland and the commencement of his Canadian commercial career form the subject of the first two chapters.

The largely rural and relatively undeveloped nature of the Ontario that greeted Timothy Eaton on his arrival in Canada in the 1850s was responsible for a commercial environment that lagged some twenty or thirty years behind that found in such large metropolitan centres as London or New York. Trade in Canada during this early period, as in much of rural Britain, continued to be founded on the close personal relationships that existed first between the wholesaler and the retailers he supplied on a regular basis and second between the retail merchant and the customers who patronized his store. Whether a merchant sold dry goods in Great Britain, Europe, or North America, change was in the air, and the retail industry everywhere manifested many of the alterations imposed by the Industrial Revolution. For this reason, chapter three provides a comparative overview of those practices still in use in the 1850s and the newer ones coming into circulation. Despite the close association between Canada and Great Britain, some of these practices were considered strange by immigrants new to the city of Toronto.

The establishment, growth, and gradual transformation of Timothy Eaton's Toronto store during the 1870s and 1880s form the subject of the next three chapters. The 1880s are regarded by some historians as the heyday of large stores, and it is during this decade that the Eaton store moved into larger quarters and began to expand to mammoth proportions. Special attention is given to the expansion of merchandise lines and to the origin and development of a concept closely associated with department stores, the mail-order service.

If the year 1886 can be seen as the point of take-off for the Eaton store, then the 1890s ushered in an era of enormous growth and the transformation of the earlier operation to full departmental store status. Chapters seven through ten deal in considerable detail with several important aspects of this decade. The physical growth of the company from formal incorporation to the establishment of subsidiary activities and the expansion of its buying operations form the subject of chapter seven. Chapter eight deals with the evolution of the store from dry goods outlet to one carrying the enormous range of merchandise familiar to present-day shoppers.

Company expansion was accompanied by a constant increase in the number of employees. From time to time the rapid addition of large numbers of new employees resulted in the emergence of severe personnel problems requiring changes in company procedures. Although this has been dealt with briefly in earlier chapters, this topic and the wider subject of Eaton personnel, both at management level and at lower levels of employment, form the focus of chapter nine. Particular attention is given to the external labour and legislative factors gaining strength in this area during the last decade of the century.

Competition, the constant goad to growth, was yet another

external factor, but because of its own aggressive activity the Eaton store during the 1890s acquired an extremely controversial profile. The animosity directed by the small merchants of Toronto at what were perceived to be the unfair practices of some retailers, and of 'departmental stores' in particular, made the Eaton store the prime target of much of this vehement hostility.

The opening of the company's first branch store in Winnipeg carries the story into the new century and the final years of Timothy Eaton's life. By 1910 the retail industry in Toronto and across Canada was vastly different from what it had been some forty years earlier, and certain conclusions can be drawn about the extent to which Timothy Eaton was responsible for the changes that had occurred in this commercial field.

Timothy Eaton was in many respects a typically Victorian businessman, and he can only be studied by setting him firmly within the social context of his own time, that of the nineteenth century. From the multi-faceted aspects that make up his life and times, certain social characteristics and human traits gradually assume greater significance than others. But these reveal themselves only as the story of his life unfolds, a life of gradual evolution from unwilling apprentice to ambitious merchant. Owing to a very real dearth of personal material relating to his life, this study has not been an easy task. With the opening of the large store at 190 Yonge Street in 1883, Timothy Eaton seems to remove himself from centre stage and to retreat into the shadows, and in the process he becomes subsumed within the larger entity. But he does not wholly disappear, for the store at all times assumes his persona, ferociously independent, aggressive in manner, practical and functional in character, blunt and abrupt in action, and progressive by nature.

The question is sometimes posed whether an entrepreneur is a passive or creative force in the historical process. Is he a self-determining entity and thereby an engine of change? Or is he a variable – himself to be explained by other independent historical factors?[4] Does Timothy Eaton, in fact, necessarily have to fit into one category or the other? In attempting to answer these questions, this study explores the reasons for his enormous success.

1
Apprentice Merchant

'This charge I commit unto thee ... child Timothy ... war
the good warfare; holding faith and a good conscience.'
1 Tim. 18–19

'Trade must not be entered into as a thing of light concern; it is called business very properly for it is a business
for life ... It must be followed with a full intention of the
mind, and full attendance of the person; nothing but
what are to be called the necessary duties of life are to
intervene; and even those are to be limited so as not to
be prejudicial to business.'
Daniel Defoe, *The Complete English Tradesman*,
1745

On 28 April 1870 Timothy Eaton wrote to his brother James in St
Marys,* 'the past 2 years has been a hard tack – and it will yet
take a long pull & a strong pull, but its all right – we are made 2
[sic] work – and as long as the Lord give me a continuation of
health and energy – I am determined to work and work with a
will.'[1] Written some four and a half months after the opening of
his Toronto store at 178 Yonge Street, these words exemplify
Timothy Eaton's attitude towards life. A firm believer in the need
for ever greater efforts, he was governed not only by the prevailing

---

* Twentieth-century practice drops the apostrophe. See Notes, chapter 2, n 1.

work ethic but also by a strong belief in a God who was willing to help those who helped themselves.

Already thirty-five years old when he opened his small store in Toronto, his life had been one of continuous effort and hard work. Timothy Eaton, the fourth son and ninth child of John and Margaret Craig Eaton, was born at Clogher, just outside the town of Ballymena in the county of Antrim, Northern Ireland, in March 1834, some two months after the death of his father.[2] Margaret Craig Eaton was thus left with the responsibility of running the farm and raising nine children – Robert, aged eighteen (born 1816), Eliza Jane, fifteen (1819), Mary Ann, thirteen (1821), Margaret, ten (1824), John, seven (1827), Nancy, five (1829), Sarah, three (1831), James, two (1832), and baby Timothy.[3] Margaret Craig Eaton, who had been born and raised in the nearby parish of Kirkinriola, could no doubt have called upon her brothers, James and Robert Craig,[4] for advice, but her sons appear to have inherited the Scottish trait of independence, and first Robert and later John gradually assumed the mantle of responsibility.

The Eaton family, descendants of Scots bondsmen taken to Ulster before 1626 by the Adair family of Kinhilt, County Wigton, in Scotland, lived and worked in Ulster for the next two hundred years. By 1833 Timothy's father was farming thirty-two acres of bad arable land at Clogher at a yearly rental of £20.9s.0d. A subsequent government valuation of lands, taken for the purpose of Poor Law support in 1845, lists the Widow Eaton as farming a similar acreage but with an increased value of £33.7s.7d., which suggests some improvement either to land or to buildings. It is possible that the latter was the case, since an Adair rent roll for 1834 has the notation 'remember the new house.'[5] The house, a large, white, two-storey building, sat on a rise overlooking the valley of the River Braid, with Mount Slemish visible in the distance.

Although an Irish acre is about one-third larger than its English equivalent, the farm was probably too small to employ or support all members of the family. But since only 4 per cent of Ulster farms were of more than thirty acres, the acreage placed the Eaton family well above the level of most Irish tenant farmers. Such a tenant was welcomed by landowners and usually granted a firm lease, in direct contrast to the bulk of the Irish peasantry who suffered under the unjust system of tenancy-at-will. Little is known about the farm on which the young Timothy Eaton grew up, but it probably followed the norm for Ulster, producing grain, potatoes, and flax, and raising both cattle and pigs.[6]

Ballymena, the small town closest to the Eaton farm, situated on the main Antrim to Coleraine turnpike, was no rural backwater. By 1840 its population numbered some 5,150, and branches of four different banks (all established in the 1830s) were located in the town. Despite the fact that the surrounding area was 'minutely subdivided into small farms,' the *Parliamentary Gazetteer of Ireland* in 1847 described Ballymena as presenting 'an aspect of cultivation and opulence [to] compare with almost any vale in England.'[7] Large quantities of agricultural and dairy produce were sold in the market every Saturday. The town was also recognized as the county's largest linen market and one of Ulster's major market centres. The arrival of the railway in Ballymena in 1848 reinforced this importance, and the town became the regional centre for the collection of agricultural produce for export.[8] The impact generated by the advent of steam transportation undoubtedly touched the lives of all local inhabitants.

A spinning mill in the town processed the flax produced by local rural suppliers and, together with the fourteen bleach greens in the district, provided a source of local employment.[9] Evidence suggests that the Eaton family were also involved in some aspects of the production of linen. The farm on which Margaret Craig Eaton had grown up had operated a scutching mill for processing the flax fibre before it was made into cloth, and Margaret probably carried this knowledge to her new home at Clogher. In a letter to James Eaton in 1870, Timothy Eaton mentions that their brother John had got the flax mill in operation and that the flax crop that year was good.[10]

Growing up on a farm in mid-nineteenth-century Ulster, Timothy Eaton was exposed to the seasonal aspects of rural life. Regular visits to the market in Ballymena effected an awareness of the urban commercial world, albeit on a small scale. Little documentation exists for his early years in Ireland, but it is believed that he attended

the local national school for several years. Following this he was
sent for a short period to an academy in Ballymena, an experience
he later pronounced somewhat unproductive, recalling that he had
'got little good out of it.' On the advice of the master his mother
removed him from this establishment some time in 1847.[11] It is
unclear whether his removal from the academy was primarily due
to his lack of interest in academic subjects or to financial problems
arising from the potato famine that had devastated vast areas of
Ireland in 1846. The failure of the potato crop had been an ongoing
problem of Irish life. From 1822 to 1844 there had been failures
in ten out of fifteen years, and in 1830 and 1831 the failure had
been sufficiently bad to cause famine conditions. Suffering in the
Ulster counties had probably been mitigated by the inhabitants'
use of oatmeal as a supplementary source of nutrition.[12]

At the age of thirteen Timothy Eaton began his commercial
career as an apprentice at a substantial general store in Portglenone
on the River Bann. The store, some nine miles distant from Clogher,
was owned by a Mr Smith, a relation by marriage to the Craig side
of the family. Some idea of the magnitude of the business can be
deduced from the fact that Smith owned and operated twelve
transport wagons and three river freighters. His involvement with
both produce and a wide variety of merchandise provided the
young Timothy with a diversified background. As he became familiar with the many different aspects of a large general store he learnt
to assess the quality of grain and linen, deal with agricultural
produce and groceries in large and small quantities, and serve
drams of liquor to farmers on their way to market. Given Smith's
obvious prosperity, it seems unlikely that Timothy had to sleep
beneath the counter, as some stories suggest.[13]

While no documentation exists for the years of Timothy Eaton's
training and apprenticeship, one can gain some insight into such a
period of service, albeit a generation later, from the notebook of
another young Irish apprentice. Harry McGee, like Timothy Eaton,
began his business career as an apprentice at a general store in
County Wicklow. It was 1878, and McGee was seventeen. Working
without wages for four years, McGee kept a daily record of his
expenditures, accounting for every single halfpenny he spent.

Appearance for an apprentice was obviously very important, and clothing in the form of suits and shirts necessitated a regular semi-annual disbursement. Food and board were provided, but arrangements had to be made for personal laundry. Large regular payments to cover this service were made to the local washerwoman. Lead pencils costing a penny, postage for letters home, church collections, and notebooks were all dutifully recorded and monthly totals noted. In four years Harry McGee spent £31.6s.4½d., or about $155, on personal items. The bulk of this expenditure was directed towards keeping himself respectably clothed, with only token amounts spent for luxuries such as fruit.[14] These years were but an extension of one's education for the real world, a time in which frivolity had little place.

Although related to his apprentice, Smith maintained a strict master-employee relationship. Timothy long remembered the unfairness of being obliged to walk the nine miles home to Clogher each Sunday to visit his family, while Smith drove by in his carriage on his way to church in Ballymena. Timothy also disliked the task of sorting the rags collected by Smith and at one point appealed to his mother to terminate the apprenticeship. Rather than forfeit the £100 bond that had been posted at the beginning of his apprenticeship, Margaret Craig Eaton persuaded him to continue.[15]

The death of Timothy Eaton's mother on 3 October 1848, when he was only fourteen years of age, undoubtedly reinforced the sturdy self-reliance already fostered in him by farm life and Ulster's Presbyterian environment.

Tradition insists that at the end of his apprenticeship Timothy Eaton received a silver watch along with repayment of the £100 bond posted by his mother. This he probably returned to his family to offset personal expenses similar to those listed by McGee incurred during the preceding five years. He subsequently worked for a short period of time for a man named Lyttle in Portglenone, presumably to acquire funds for his move to the new world, a step that seemed increasingly necessary.[16]

Rapid population growth in the late eighteenth and nineteenth centuries created a special problem for Ireland, where underemployment and unemployment were both constant and severe. The political, social, and economic instability within the country led to great uncertainty with regard to investment. This uncertainty, combined with the shortage of land and high rents, was responsible for much of the pre-famine migration to North America and Australia. That this movement had early roots can be seen from reports demonstrating that between 1769 and 1774 some 43,700 people sailed from five Ulster ports to various settlements on the Atlantic seaboard.

With the introduction of the Corn Laws in 1815 hundreds of displaced farmers swelled the ranks of those leaving Ireland. The majority of these were Ulster Presbyterians anxious to better their condition, the only ones who could at that time afford the transatlantic fares. Accepted as a fact of Irish life, emigration paralleled the drift to the cities in Great Britain and most other European countries. With the gradual move by the British Parliament toward free trade and the subsequent inflow of English-made goods, the displaced artisan was forced to join the displaced farmer in the ranks of those seeking a livelihood elsewhere. Evidence given before the Devon Commission and the Ordinance Survey of Antrim of 1840 substantiates this: 'In this as in most districts, the industrious and well conducted are almost the only emigrants, while the able-bodied idlers and disorderly characters are but rarely known to leave the country.'[17]

Emigration received encouragement and added impetus from press reports and advertisements and from activities undertaken by shipping companies. In the first decades of the nineteenth century, Irish newspapers throughout the country not only publicized the offers of land and aid made to settlers in Canada but contained regular advertisements urging passengers to take advantage of the free crossing to Liverpool. Each spring, shipping agents visited principal towns on market days to make the necessary arrangements for prospective emigrants. The westward migration continued steadily throughout the 1830s and into the 1840s. In 1846 it became a flood that lasted until 1854, when more than 150,000 Irish emigrants left Ireland to seek a new life elsewhere.[18]

Timothy Eaton, perhaps unable to obtain a position suited to his qualifications, responded as others had done to the push-pull influences common in the migratory movements of large numbers of people. The material published in abundance regarding prospects for emigration was supplemented by firsthand impressions from relatives and friends who had already made such a move. And the Eaton family, like hundreds of others, had no need to look beyond their extended family for examples. Agnes Craig Reid, Timothy Eaton's maternal aunt, left Ireland in 1833 with her family of seven children to join her husband, William Reid, then farming in the Georgetown area of Upper Canada.[19] The Reids became a focal point for family members who came later. Robert, Timothy's eldest brother, emigrated in 1840 and was eventually followed by his brother James and sisters Margaret, Nancy, and Sarah. Some time in 1854, Timothy Eaton, taking a by now well-trodden path, followed his older brothers and sisters to Upper Canada. He later recalled earning a shilling by obtaining a ticket for a man struggling to get through the crowd of emigrants on the Liverpool docks.[20]

Although steam was coming into use by the 1850s, most emigrants continued to travel under sail. The journey, despite attempts by the British government to improve conditions on the ships, remained both arduous and hazardous. A Mrs Ellen Stewart, who arrived in St Marys in 1854 after travelling from Ireland via Liverpool and New York, recalled that the journey took a month. Another emigrant who sailed from Liverpool in October 1853, described a voyage of thirty-seven days during which sixty-five of the passengers died and were buried at sea. He consoled himself with the knowledge that a similar ship had lost nearly one hundred passengers.[21]

Very little is known of Timothy Eaton's first two years in Canada, but it seems likely that he travelled first to Georgetown to stay with his sister Margaret (recently married to a cousin, Robert Reid) and Robert, the brother he had last seen some fourteen years earlier. After helping with family chores on the Georgetown farms, Timothy Eaton began his Canadian career as a junior bookkeeping clerk at a small general store in Glen Williams, a village just outside Georgetown.[22]

The demand created by both railway construction and the Crimean war made the period 1853 to 1856 one of booming prosperity for much of Canada West. Earning possibly $75 to $80 a year during this time,[23] Timothy Eaton was at the same time learning about life in the new land and generally coming to terms with the nature of life in a Canadian community that was smaller than either Ballymena or Portglenone. The excitement generated by the coming of the Grand Trunk Railway perhaps revived memories of a similar event in Ireland and suggested the possibility of greater opportunities elsewhere.

By the fall of 1856 the Grand Trunk Railway extended from Montreal to Toronto and onwards through Georgetown and Guelph to Stratford. The Huron Tract, which had acted as a magnet for many settlers both new and old, was by this time largely settled; but several areas, Blanshard and Usborne townships, for example, still offered opportunity. Advertisements by the Canada Company posted in post offices and stores across Canada drew attention to this area for settlement.[24] The three Eaton brothers, Robert, James, and Timothy, no doubt encouraged by the possibility of greater local development and the corresponding opportunities for personal success, moved from Georgetown to the Huron Tract some time in 1856 with the intention of establishing themselves in business.

In December 1855 Robert Eaton sold the forty-five acres he had been farming in Georgetown and, accompanied by his wife and four children, moved to the village of St Marys, the largest centre in the township of Blanshard. Here, in partnership with John Neelon, he purchased two pieces of property, and early in 1857 he and Neelon opened two stores, a grocery and dry goods store on Queen Street and a book store in the Post Office Building on Water Street.[25]

For reasons that are not altogether clear, however, Timothy and James chose to begin their commercial life in the less settled environment of Kirkton some ten miles northwest of St Marys. Early in the spring of 1856 the two brothers, operating as 'J. & T. Eaton,' opened a small store housed in a log cabin on the banks of Fish Creek in Kirkton.[26] Given the rather acrimonious discussions regarding the location of the rail depot in St Marys in early 1858, it is possible that in 1856 the western route of the Grand Trunk

Railway had not yet been finally determined.[27] Hopes may have been high that the railway would travel along the valley of Fish Creek, passing through Kirkton on its way west.

Named after the six Kirk brothers, Irish immigrants who had settled in the area, the small hamlet of Kirkton acquired its initial inception from the establishment of the small Eaton store, probably the first place of business to be set up at the intersection of what is now Highway 23 and County Road 24. The Post Office, undergoing rapid expansion under new provincial jurisdiction in the years after 1851, took advantage of the location of the Eaton store to establish an agency in the village, and on 1 July 1856 James Eaton was appointed local postmaster. He was also awarded the contract for the weekly mail service between Kirkton and the town of St Marys.[28]

Although not far removed from its earlier wooded condition, the little village of Kirkton may have appeared to its residents to hold potential for growth, situated as it was on the boundary concession between townships. Both Stratford and London had commenced in similar fashion, and the residents' hope was reflected in the sales of some village properties. In the late summer of 1858 James Eaton paid $375 for three acres on the southeast corner of the village intersection. Since the store and post office, both housed in the same log cabin, occupied only a small corner of these three acres, some income was raised by leasing space to other small tradesmen.[29]

The area offered the added attraction of congenial fellowship, for much of the surrounding countryside had been settled by immigrants of Irish and Scottish background. Many of these settlers were not recent immigrants, but had spent several years elsewhere in British North America – for instance, in Lanark County, where the land had proved too poor for productive farming.[30] The pool of potential customers for the new store was large. Many of the settlers, while raising their own corn, grain, vegetables, fruit, cattle, hogs, and poultry, and producing such things as flour, maple sugar and maple syrup, candles, and soap, relied on the local general store for salt, spices, dried fruit, kerosene, boots and shoes, dry goods, patent medicines, crockery, and hardware, the latter term covering everything from chains and ropes for farm equipment to cooking pots and pans.

Both James and Timothy Eaton were probably aware that such personalities as Milner Harrison in St Marys, John Cory Wilson Daly in Stratford, and George Jervis Goodhue and Adam Hope in London had all achieved considerable success from similar small beginnings in frontier situations.[31] The general merchant occupied an important and influential position in pioneer society, for as Mary Quayle Innis observed, he received the 'produce from the inhabitants and sold them imported goods in comfortable excess of the value of the goods they had to offer.'[32]

Although the store operated as J. and T. Eaton, it is evident that Timothy Eaton was the active partner, with overall responsibility for the business. A notation regarding stock bought from James by Timothy amounting to $1,177 on 16 September 1857[33] suggests the latter's direct accountability for the whole financial operation of the Kirkton store. As the person most closely involved in the day-to-day running of the store, Timothy Eaton collected the produce from local farmers as he travelled around the countryside advertising his small stock of goods and then transported the grain to the mill in St Marys to be ground into flour. James Eaton meanwhile took advantage of the opportunity to involve himself in other commercial activities and, for several months during the winter of 1858–9, was occupied in an unprofitable business venture with his brother Robert in St Marys. Timothy Eaton then served as acting postmaster.[34]

As merchant and acting postmaster in Kirkton, Timothy Eaton would have played an important role in the daily lives of his neighbours. This influence probably extended beyond the townships of Usborne and Blanshard into Hibbert, Fullarton, and Biddulph. By 1851 the population of these five townships totalled well over 7,000, and by mid-decade this had undoubtedly increased still further as more settlers moved into the area.[35] At first Timothy Eaton seems to have traded solely in groceries and dry goods, with necessary staples probably forming the bulk of his stock. For the last half of 1859 groceries and dry goods formed almost parallel totals in his list of purchases – Dry Goods $540.04, Groceries

$562.17. Nevertheless his stock, according to one contemporary source, 'was very small indeed, and any two of his pioneer neighbours might have carried off the whole outfit of the commercial venture on their shoulders.' In 1860, no doubt in response to customer demands, a narrow selection of hardware ($146.51 as opposed to $1,147.51 for dry goods) was added to the stock of goods.[36] Towards the end of his stay in Kirkton, possibly in an attempt to attract more customers and perhaps as a means of using up some of the produce he had acquired in exchange for store goods, Timothy Eaton began selling baked goods in his general store.[37]

The bulk of the merchandise sold in the store was supplied by the London wholesale house of Adam Hope, then in close business relationship with the Buchanans in Hamilton. Sketchy evidence suggests that Timothy Eaton may have dealt initially with Kerr McKenzie and Company, also located in London.[38] Deliveries of goods were usually made by suppliers twice a year, in late March and September, and advertisements of the period commonly drew attention at these times to importations of new goods or the opening of fresh stock. However, retailers could and did acquire smaller orders of necessary merchandise throughout the year. Payments for merchandise were spread over a very long period, with suppliers accepting paper dated twelve and fifteen months ahead.

The Kirkton business followed the contemporary practice of allowing merchandise to local farmers on credit. By January 1859 such accounts standing on the Eaton books amounted to $723.50. At $1,588, liabilities, presumably to suppliers, totalled more than double that figure.[39] Given the habits and attitudes of rural inhabitants, the general state of the farm economy, and the very real shortage of specie within the province during this period, there was little that a rural merchant could do about the credit system. Most farmers were neither prepared nor in a position to pay for store merchandise until their own produce had been harvested. The largest cash remittance ($1,103.62) made by Timothy Eaton to Adam Hope, for instance, was in October 1860, although attempts were made to forward some payment, no matter how small, every month (see Appendix, Table 2).[40] Many retailers urged their customers to settle their accounts at the beginning of the New Year, and newspapers regularly carried advertisements to this effect throughout the month of December.

This system of long credit, while allowing for a reasonable flow of supply and demand, depended in very large measure on the continued prosperity of all parties involved. The increased demand for wheat and timber during the Crimean War and the resulting high financial returns had encouraged a high degree of speculative expansion in both rural and urban sectors. The period of crisis, uncertainty, and instability that followed the termination of the war undermined this somewhat tenuous prosperity. All levels of society experienced distress, from the failed wholesale houses reported in Toronto by Henry Scadding to the unemployed clerk who complained of having gone through the entire country from Niagara to Barrie in June 1857 without finding work.[41] A drop in the prices of both land and produce destroyed fortunes that, in many instances, had existed only on paper. Those who had financed their speculation by credit were hardest hit. The overwhelming dependence on credit at all levels of society fuelled, directed, and ultimately mauled the fragile economy of mid-nineteenth-century Canadian pioneer society.

Economic hardship was aggravated by a growing depression in Great Britain and an acute financial crisis in the eastern United States. In Canada the crisis was intensified by the collapse of several Upper Canadian banks. In the fall of 1857, refusal by the banks that remained in business to provide the usual financial accommodation brought the movement of agricultural produce almost to a standstill. Wheat, which had sold for two dollars a bushel in 1854, dropped in 1857 to fifty cents. Canadian imports through the ports of Toronto and Hamilton fell drastically from abnormally high levels in 1856 to rates more in line with the prewar figures of 1853. This was particularly noticeable in the area of cotton goods. The failure of several American banks in the winter of 1857–8 created additional difficulties for those who traded across the border in wheat or lumber, since notes on these institutions were immediately rendered worthless.[42]

During this period, whether because of the state of the economy or as a result of other financial circumstances over which they had no control, the personal fortunes of both Robert and James Eaton underwent significant changes. In 1858 the partnership between John Neelon and Robert Eaton in the operation of two establishments in St Marys was dissolved by mutual consent. Robert Eaton withdrew from the book and stationery establishment, leaving Neelon in sole ownership, and combined instead with his brother James to run the general and dry goods store, also formerly run in partnership with Neelon.[43] Owing to a lack of capital, the general and dry goods store operated by Robert Eaton and John Neelon had never been very successful and, although Robert was reported to be honest and prompt, he was not considered a very good businessman.[44] In order to assist this new venture, James Eaton in October 1858 raised a mortgage of $500 on property purchased in Usborne. Despite this influx of capital, some three to four months later the new firm of R. and J. Eaton was experiencing severe problems with creditors and was compelled to seek further help from another family member to stave off the threat of bankruptcy. Early in March 1859 its entire stock was acquired by brother-in-law Robert Reid, and the business continued under his name at least until the summer of 1860.[45]

Timothy Eaton fared slightly better in Kirkton, although the limitations imposed by the merchandise available and the general financial situation made the early months of trading far from easy. His difficulties were probably aggravated by the fact that the old stock purchased from James had to be worked off at reduced prices.

A primitive balance sheet for January 1859 demonstrates the attempts made to arrive at some assessment of these early months. While the calculation does arrive at a profit of $134 for the fifteen-month period of September 1857 to January 1859, it seems obvious that this was only a figure on paper, since the asset side of the balance sheet contained only two items, one comprising stock amounting to $999 and the other covering amounts owing to him by his customers on the book account.[46] No mention is made of wages or salaries, so it must be assumed that both Timothy and James drew only sufficient funds to cover living expenses. The rental payments received from other tradesmen located on the three-acre lot and revenue from the mail contract, which yielded £20.0s.0d. per annum, while furnishing additional income, were probably used by James Eaton to assist him in his own business dealings.

With trade and commerce severely confined by the depression, circumstances would not allow for excessive credit limits. Intense competition among importers and their retail clients had led to the chronic over-importation of merchandise, much of it financed by long credit. The subsequent rate of commercial failure, as might be expected, reached a high level. Those who remained in business were compelled to enforce severe measures of retrenchment and reorganization on both their internal and external methods of operation. Adam Hope, in a letter to Peter Buchanan on 8 August 1857, noted that 'There is a great falling off in the cash receipts. Times are very hard. Money was never scarcer in my recollections, certainly not since 1853.'[47]

As the Buchanans struggled to reduce overdue accounts and swollen inventories, they became more careful and restrictive in dealing with their own customers, in many cases shortening credit or else requiring security on strictly limited quantities of goods in the form of mortgaged property or life insurance policies. This practice was continued at least until the early 1860s. Timothy Eaton, for example, in April 1860 received a $300 mortgage from Adam Hope and Peter Buchanan, no doubt in the form of merchandise, giving as collateral a fifty-six-acre property in Kirkton purchased just three months earlier. Of the fifty-six acres on this lot, ten were cleared, as were ten acres of the twenty-five rented on an adjoining lot.[48] At first glance these transactions could be taken as expressions of confidence in the future of the village, but it seems likely that the land not only provided some kind of security, but also allowed for the production of a crop that could be converted into cash. However, Timothy Eaton, possibly referring to this period of his life, later stated that he was 'not fond of much plowing, or selling wheat at 68 cents a bushel.'[49]

The lessons learnt in this initial foray of running a business, when combined with Timothy Eaton's own natural caution, provided the foundation on which the later successful undertaking was built.

The fact that the mortgage with Adam Hope and Peter Buchanan was discharged several months before it became due is perhaps an early manifestation of his later abomination of credit and its attendant interest payments. Furthermore, he did not rest wholly content until he had received from both Hope and Buchanan the duly authorized mortgage discharge, which was somewhat delayed by the latter's illness and subsequent death. Since this $300 represented only a fifth of the payments made to Adam Hope in October 1860, Timothy Eaton obviously wished to demonstrate to his supplier that in his case it was totally unnecessary to demand security for loans made. The land on which the mortgage had been given was sold, possibly to discharge this debt. In a letter from Adam Hope to Isaac Buchanan regarding this mortgage, Hope noted that 'Eaton sold the place; got the money and paid it over to us.'[50].

It seems obvious from subsequent evidence that plans were underway for a move and that Timothy Eaton wished to free himself from all past obligations before establishing himself in a new venture. Life in Kirkton, while it offered a considerable degree of freedom and some opportunity along with a new sense of independence, probably presented striking contrasts with both Ballymena and Portglenone. The three or four years spent in a small village surrounded by farm land still not entirely cleared were sufficient to demonstrate to Timothy Eaton that development in that location would be slow. Moreover, competition in the form of another general store established just across the township line from his own small establishment posed further difficulties. The new store, operated by a Gregg Nealan, contended for the custom of a neighbourhood formerly served only by the Eaton store.[51]

In spite of the restricted nature of the times and the attendant uncertainty, a comparison of the merchandise purchased for fall openings from Adam Hope shows that Timothy Eaton's commercial reputation had undergone some improvement. In September 1859 he purchased groceries and dry goods amounting to only $43.65 and $214.43 respectively. In September 1860 these amounts rose to $375.40 and $1,031.61. Although for most months the amount of goods purchased usually exceeded the remittances, attempts were made to forward cash as and when it became available. Since these figures represent only a very incomplete picture of Timothy Eaton's early business career, it is difficult to arrive at a full interpretation. In February 1860 stock on hand amounted to $663. This appears to be somewhat on the low side when compared to the higher figures of previous years (see Table 1). From the limited evidence available it seems unlikely that this low figure was wholly due to financial restrictions. Instead it can be assumed that it was due to a deliberate reduction of stock prior to a move to a new location. The larger purchases in September 1860 perhaps represented stocks of merchandise for the opening of a store in a different location. In addition, the remittances forwarded in October and November 1860 and January 1861 were greatly in excess of amounts purchased in those months – further evidence of a desire to settle accounts before starting afresh elsewhere.[52]

Although Timothy Eaton's energies were directed towards the establishment and maintenance of a successful commercial enterprise, this did not prevent his regular attendance to the duties relating to the spiritual side of his life. Both Timothy and James Eaton, as Presbyterians, became active members of the Blanshard and Usborne Union Sabbath School in Kirkton. Serving both Presbyterians and Methodists, the sabbath school was attended by all members of both denominations, although separate catechisms were purchased for distribution to the two groups of members. Such gatherings were common in the early days in many small communities. On 7 July 1856, at a monthly meeting held in the village schoolhouse, James Eaton was appointed a sabbath school teacher, and at a similar meeting in February 1858 was joined in this endeavour by Timothy. Meetings were held in the schoolhouse, and the exercises of the sabbath school consisted of 'repeating from memory passages of scripture and scriptural catechisms, reading of the scriptures and oral instruction founded on these.'[53]

During the 1840s and 1850s the Methodists throughout Upper Canada had been swept along on a wave of religious revival. At one such revival meeting or 'love feast' held in James Kirk's grove some time in the late summer of 1858 and led by the pastor of St Marys' Methodist Church, the Reverend Alexander Campbell, Timothy Eaton made the decision to become a Methodist, following a path already taken by Robert and James Eaton.[54] Possibly his position as a sabbath school teacher, which required him to convey his beliefs to others, had prompted more serious thought. Accustomed from childhood to regular church attendance, Timothy Eaton had earlier probably accepted his father's faith without question. He may now have come to feel that Methodism, with its stress upon individual personal salvation in both the present and the hereafter, afforded a more positive doctrine for life in a new environment than Presbyterianism, with its Calvinistic stress on predestination. Imbued with the principle that God helps those who help themselves, Methodism offered a dogma that would comfortably allow for the integration of both the spiritual and temporal sides of life. Timothy's appointment as secretary-treasurer from September 1858 until 9 March 1859, in which position he was responsible for the purchase of both testaments and books for use by the pupils, nicely incorporated both interests. This involvement with the Methodist and Presbyterian congregations and the Union Sabbath School undoubtedly drew him into closer association with the small community and augmented his commercial position.

2

The Eaton Store in St Marys

> 'Nothing can give a greater prospect of thriving to a
> young tradesman, than his own diligence; it fills him
> with hope, and gives him credit with all that know him.'
> Daniel Defoe, *The Complete English Tradesman*, 1745

The small town of St Marys, located on the northwest branch of
the River Thames ten miles east of Kirkton, was situated in the
centre of rich grain-growing country and was further blessed with
an abundance of the finest limestone. The first settler to take up
land in St Marys did so in 1841, and by 1855 fairly rapid growth
had transformed the town into a separate municipality with a
population of about 2,000. St Marys contained churches of all the
predominant faiths and, in addition to the usual service trades
commonly found in small rural centres, was also home to a mechanics' institute, three carriage factories, three iron foundries, and two
woollen factories, as well as several flour mills, tanneries, and saw
mills.[1] The arrival of the Grand Trunk Railway in the late summer
of 1858 gave the town a temporary ascendancy over other local
trading centres. Continued development was expected, and it was
commonly believed that St Marys would soon outrank Stratford.
The local paper, the St Marys *Argus*, regularly bore witness to this
fact by constantly citing comparative evidence ranging from the
price of grain to the growth in the two towns' respective popula-
tions. Although the *Argus* regularly carried the advertisements of
London stores, it denounced both the principle and practice of

shopping there, and urged local shoppers to encourage home enterprise by patronizing local dealers.[2]

The depression of 1857 and the attendant restriction of credit had compelled many retailers to consider other ways of doing business in order to survive. Toronto grocer William Davies's ability to survive this depression, for instance, was due in large part to the fact that, as a new arrival on the business scene in Toronto, he was compelled to operate very largely on a cash basis.[3] One general store in St Marys in January 1857 offered discounts on cash purchases of more than five dollars and drew attention to the fact that the prices of all goods were marked in plain figures.[4]

In October 1857 the merchants of St Marys, several of whom were in severely straitened circumstances, banded together and unanimously adopted a resolution abandoning the old system of long credit and adopting instead the cash and short credit principle. The announcement cited the general depression of trade as the reason for this action and was signed by twenty-one merchants, one of whom was Robert Eaton. The fact that no account would be allowed to run longer than three months would seem to suggest an attempt to implement shorter credit terms than the generally accepted practice, rather than an intention to establish cash only.[5]

Whether these changes were imposed by supplying wholesalers is not entirely clear. During this same period Peter Buchanan certainly attempted to salvage some debts incurred by retail dealers by employing many former store owners as managers in their old establishments. Such retailers were ordered to sell for cash only, thereby ensuring that no further funds would be locked up. Isaac Buchanan was convinced that some retail businesses, at least in the cities, could attract cash customers by offering lower prices, thus placing both the retail and the wholesale business on a more secure footing. Another contemporary observer, a retail clerk familiar with the business, stressed that, although this sometimes meant operating with a smaller stock, the payment of cash allowed for a cheaper price on the goods.[6]

Despite their stated published pronouncements, several St Marys merchants continued to grant long credit terms to many of their rural customers.[7] In Adam Shortt's view such lengthy credit was totally unnecessary since many farmers either put their money out in mortgages or bought more land rather than paying their debts.[8] However, a bad harvest or a long cold summer could wreak havoc on a farmer's crops, leaving both his barns and pockets empty and placing him at the mercy of high-interest money lenders or a trusting general store owner.

The whole matter of financial transactions was further complicated by the uncertain nature of colonial currency. Although Canadian currency converted to the decimal system in 1858, the country continued for several years to utilize a wide variety of specie, ranging from Spanish doubloons to English shillings. The introduction in 1858 of several million dollars' worth of new Canadian coinage in denominations of twenty-, ten-, five-, and one-cent pieces did little to resolve this problem, and specie continued to be in short supply.[9] To add to the problem, paper currency was never popular with the rural population, for the general practice of discounting paper notes throughout the country rendered its value uncertain. Most banks refused to accept even their own notes at par, much less those issued by competitors. The fact that many Canadian farmers hoarded large sums of money in their homes only aggravated an already difficult situation in the post-Crimean War period.

The Bank Act of 1858 attempted to ease the continuing shortage by allowing banks to give credit on bills of lading and warehouse receipts and to acquire ownership of the goods so pledged. This was in contrast to the earlier bank practice that had advanced capital on personal security only, with landed property as the sole item of collateral.[10] William Davies, in a letter to his brother in March 1860, explained how this system worked:

Suppose I have cured a 100 hogs which I can do in a week and they cost say £300. I ship them and insure, take the Bill of Lading to the Bank and draw at 60 days on my consignee, & if he be a good man and the Bank have made enquiries about him & find he is A1, and I have instructions to draw on him showing Bill of Lading at Bank, I can get £300 to go on with and can repeat the operation to any extent.[11]

Similarly a retailer who had taken farm produce in exchange for store merchandise could pass on the produce to the produce or commission merchant and receive a bill of lading for it. Such paper was accepted by the bank either as security for a loan or, if necessary, to be discounted immediately for personal credit. The movement of such paper undoubtedly facilitated much business in this period and served to lessen the retail merchant's dependence on his wholesaler for financial accommodation.

By 1858, largely due to the arrival of the railway, St Marys appeared to have recovered some of its earlier vitality and, in the eyes of a recent immigrant, presented a picture of vigorous activity:

St. Marys grain market was far in advance of any surrounding business centres. On the streets could be seen every day a dozen of grain buyers, all busy, with long strings of loaded waggons pouring into town from all directions. During autumn the market square was for several hours each day blocked with teams, and extending down Queen Street as far as Wellington was a mass of men and horses, with wheat and other products awaiting an opportunity to move onward.[12]

Some time in the fall or winter of 1860, Timothy Eaton, no doubt also impressed with the town's obvious burgeoning activity, moved from Kirkton to St Marys, where he endeavoured to launch himself by establishing a bakery. Information relating to this venture is extremely limited, but the advertisement in the *Argus* of 19 December 1860 requesting the settlement of all accounts on or before 15 January 1861 suggests that T. Eaton's Bakery had been in operation for at least three months. Contemporary census statistics list an investment of $2,000 in the business, ownership of two horses valued at $100, and three carriages, two for hire and one for pleasure, evidence of some business viability. Timothy Eaton, grocer and baker, was listed as head of the household, and four other adult males lived on the premises – James Eaton and William Gilpin, clerks, T. Mitchell, teamster, and James Oliver, baker. Oliver, who with his family resided in the two-storey frame house, had no money invested in the business; his sole assets were two pigs worth eight dollars. It is possible that Timothy's sister Nancy normally acted as housekeeper for the four Methodist bachelors, but at the time of the 1861 census she was in Georgetown visiting her sister Margaret Eaton Reid, who was expecting her fourth child.[13]

Given the disruption that had occurred in the businesses operated by Robert and James Eaton in 1859 and 1860, perhaps it was thought wise to place the bakery in Timothy's name to reduce possible problems with suppliers and creditors. The enterprise may have been a means of gaining a more secure footing in the larger centre while utilizing this period to clear outstanding obligations relating to Kirkton. The cash remittances of $550.00 to Adam Hope for the month of January 1861 certainly exceeded the total billings of $85.23 for that month. Timothy Eaton also had sufficient capital to allow him to take over a mortgage of nearly $500.00 from James Stephen to John Sutherland in February 1861, further indication of a firmer financial standing and evidence of available cash for investment.[14]

Timothy Eaton had, however, entered a market fraught with competition. During the period 1856–60 three bakery ventures had succeeded each other in St Marys with some rapidity. The bakeries in St Marys, like their counterparts elsewhere, not only supplied customers with their daily bread, but also, as their advertisements indicate, offered catering services for the large soirées and church teas that were a regular part of the Canadian social scene. The one viable bakery in town, owned by Levi Wilson, had been in operation for some time and appears to have been sufficient to meet the necessary demand.[15] T. Eaton's Bakery remained in business for a few months only, perhaps just long enough for its proprietor to see where future opportunities might lie.

On 1 May 1861, the *Argus* carried a small but important advertisement calling the attention of Timothy Eaton's 'old customers in Hibbert, Fullarton, Usborne, Biddulph and Blanshard townships to his new stock of goods.' The new store, established in rented property in a central location in St Marys, on Queen Street between Wellington and Church streets, carried a large variety of dry goods, boots and shoes, hardware, kitchen utensils, farm tools, crockery, and patent medicines, all of which were to 'be sold Cheap and for Cash.'[16] The *Argus* of 1 May also carried the advertisements of eight other dry goods stores in St Marys, the coverage for all of which was much larger and more pretentious than Timothy Eaton's modest insertion. McIntosh and Robinson, calling themselves the 'Cheap Cash Store,' for example, spread their wares in detail over fifteen inches of paper in two columns.

Timothy Eaton has sometimes been considered the first Canadian to offer goods for cash on the principle of one fixed price, but even a cursory study of a small local paper such as the *Argus* during this period indicates that this was not the case. One general merchant, extolling the virtues of small profits and quick returns, announced in May 1857, before the adoption of the resolution by many of the St Marys merchants, that he was 'determined to sell for cash or produce as cheap as any retail house in the city of London.' Paton and Company Dry Goods announced cash terms in December 1858 and further declared that every article was marked the lowest price in plain figures. The Paton store was still advertising this principle in January 1861. Nevertheless, such expressions of policy did not prevent these and other merchants from continuing to accept butter and other farm produce in exchange for goods at cash rates. Presumably a straight exchange then took place, and nothing was charged to the account of the customer. One St Marys customer, for example, paid for the purchase of a kettle and some cutlery with a supply of maple sugar.[17]

In spite of the firm note sounded by such advertisements, it is obvious that the words 'cash only' were included more in hope than as an expression of realistic possibility. A cash system required a financial environment where the supply of currency was both adequate and regular, and in rural Canada in the 1850s and 1860s this was neither possible nor practicable. In expressing his intention to adhere to a concept then coming into circulation, Timothy Eaton no doubt hoped to encourage customers where possible to pay cash and by this means steer clear of the problems encountered by his brothers.

Despite his announcement that all goods would be sold for cash, Timothy Eaton's accounts show that this was not the case. It was probably not a one-price-only business either, although lower prices were given for cash. The Eaton store followed a system commonly practised in St Marys, and one that Timothy himself had become familiar with as an apprentice in Ireland, of marking goods with a code understood only by the owner and his assistants.[18] This system allowed employer and salesmen to ask a higher price than that marked and then come to some compromise with the customer, in effect haggling or bargaining over the price of the merchandise. While many shoppers relished the opportunity of securing a lower price than that first asked, many felt cheated since they could never be sure that other shoppers paid similar prices.

During the 1860s only two advertisements for the Eaton store appeared in the *Argus*, and both carried only the name T. Eaton.[19] However, the business was a partnership of James and Timothy Eaton, and most financial arrangements were handled jointly.[20] As with the business in Kirkton, Timothy Eaton was involved with the day-to-day operation of the store, both as acting manager and full partner, leaving James free to investigate opportunities elsewhere. On at least one occasion James Eaton made use of this relationship to finance other ventures. Early in 1863 he attempted to establish a business in Mount Forest, some seventy miles from St Marys. By discounting customers' paper at the St Marys branch of the Bank of Montreal, he purchased for $800 the bankrupt stock of J.N. Yeomans, a Mount Forest merchant. Chances for success there were very limited. Competition was strong, and the business lasted only a short time.[21] The fact that such a venture could be contemplated is an indication that the St Marys store was experiencing a fair degree of success. This impression is reinforced when one compares Timothy Eaton's financial actions with those undertaken by another St Marys merchant, Adam Lambie, also one of Adam Hope's customers. Lambie's purchases of dry goods, hardware, and groceries by 30 June 1861 amounted to $11,543.91, but in the three-month period from March to June 1861 this debt was reduced by only $748. Timothy Eaton's total purchases for the same period amounted to $4,811.53, against which payments of $2,124 were forwarded.[22]

By the spring of 1863 Timothy Eaton was reportedly operating a fairly large business, although it was felt that his practice of stringently cutting prices produced but small profits. The Dun Credit Agency therefore rated the business as weak and recommended only trifling credit terms. By the following year the Commercial Bank of Canada reported that business for the Eatons was brisk and that the store was meeting 'moderate outside engagements promptly.' Despite his limited financial resources, it was felt that, provided he did not overtrade, Timothy Eaton was likely to succeed, although it was noted that he continued to depend very largely on credit.[23] Accounts carried on the Eaton books rose from $723.50 in 1859 at the Kirkton store to $7,866.00 in 1866 at St Marys. By January 1868 these had dropped to $5,000.00 while the value of stock on hand had increased to $11,000.00, a further indication of financial improvement.[24]

Continuing a relationship with the Bank of Montreal that had begun several years earlier in Stratford, James and Timothy Eaton were among the first businessmen in St Marys to open an account when this bank opened its new branch on 13 October 1862. Despite what seems to be a fairly heavy customer reliance on credit, the bank folios indicate regular deposits of cash, sometimes on an almost daily basis. During the traditionally slack months of March, April, July, and August, revenues were generally low and deposits infrequent, but reference to Table 6 demonstrates that from September through to January there was a noticeable increase. In 1863, when the first full year of figures are available, cash deposits were $14,156.13; by 1867 they had risen to $25,148.66.[25]

Like many other rural businessmen, Timothy and James Eaton made full use of accommodation offered by the bank. Since all such transactions are simply listed as discounts, it is difficult to ascertain which discounts represent loans from the bank to cover immediate expenditure and which straight credit in the form of bills of lading for produce, personal notes, or notes from other banks. What is apparent, however, is the fact that the proportion of discounts to deposits decreased over the period from 1864 to 1868, an indication that business was on the increase and that definite attempts were being made to encourage customers to pay in cash rather than in kind or on credit. In 1863 at least 40 per cent of the revenue deposited by Timothy or James Eaton was in the form of discounted paper, but by the beginning of 1868 this proportion had decreased to 30 per cent. As well, the increase in deposits allowed the Eatons to finance 70 per cent of their own payments in 1867 as opposed to only 46 per cent in 1864, when the cash deposits amounted to only $12,700.48. Thus, for the five years for which bank figures are available there does seem to have been some reduction of dependence on bank credit.

There also appears to have been a growing reluctance to accept notes from customers in payment for merchandise. Listed in 1864 as amounting to $1,291 and rising to $1,739 in 1866, these were reduced by 1868 to $550,[26] representing then only 11 per cent of outstanding debt, as opposed to the earlier figures of 31 per cent and 22 per cent respectively. It is possible that notes were taken in exchange for merchandise and immediately passed to the bank at a discount; but it can be assumed that they were either disposed of rapidly or accepted only reluctantly by the Eaton brothers. It is also feasible that long overdue notes were sold to the bank at a great discount, thereby ensuring at least some return on the debt.

Operating in a rural community, Timothy Eaton was occasionally obliged to take farm produce in exchange for store merchandise. The produce could be disposed of to a produce or commission merchant and the note from such a source then either retained as negotiable paper or sold to the bank. In the early 1860s Timothy Eaton occasionally paid for part of his supplies by handing over shipments of wool or butter, but this does not appear to have been a general practice. The difficulties involved in handling small amounts of farm produce whose quality was at best uncertain[27] and Timothy Eaton's professed dislike of selling wheat at low prices are perhaps indications that, where possible, he discouraged payment in kind.

Continuous efforts were made to ensure complete and full collection of amounts owing to the Eaton store, and printed notices were mailed to all customers in December. Customers whose accounts were not paid within a given period received a personal call. Interest at the rate of 7 per cent was then charged on overdue accounts.[28]

Although the credit system ensured customers' loyalty by tying them closely to one specific retailer, Timothy Eaton wished to progress beyond this and to attract customers to his store by appealing to their instincts for quality and value. One old resident described how Timothy once compelled a clerk to travel several miles after a customer who had just purchased a spinning wheel to inform him that the wheel had a small crack in it. It was his belief that an honest storekeeper should promise his customers 'not only bargains, but that every article will be found just what it is guaranteed to be ... use no deception in the smallest degree ... no nothing you cannot defend before God or man.'[29]

The pressure of business combined with a natural disinclination to draw attention to himself personally kept Timothy Eaton from participating in the public life of St Marys. While the names of both Robert and James Eaton can be found on property deeds and mortgage agreements in connection with the Methodist church in St Marys, Timothy seems only to have acted as a Sunday school teacher there.[30] James also held the position of town auditor for several years and later was actively involved in the Board of Trade in London, while Robert Eaton served on the St Marys Board of School Trustees.[31] Timothy, on the other hand, appears to have been totally committed to the development of the business. One old resident recalled a remark made by Timothy to the resident's father: 'You know, Charlie, that we never close the store in the evening while there is anybody on the street.'[32]

The Reverend Andrew Baird, who as a child had been treated to raisins and candy while his father talked business with Timothy, related that since Timothy Eaton's only free day was Sunday, and since he had no taste for pleasure driving on the sabbath, a driving horse that had been given to him by his father-in-law was loaned to the Bairds for two years.[33] Holding very strong views about sabbath activities and behaviour, Timothy Eaton followed the biblical injunction to regard Sunday as a day of rest to be devoted to church attendance, consideration, and Bible study. He had a very firm conviction that the righteous would prosper, and in his view this applied to matters both spiritual and temporal. He would later assure his Toronto employees that those who put aside their own thoughts and words and called 'the Sabbath Day a delight' would have their reward and would 'ride in the high places of the earth.' One of the texts inscribed in his notebook read: 'Trust in the Lord and do good and verily thou shalt be fed.'[34]

If such honesty and service were responsible for both the increase in customers and continued business, it would in part explain Timothy Eaton's apparent reluctance to utilize at this time what one later writer regarded as the secret of his success, namely his 'enlightened faith in printer's ink.'[35] Although the rates for advertising in the weekly *Argus* were minimal (one square inch for three weeks for one dollar and one column by the year for forty dollars), only two advertisements appear to have been inserted in the eight years Timothy was in business in St Marys.[36] The initial advertisement placed on 1 May 1861 ran without change until 11 July 1861, and the announcement of fall stock advertised on 24 October 1861 was still being carried in the *Argus* of May of the following year. While this was the practice of many retailers, several in St Marys went to great lengths to introduce new material in their advertising each week. The regular Eaton flyers, distributed by hand or by mail, probably reached a wider audience than a newspaper whose circulation was perhaps limited to those subscribers who supported the Reform platform. A list of 'Rules for Business Success' in Timothy's notebook included one that noted 'Advertise your Business line within your income.'[37] This certainly seems to have been the policy followed where the St Marys store was concerned.

Timothy Eaton's retailing methods ensured the success of the enterprise. Depending in the early years on Adam Hope for the supply of dry goods, groceries, and hardware, his account by total purchases ranked in the top 10 per cent of the more than 250 outlets supplied by Buchanan and Hope. In a one-to-five ranking of customers in 1868, J. and T. Eaton, according to Adam Hope's considered estimation, were classified in the top grade.[38] Although there were several occasions on quarterly statements when large amounts were marked overdue, there does seem to have been a determined attempt to maintain this rating. Timothy Eaton, while utilizing Hope's credit accommodation to the fullest extent, constantly forwarded funds, at times exceeding the expected sum, possibly in an attempt to offset those months when income at the store was down. The goods purchased from Hope amounted on one quarterly statement in 1862 to $8,608.74. This dropped in subsequent quarterly statements to the $5,000 level.[39] However, in the same period the level of stock at inventory rose from $3,915.82 to $6,285.00, indicating not only a greater investment in store merchandise, but also the likelihood that goods had been secured from another supplier.[40] This new supplier was probably John Macdonald, the Scottish wholesaler in Toronto, who, like many of his colleagues, took advantage of the expansion of the dry goods trade in the 1860s to secure new customers in western Ontario.

The period from 1860 to 1867 was on the whole one of prosperity and agricultural plenty. Between 1863 and 1866, retailers and wholesalers alike flourished in an environment conducive to the rapid accumulation of fortunes. The three Eaton brothers benefited from an active retail market and shared in this prosperity. Robert Eaton's fortunes underwent a change during this decade, and some time during 1863 he opened a store retailing groceries and furniture[41] that remained in operation in St Marys down to the late 1880s. As an early demonstration of his later expansionary tactics, Timothy Eaton enlarged his store in 1867 with the addition of a new building for a clothing store.[42]

The three brothers followed the practice, traditional in a society where speculation was rampant, of investing spare funds either directly in property or indirectly as capital in property mortgages. From time to time purchases were made of small parcels of land in and around St Marys. In 1863, for example, Timothy purchased property owned by Adam Lambie on the south side of Queen Street, for which he acquired a mortgage of $800 at 7 per cent interest. This was discharged in full in 1867.[43]

Given the town's relative prosperity at this time, it seems likely that much of the property so purchased consisted of stores or shops that were rented to dealers or craftsmen in much the same way that space had been rented to the shoemaker and blacksmith at Kirkton. However, as long-term investments few proved profitable. In terms of lending money out on mortgages, the timing of some of these ventures occasionally proved unwise. The mortgage of $500 given to William Vickers by Timothy Eaton in January 1865, for instance, had to be assigned to Milner Harrison in September of the same year.[44]

Although the period in St Marys afforded both Timothy and James Eaton some satisfaction and a measure of success, it seems obvious that it did not wholly satisfy their ambitions and expectations.[45] The increasing ease of travel throughout the province gradually encouraged thoughts of greater possibilities. The industries then in existence in the town – primarily woollen factories, iron foundries, and several small mills – employed only a limited number of workers. The actual pool of workers receiving a weekly cash wage, even including those employed by skilled tradesmen, was probably very small in relation to the total population of the town and the surrounding farm community. If the business had grown in such a setting, what might not be achieved in an even larger centre with an almost unlimited pool of workers receiving regular cash wages and who were beginning to demonstrate definite preferences for goods that had earlier been affordable only by the upper and middle classes?

The preceding eight years had supplied Timothy Eaton with valuable experience; more important, they had provided the capital necessary to open a business elsewhere. With the completion in the late 1850s of the Grand Trunk Railway from Montreal to Sarnia, the urban pattern of southern Upper Canada was, as Douglas McCalla points out, largely determined. It was then relatively clear which would be the significant centres.[46] As well, the arrival of the London, Bruce and Huron Railway in the 1860s gave easy access to the major centres of Stratford, London, and Toronto and further diminished the possibility that St Marys would achieve any great dominance. By encouraging manufacturing industries to locate and develop within their environs, cities such as Stratford were able to enhance and even increase their growth so that they soon outstripped smaller centres like St Marys. Moreover, after the completion of settlement in the Huron Tract, the rural population would increase only marginally; indeed, net emigration from the area would become the trend.

A picture of Timothy Eaton taken in 1863 shows a determined-looking young man without the full beard and moustache that later concealed the strong jaw line and full lips. His countenance seemed to reconcile both the intensity and the caution with which he addressed life. On 28 May 1862, at the age of twenty-eight, Timothy Eaton married Margaret Wilson Beattie, a dark-haired, vivacious girl of twenty-one from Woodstock, the daughter of Joseph and Elizabeth Tilt Beattie.[47] Surrounded by family and close friends, Timothy and Maggie would both look back on the period in St Marys as the happiest of their lives. These years were not marred by the tragic infant deaths that were to haunt their early years in Toronto. Their first three children were born in St Marys: Edward Young on 30 September 1863, Josephine Smith on 4 December 1865, and Margaret Beattie on 6 December 1867. As always, Timothy Eaton looked to tried-and-true proverbs and texts for comfort and counsel. One such, noted in his own hand, advised: 'Let hope predominate but do not be visionary.'[48]

3

Shops and Shopping

'Shopping is very demonstrative.'
Lord Melbourne to Queen Victoria

Timothy Eaton's later career cannot be fully understood unless
some attempt is made to examine the character of the retail industry
in the late 1860s and to discover the extent to which it had been
changed by the Industrial Revolution.

The spread of new ideas and technological progress that gave
rise to the Industrial Revolution was also responsible for enormous sociological changes. Many such changes, originating in
the humanitarian conscience of the age, ameliorated the harsh and
unhealthy aspects of the trend towards urbanization. Other
changes, drawing on the innovative spirit of the century, attempted
to come to terms with the growth of urban communities by providing consumer services in the form of improved distribution and
supply. The transformation of society from small communities of
people living in rural, self-supporting towns and villages to large
concentrations living in expanding urban centres generated new
demands and pressures that required original and revolutionary
responses. Although such innovations have not received the wide
attention accorded to the larger and more visible 'revolutions' of
industry and agriculture, it has been recognized by several historians[1] that the revolution in retailing during the nineteenth and early
twentieth centuries was both dynamic and widespread. Its dramatic
impact upon society in meeting the needs of the new working class

had important consequences for succeeding generations at all levels of society. Rosalind Williams, in a study of the growth of consumer society in eighteenth- and nineteenth-century France, discusses the change from a society where the availability of consumer goods had been limited to a few kitchen utensils, essential tools, and 'several well-worn pieces of furniture and clothing, [with] sometimes one outfit for special occasions,' to one that provided access to a 'seemingly unlimited profusion,' of standardized goods, produced and sold in large volume. In her opinion, this change represented 'a pivotal historical moment,' in the material and mental evolution of society.[2]

In the past, the rate of consumption was constrained and restricted by contemporary living standards. The gradual increase during the nineteenth century in the number of workers, both male and female, drawing a steady weekly wage allowed for a corresponding increase in the consumption of the goods and merchandise pouring out from manufacturing establishments. For one historian, the newly solvent, working-class female consumer represented the most important link between the production end and the demand side of the economy. Her overwhelming desire to emulate her social betters is one factor that cannot be underestimated.[3] This increase in consumption was motivated and propelled by burgeoning population growth in all urban centres, whether in Europe, Great Britain, or North America.

To meet the growing consumer demand many merchants first increased the size of their stock and then expanded this to include the many different categories of merchandise coming onto the market. Others moved towards a degree of specialization, both at the wholesale and retail level, not only for the purpose of survival through conspicuous expansion, but as an effective method of dealing with the increase in the volume of business. Improvements and specialization in the manufacture of numerous products resulted in a lowering of costs that, together with improved methods of transportation, placed goods ranging from iron pots to lacy parasols on the counters of stores throughout the western world. Improvements made on earlier innovations vastly increased the marketability of some items. The introduction by Isaac Merritt

Singer of a sewing machine suitable for home sewers in the early 1850s is but one example. The subsequent distribution of paper patterns in ladies' magazines then allowed for the growth and spread of classless clothing.

Expansion was further stimulated by the production of more attractive goods as manufacturers themselves refined the actual manufacturing process. Early factory-produced shoes, which were frequently poorly made and did not distinguish between the right and the left foot, led to the creation of an active secondhand market for shoes made by hand. Lack of demand by both retailers and customers for manufactured shoes compelled stringent improvements in this line of merchandise. The aesthetic movement of the 1860s rejected the crude dyes and machine-made finishes of the 1850s and encouraged the reproduction of the superior colours and patterns imported from the Middle East and the newly opened areas of the Far East. International exhibitions revealed the artistic shortcomings of British goods and encouraged a new interest in craftsmanship and an improvement in public tastes.[4] Manufacturers such as John Horrocks, Josiah Wedgwood, and Samuel Courtaulds recognized the advantages that could be gained from establishing a reputation closely tied to the excellence of a product. The manufacturers who were most successful achieved their results by catering to the whole spectrum of the market-place. Wedgwood, for example, produced both highly ornamental hand-painted dinnerware for Catherine the Great and inexpensive, high-quality useful china for the growing class of British urban workers.

The increase in the supply and variety of goods kept pace with and at times outmatched the growth of consumer demand, creating new openings or niches for those blessed with either foresight or luck. As prices became more competitive, merchants were compelled to introduce new ideas, concepts, services, and novelty goods with which to retain the custom they had already acquired.

In a period of rapid change, the old and the new continue for some time to exist side by side. However, as Ralph Hower noted, while the old appears to retain a considerable hold because of its wider visibility, the new occupies a strategic position and ultimately wields the dominant influence.[5] Numerous examples of this can be found in the career of a retailer such as Timothy Eaton or that of any other enterprising merchant during the middle decades of the nineteenth century. Both the shopping habits of the consuming public and the practices of wholesalers and retailers demonstrate similar patterns of development as merchants on either side of the Atlantic sought to gain an advantage over their competitors.

In England and Ireland by the 1820s and 1840s, for example, several enterprising retailers were in the habit of ordering goods direct from the manufacturers. This was the exception rather than the rule, and most continued to deal either with local wholesalers or with commission merchants. Nevertheless, this practice demonstrated the lengths to which some retailers were prepared to go to maintain their ascendancy. Owners of the larger American retail stores began to travel to Europe on buying trips, seeking ways to respond to the growing demand and increasing competition by effecting a reduction in the costs of buying and selling. A.T. Stewart, the proprietor of the first American department store, was an early pioneer in this activity, although it could be argued that, as the owner of a wholesale business, he was simply following the accepted practice of the day. Whether he dealt with the actual manufacturers of the goods or simply with wholesalers or commission merchants is not clear; but, after his first buying trip overseas in 1839, he quickly established an office in Europe (in 1845) to deal with the bulk purchase of merchandise for his retail store. In this way he successfully eliminated one unprofitable link in the distribution chain. With the establishment of his own manufacturing plants in many parts of the United States and Great Britain, Stewart by the 1860s had achieved almost complete vertical integration for some of his merchandise. By the early 1870s the annual sales volume at Stewart's New York Marble Palace was in excess of $12 million, concrete evidence of the effectiveness of his methods.[6]

Similar success was achieved by William Whiteley in London, John Wanamaker in Philadelphia, Rowland Macy and Lyman Bloomingdale in New York, and Aristide Boucicault in Paris. All began in a relatively small way as dry goods merchants and, by meeting the demand for high-quality, low-cost merchandise, then captured a developing market. The Victorian emphasis on respectable domesticity extended not only to the clothes one wore, including the best black and broadcloth for the Victorian Sunday, but also to such things as well-draped horsehair sofas, antimacassars, and flower stands for the front parlour, and a well-stocked linen cupboard. The Victorian predilection for cleanliness, domestic sanctity, and respectability, combined with the fact that practically every item for household use and personal wear was stitched at home, accounts for the drawing power exerted by stores offering high-quality bargains on all lines of dry goods.

As businesses mushroomed towards the end of the century, they were forced to expand further to meet the demand not only for material and articles of wearing apparel and household linens but also for more and more items of a less utilitarian nature. Indeed the gradual increase in purchasing power encouraged what might be referred to as the democratization of luxury. The ceaseless introduction of new products and the production of standardized merchandise in large volumes combined with the seductive power of advertising to animate a growing desire for goods that had previously been within the reach of the upper and middle classes only. As David Alexander points out, nowhere was this more evident than with the two most important commodities – food and clothing. Toronto grocer William Davies complained to his brother in 1855, for example, that the demand in Toronto for his provisions constantly outpaced his ability to prepare and supply them. The enormous working-class demand for cloth and clothing exceeded that for any other manufactured commodity[7] in Great Britain, Europe, the United States, and Canada. This need remained largely unrecognized and unmet by merchants catering to a traditional clientele of middle and upper-class shoppers accustomed to purchasing goods on credit. In the past, the small independent shopkeeper supplied the needs of a limited market, dealing only with those customers known personally to him. With the expansion of supply and demand, many such shopkeepers began to lose ground, for they could no longer handle all the goods flooding onto the market. In addition they were neither prepared nor willing to offer their services to the enlarged market-place. Some small dry goods merchants, blessed either with foresight or luck, sought to create a demand among the newly solvent members of the industrial working class and, by feeding the growing hunger of these consumers for low-cost, good-quality merchandise, captured a developing market.

As early as the 1840s, William Hancock remarked that the principal supporters of large shops in Dublin were the servants, work people, and ladies in the community: in other words, those who had the least amount of money to spend and who attached the greatest importance to small differences in cost.[8] In catering to these consumers, merchants from David Lewis in Liverpool, with his slogan 'Friends of the People,' to Lyman Bloomingdale in New York, generated changes that were widely visible in society. One old draper contrasted 'the abundance of clothing that even servant girls' possessed in the 1870s with 'the scanty equipment that the poorer people of decent station had to put up with' some decades earlier, when even the hessian wrappers in which merchandise was packed were put to good use. William Davies noted in 1855 that 'every Butcher Boy, Snip & Snob' in Toronto was 'excessively given to dress' and 'wearing rings & such foolery.'[9]

The constant stress on quality and low cost was indicative of the unprecedented purchasing power of both the new industrial wage earners and the growing class of lower-middle-class white-collar workers. According to Dorothy Davis, the wives of such workers 'were gradually switching the emphasis of their housekeeping expenditure from foods to other kinds of things.'[10] This was also true for the wives of those employed by the countless large manufacturing plants of the industrial world. These consumers were further supplemented by the rapidly increasing class of female domestics. By 1891, for example, domestics in Canada accounted for 41 per cent of the female work-force.[11] Most domestic workers were provided with the uniform necessary for the position, with board and lodging, and with a small weekly wage. The latter could be used to purchase goods for wear and use during leisure hours. 'Window shopping' servant girls were considered 'a great trial' to dry goods men and their assistants, but were 'recognised as an important group of customers.'[12]

The enormous demand for consumer goods in Great Britain in

the early decades of the nineteenth century gave rise to considerable modifications in the character, physical size, and capacity of many of the nation's dry goods shops. Some retail outlets expanded so extensively that, as early as the 1820s, they became known as 'monster shops.' Generating energetic competition with their smaller colleagues, they were reported to transact so much daily business 'as almost to exceed belief.' To assist customers in making selections and perhaps to simplify inventory control, merchandise was segregated into distinct departments. In most cases each department was managed by a separate buyer. Bainbridge's in Newcastle in 1849 listed twenty-three separate sets of undertakings by departments, and this is just one such example.[13]

Plate-glass windows proliferated as merchants acted to attract new custom rather than waiting for it to come to them. Charles Dickens, writing in the 1840s, regarded the 'inordinate love of plate glass' as a disease that, in his view, had reached epidemic proportions.[14] There was also a greater awareness of the profitability of rapid stock turnovers. In the past it had not been uncommon for a roll of fancy ribbon to remain in stock for up to five years. The introduction of muslins and other light-weight fabrics in the Napoleonic era and its impact on what would become the world of fashion generated enormous changes. Charles Knight, writing in 1851, declared that the high cost of woollen goods before the Industrial Revolution had effectively prevented much competition. A careful woman fully expected a good merino (wool) dress to last for many years.[15]

Because of the universal demand for their goods and the fact that they operated in a trade free of guild restrictions, haberdashers and dry goods merchants had long been in the forefront of innovations in retailing. The resulting competition had both sharpened their salesmanship and bestowed a reputation for less than honest dealing. As early as the fourteenth century Piers Plowman speaks of being 'drawn into drapery and by devious tricks [learning] to lay out linen so that it looked longer. Till ten or twelve yards told out thirteen'. Consumer attitudes may have encouraged this behaviour. Early-nineteenth-century observers were frequently annoyed and offended by the customer's mistaken ideas regarding the true value and quality of cloth. Robert Owen related how exasperated sales clerks got their revenge on such customers by offering cheaper goods at inflated prices.[16]

To counteract such practices some merchants tried to introduce a greater measure of honesty in their dealings with the general public. The system of cash and one price had a fairly lengthy history but had fallen into disfavour. George Fox, a Quaker, urged his followers in the seventeenth century to eschew sharp bargaining practices and to make retailing so straightforward that a child could be sent to shop. William Stout, another Quaker, detested the practice of asking more for goods than they were worth. John Morton introduced the principle of cash and one price in his London shop as early as 1712. Many customers disliked the one-price system, however, since it was commonly believed that it was not possible to get a good buy without haggling over the price. For this reason many Quaker shopkeepers had, according to Daniel Defoe, gradually been obliged to revert to the practice of abatement. It is interesting to note that Defoe considered this a return to the more honest practice of shopkeeping.[17]

Some merchants continued to swim against the tide, however. Flint and Palmer, a haberdashery and drapery shop on London Bridge, dealt only with customers willing to purchase with ready money. Furthermore, since bargaining was strictly forbidden, fixed prices were quoted for every item of merchandise. As Robert Owen recalls, the store was generally full from morning till late in the evening.[18]

As both contemporary and later observers have pointed out, the two concepts – cash sales and fixed prices – were almost always inextricably entwined. Neither practice was widely known on either side of the Atlantic until the early decades of the nineteenth century. Where used, they were often disliked because of the inferior clientele they attracted. Such stores obviously directed their appeal to a different class of customer and, by attracting the newly solvent industrial worker, brought increasing numbers into contact with consumer society. Robert Owen considered the mass of customers at Flint and Palmer to be highly inferior to the upper-class patrons of his former place of employment. He also complained that fixed prices encouraged a somewhat disrespectful attitude in sales clerks. Customers who hesitated over prices were rapidly ignored, and the sales clerk would turn almost immediately to the next customer. For Owen, trained in and accustomed to the traditional manner of dealing slowly and solemnly with each genteel customer in turn and returning each bolt of cloth to its rightful place before displaying the next, the change was, as he put it, almost more than his constitution could support. Both Flint and Palmer and Lackington, the London bookseller who introduced the concept of cash sales in 1780, were regarded as eccentrics rather than innovators to be imitated.[19]

By the early decades of the nineteenth century the practice of cash sales began to spread throughout Great Britain, especially in larger retail drapery outlets where the sheer number of customers made any other system impracticable. David Alexander identifies several, ranging from Campbell's in Glasgow in 1824, Harvey's in Dublin in the 1830s, to Shoolbred's in London in the 1840s. All were dubbed 'monster shops' by their contemporaries. Catering to the large urban market where personal subsistence expenditure became increasingly less important, such stores enjoyed a sales volume that encouraged the small shopkeeper gradually to adopt the same principles.[20]

Price ticketing, on the other hand, especially if ticketed items were placed in the store windows, continued to be regarded as less than genteel. As one witness told the Select Committee on Manufacturers and Trade in 1833, price ticketing was 'not a practice that would be resorted to by those who would seek their custom from the higher class of the community ... it is much more resorted to where they seek principally customers among the lower and middling classes of people.'[21] The 'No Abatement' sign hung in the window was intensely disliked by one employee, since it indicated a pushing and ticketing shop. Charles Dickens, writing in the 1840s, reported that only faltering merchants resorted to such techniques; price tickets in the windows were a sure sign of decay. Those stores that did resort to price ticketing endeavoured to maintain at least an illusion of dignity by refusing to make use of any 'puffery adjectives' on the sales labels. However, the practice of fixed price appears, like cash sales, to have been firmly established well before the middle of the nineteenth century. Indeed, in the 1855 Paris Exposition all displayed objects carried price tags. As both contemporary and later observers point out, fixed prices increased both labour productivity and stock turnover, for the salesman could sell more than double the amount of goods in the same time. Furthermore, by diminishing the cost of selling, the retailer could offer a lower price to the buyer, thereby 'pursuing a nimble sixpence before a slow shilling.'[22]

A long complaint written in 1846 by a draper's assistant railing against the practice of haggling or bargaining over the price of goods suggests the distance travelled by the retail industry.[23] By the 1850s the transition in England was more or less complete. Francis Wey, a Frenchman on a visit to England in 1856, described the response met by a shopper who dared to question the price of goods:

The assistant thinks at first that you have misunderstood him, but when he realises what you are driving at he stiffens visibly like a man of honour to whom one has made a shady proposal. He gives you to understand, politely but plainly, that his prices being equitable cannot be reduced. His resolute bearing is so unmistakable that only a fool would insist. Hawkers, dealers in booths or stalls, or small nondescript shops are the only tradespeople that you can drive a bargain with. In fact the higher the commercial class the more conscientious is the price quoted.[24]

Despite these visible changes in the character of many dry goods stores, the behaviour of the traditional merchant towards his customers had remained the same. No customer was allowed to leave a shop until satisfied or served. One draper's assistant complained bitterly of the great evil perpetrated by the members of society who habitually went 'a-shopping' without any intention of buying. It was generally assumed that no person entered a store except with the intention of buying. It was further assumed by the merchant that his managers carried everything the general public required. To secure compliance with this edict, shop assistants in many

British stores, even as late as the 1890s, were fined by their employers if a customer left a store without purchasing anything. As the merchant in a *Punch* cartoon informed his sales assistant, 'I keep you to sell what I've got, and not what people want.'[25] One contemporary, remembering his own sales experience, recalled that 'The ladies ... came with their lists all prepared and were shown from department to department till all was selected ... there was no time for bantering as there was no idea of anything but a fixed price ... No person was allowed to remain in the business who violated any rule, and no allowance was made for even the slightest delinquency.'[26] In many of the older stores customers were 'received at the door of the shop by a solemn gentleman in black, who in due time delivered one over to another solemn gentleman ... who found one a chair, and in a sepulchural tone of voice uttered some magic words such as "Silk, Mr. Smith." '[27] Customers were never left unattended. Even small stores, such as that operated by Timothy Eaton in Toronto in the early 1870s, employed a floorwalker to greet customers on arrival and to secure the services of a sales assistant. As one Victorian observer wrote of Whiteley's emporium:

It is difficult nowadays to realise how very personal was then the relationship, even in London, between shopkeeper and customer and the enormous importance, comparable almost to that attained by rival churches, which late Victorian and Edwardian ladies attached to certain stores. All my female relatives had their own favourites, where some of them had been honoured customers for more than half a century and their arrival was greeted by frenzied bowing on the part of the frock-coated shopwalkers, and where certain of the older assistants stood to them almost in the relationship of confessors.[28]

All goods and merchandise were kept carefully out of harm's way either on shelves behind the counter or in closed drawers and boxes, accessible only to the sales clerks. Shopping in such an atmosphere was considered an occasion of some dignity. One English lady, referring to the 1870s, considered 'an afternoon's shopping ... a solemn and dreary affair. One bought what was wanted and nothing more, and having secured one's goods left the shop as seriously as one arrived. The whole performance left an impression of responsibility and sadness on one's mind, and whether desiring wedding or funeral garments the same solemnity characterized it, and with a great sense of relief the large doors closed behind one.'[29]

Gordon Selfridge, coming from the free-wheeling and unrestrained atmosphere of North America, found this system somewhat of a surprise when he arrived in London in 1909. Indeed the London magistrates accused him of encouraging shop-lifting when it was realized that he allowed both unlimited entrance to his department store on Oxford Street and also free access to the actual merchandise.[30] Selfridge, however, only wished to implement what had long been general practice in North America.

The pace of retail change tended to be greater in the United States. This was true not only for those merchants who would come to dominate the market, such as A.T. Stewart, Rowland Macy, and John Wanamaker, but also for numerous small dealers. One Chicago merchant, L.D. Olmstead, declared in 1852 that he would cheerfully: 'guarantee our prices in all cases to be as low as the same quality of Goods are [sic] sold, at the time, by any one in the city. If it should prove otherwise, in a single instance, we will make it satisfactory or refund the money.'[31]

Potter Palmer, the founder of what later became Marshall Field and Company, initiated a cash system when he opened his business in Chicago in 1852. He also allowed customers to take goods home on approval and, if the purchasers were not satisfied, he cheerfully refunded their money. This promise was echoed by other merchants in centres both large and small.[32] Within a decade many retailers were announcing that money would be refunded to customers not satisfied with merchandise.

Retailers like John Wanamaker recognized that to attain success it was not enough to offer honest quality. Retailing should be regarded as a science, with service to the public as its goal. To this end every effort had to be made to ensure the close margin necessary for profits. This entailed going beyond the concepts of cash sales and fixed prices. As early as 1823, A.T. Stewart stated that not only were his goods sold for cash, but that all store merchandise had been bought for cash. In this way he could afford to place his goods on the market at rock-bottom prices and still secure a reasonable profit. Substantial sales then enlarged a business whose multiplication of small profits resulted in a large accumulation of capital. Already by the late 1830s Stewart's sales totalled more than $5,000 a day. Rowland Macy, who had espoused the ideas of cash and fixed prices at his Haverhill store in 1851, by 1870 had an annual sales volume of $1 million.[33]

Activities of this size and scope advanced at a somewhat slower pace in Canada and did not appear until both population and demand also increased. Henry Morgan established his business in Montreal in 1845, but by 1874 employed only 150 clerks, a fraction of Stewart's work-force of 1,000. Still, by the 1870s Morgan had departmentalized his store from a merchandising and accounting point of view. Robert Walker, who established his Toronto whole-sale and retail business in the late 1830s, was reported by the early 1860s to be doing the largest cash retail trade in the city, taking in nearly $300,000 over the counter, $60,000 of which was for the retail side of the business. Though this was but a fraction of the business done by Stewart's Marble Palace, the Walker store was considered the most prosperous in Toronto. By the late 1850s Walker's success allowed him to open branch stores in London, Hamilton, and Galt.[34]

Toronto did not rank in size with centres like London, New York, and Paris; but when compared to a town like St Marys, it could quite justifiably be included among those cities experiencing rapid growth. The population rose from approximately 45,000 in 1860 to nearly 70,000 in the early 1870s. Although the increase in living standards, mass production, and consumption of goods and merchandise occurred somewhat later in Canada than in Britain and the United States, the general trend was similar to that experienced in most western nations. The steady increase in the number of people residing in Toronto introduced and advanced needs at once greater and more diverse than those required by the earlier population. The gradual expansion of the provincial railway system also reinforced the drawing power of the developing city, as rural inhabitants supplemented and enlarged the market available to Toronto retailers.

Toronto, like many other North American cities, retained many of its original characteristics, but change was visible and nowhere more so than in the retail industry. Charles Dickens, when he visited the city in 1842, found the town itself 'full of life and motion, bustle, business and improvement.' The shops he noted were excellent, and he further observed that 'Many of them have a display of goods in their windows, such as may be seen in thriving country towns in England: and there are some which would do no discredit to the metropolis itself.'[35]

The supply and distribution of food during this period probably underwent the greatest change. Although multiple grocery stores did not develop as early in North America as in Great Britain, in 1855 retailers such as William Davies began supplying Toronto residents with provisions – sausages, bacon, ham, butter, lard and cheese – that were both reasonable in price and superior in quality. The demand for items that had earlier been either produced or raised at home or regarded as attainable only by the middle and upper classes increased at an astonishing rate as the working class added such things as store-bought jam, bacon, tea, and other provisions to their weekly shopping lists. In 1847 Toronto's population of 19,706 had been served by only seven wholesalers and four fixed retail grocers. A large proportion of the population at that time patronized the stalls in the daily and weekly market for their supplies of fresh meat, produce, and staple provisions, but shopped only occasionally for such items as tea, coffee, and other luxury comestibles.

By 1871, however, the number of fixed-shop retail grocers had risen to seventy-seven and in the next decade or so increased almost sevenfold. By 1894 the number had risen again, to 794. A shop that in 1847 had catered to an average of 4,926 members of the population, in 1894 served only 252; indicating not only increased demand but also competition for this market. These statistics of course do not include the vast number of specialized stores that distributed only individual items such as meat and bread.

The dry goods trade demonstrated similar growth, and its expansion was accompanied by structural changes. Because of the greater reliance by Toronto residents on external suppliers for household and personal linens, by 1847 there were some 15 wholesale and 21 retail stores catering to this trade in the city. During the boom years of the mid-1850s, the city was served by 12 wholesale and 59 retail dry goods stores. The depression of 1857 brought a slight temporary decrease in these numbers, but by the 1860s trade was once more in a vigorous condition. By 1871 more than 57 retail outlets served a population of just over 66,000. This number rose to more than 150 in 1881, the highest number at any time in the late nineteenth century. The *Monetary Times* constantly makes reference to the excessively large numbers of traders in dry goods, encouraged by access to easy credit and by the general belief that neither a large amount of capital nor experience was necessary for entrance into this business.[36]

By 1860 the Toronto wholesale and retail trade no longer operated exclusively on the lines of the rural general store, but had begun to specialize to some degree as the demand for less necessary items increased. Wholesalers by the 1850s were beginning to departmentalize their houses in an attempt to deal more efficiently with both the rising demand and the expansion of stock. By the 1870s departmentalization was well established. As Gene Allen points out, firms that adopted this method were able to keep up with changes in both fashion and supply. Furthermore, with each department controlled and managed by a skilled buyer, such wholesalers could then compete as effectively with the more specialized houses, for the 'stronger capital position' of the general firms 'gave them an advantage their smaller competitors did not possess.'[37]

On the retail side of the industry, demand and expansion encouraged the establishment of highly specialized stores. Ralph Hower noted that in 1800 it was practically impossible to find a specialized store in the United States, but by 1850 the cities were filled with them.[38] Although this trend occurred somewhat later in Toronto, by the 1880s enterprising merchants within the city were specializing in goods as varied as hoop skirts, baby and infant's wear, imported buttons and Nottingham lace, Ontario-manufactured iron stoves, and underwear produced by the Toronto Knitting and Yarn factory.

Toronto's ability to keep pace with other large retail centres was chiefly due to the constant movement of Canadian wholesalers travelling to the centres of supply on both sides of the Atlantic. Regular Atlantic crossings undertaken by Canadian buyers were responsible for the flow of merchandise to Canadian stores. The value of imports arriving at the port of Toronto increased from $3,530,198 in 1858 to $18,634,451 in 1883, with dry goods representing a large proportion of these totals. As the *Monetary Times* observed in 1869:

The normal demand for dry goods from consumers has increased much faster than the increase of population. This arises from the increase of wealth, and hence the purchasing power, giving rise to a desire for more expensive and stylish goods; so that Canadian factory made and imported cloths, yarns, blankets, etc., have been largely substituted for the coarse woolly homemade articles ... which every well-to-do farmer formerly produced.[39]

Importing at this time was undertaken primarily by wholesalers, although several of the larger retail stores tried to create the impression that they also took an active role in this transaction. Many dry goods stores, for example, carried the term 'importer' over their doors, but as C.C. Taylor (that ubiquitous commentator on nineteenth-century life in Toronto) noted, this was not a direct business involvement. Large orders may on occasion have been delivered to the retailer in the original packages, but the initial orders would have been placed with the wholesalers. Some retail stores – such as Robert Walker and Company – were sending their own buyers to Great Britain and Europe as early as the 1860s.[40] Nevertheless, it seems clear that most Canadian buyers continued to deal primarily with wholesalers and commission merchants during such overseas visits.

Although King Street retained its long-established reputation as Toronto's fashionable centre of commerce, the expansion and development of the city and the opening of the Toronto Street Railway in 1861 led to the gradual extension of the retail trade's centre of operations. One observer noted in 1870 that: 'The buildings on King Street are greater and grander than their neighbours on Yonge: the shops are larger and dearer and last though far from being least, King Street is honoured by the daily presence of the aristocracy, while Yonge is given over to the business man, the middle class and the beggar.'[41] Nevertheless old engravings and lithographs clearly indicate that some of the buildings on Yonge Street were no less imposing than their counterparts on King Street. In 1856 commercial property had not extended northwards much beyond Trinity Square on Yonge Street, but even at that time twenty-nine of the fifty-nine dry goods stores were located on this thoroughfare. Some thirteen years later retail stores of one kind or another stretched northwards on Yonge Street as far as Hayter and McGill streets. However, the daily afternoon parade by the fashionable along the wooden boardwalks of King Street continued into the 1870s and was recognized as a venerable Toronto institution, known as 'doing King.'[42] The promenade was undoubtedly enhanced by the North American practice, already well established by the 1840s, of 'shopping' either for amusement or to compare prices before purchasing. According to C.C. Taylor: 'The custom was almost universal to go from Yonge Street to the market before deciding on what or where to buy. The common expression was "We will look around, and return if not better suited elsewhere." '[43]

C.C. Taylor, who had worked for a Quaker dry goods house in Dublin, found the store of A.T. Stewart of New York lacking in the refinements of the Irish store with which he was familiar. Stewart has been credited as the first merchant to establish the free entrance system whereby one could enter a store, inspect and price the goods, and then leave without being importuned to purchase. It seems likely, however, that in North America the earlier dependence of rural inhabitants on the village or small-town general store did much to remove 'old country' attitudes towards shopkeepers. One would not expect a general store to carry absolutely everything, and since many such stores also functioned as the local post office, the merchant would not expect every customer to purchase merchandise on every visit. As well, the relative lack of pedlars, scotch drapers, and tallymen in Canada forced people into a relationship with the local storekeeper and helped eliminate much of the timidity in commercial affairs that had earlier existed among the lower ranks of society.

Nevertheless, for immigrants accustomed to the unhurried and professional atmosphere of many British shops, the customs of 'shopping' and of haggling or bargaining found in the thriving stores of Toronto came as something of a shock. As C.C. Taylor observed: 'In consideration of my previous experience, the principal of the business, in which I had made a temporary engagement, immediately took charge of a customer where any deviation from the marked price was asked, well knowing that on no account would I condescend to such a practice ... the anxiety to press sales ... was painfully apparent, the offer of a reduction in price being the principal inducement held out.'[44]

Many Toronto retailers, like their counterparts in St Marys and elsewhere in Canada, had begun to adopt the concept of cash sales. The earliest recorded instance of this practice in the town of York was in the 1820s when several minor retailers were reported to be prospering by selling goods for cash. The *Colonist* in the 1830s carried advertisements announcing cash sales. In the late 1840s one merchant, a J.R. Mountjoy of the Golden Fleece, plainly stated in the city directory, 'Terms Cash – No Abatement.'[45] Given the contemporary state of the currency and the economy, the hope for that type of business must have been greater than the actuality. One of the primary requisites for a successful cash trade was a large urban centre whose inhabitants were employed in factories or industries and were in receipt of regular cash wages. Although circumstances in the late 1850s did not allow for the full application of the cash sales principle, the depression of 1857 and the attendant restriction of credit undoubtedly compelled many merchants to attempt its introduction.

By the late 1850s several large Toronto houses – Robert Walker has already been mentioned – were reported to be doing a good cash trade. One merchant went so far as to list prices in the *Globe*, informing his customers that 'as our business is done exclusively for cash' it was not necessary to allow a margin for bad debts. But old attitudes continued to linger, and this practice did not find universal favour. Walker, for instance, in the late 1850s was censured on two occasions for resorting to similar tactics. The credit agency did not approve of 'forcing off sales by news paper puffs.'[46]

By 1869 comments in the *Monetary Times* indicate that older attitudes were beginning to change. One writer suggested that cash sales might effectively prune out the rubbish of the retail trade: 'selling goods on credit is not necessarily making money ... [cash sales] will tend to lessen corruption and give those who do sell goods in future, a chance to make fair profits, and lessen the danger of losses.'[47]

By the late 1860s the relationship between the Toronto retail industry and the consumer exhibited many characteristics that were wholly North American. But innovation proceeded slowly. Many of the traditional merchants had not yet directed their appeal to the city's growing class of industrial workers, but continued to concentrate on their regular middle- and upper-class clientele. The activities of a retailer who undertook to serve a different market that was ripe for exploitation are the focus of the rest of this study.

4

A New Beginning: Toronto

'Keep thy shop and thy shop will keep thee. Light gains
make heavy purses.'
George Chapman, *Eastward Ho*

'The diligent hand maketh rich.'
Prov. 10:4

Despite a financial crisis in the mid-1860s that resulted in the
failure first of the Bank of Upper Canada in 1866 and then of the
Commercial Bank in 1867, Toronto by 1869 had experienced
sufficient change and growth to offer at least the appearance of
greater opportunity than the rural centre of St Marys. The growth
and development of financial institutions in the form of banks,
insurance companies, building societies, and savings banks greatly
assisted this development and added to the general prosperity that
appears to have been experienced at all levels of society. The *Globe*,
commenting in October 1866 on the amount of funds deposited in
the three savings banks in Toronto, regarded this as a sure indication of the increased earning power of the working classes. The
manufacturing establishments within the city were largely responsible for this affluence, for they employed nearly 10,000 workers
whose annual wages amounted to more than $2.5 million.[1]

Some time in 1869 Timothy Eaton moved to Toronto and set up
shop on Front Street West, a downtown thoroughfare where large
imposing buildings existed alongside smaller commercial proper-

ties. The American Hotel, a substantial three-storey building erected in 1844, was located at the intersection of Front and Yonge streets across from Kivas Tully's Bank of Montreal building erected in 1845 and the old Customs House designed by John Tully in 1840. The harbour master's office and the Military Hospital (formerly the residence of William Warren Baldwin), Jacques and Hay's furniture factory, a wood yard, and a paper making plant separated by several large vacant lots could also be found on Front Street between Yonge and Bay streets. The area would soon experience considerable development with the construction in 1871 of McMaster's large new warehouse and the replacement in 1876 of the Customs House by an impressive new building.

Timothy Eaton's choice of location at first appears somewhat strange, for Front Street, even in 1869, was not patronized by the casual shopper. If the business was a wholesale venture, then the location offered some potential. According to Nasmith, Timothy Eaton established a wholesale dry goods business in partnership with a Mr Allison. A family member later stated, however, that Timothy began by specializing as a wholesaler in woollen goods and that Allison was only an employee, not a partner.[2] If this was the case, then Timothy Eaton was following a practice traditional among retail merchants of moving from retailing to the far more profitable sector of wholesaling. This had been the route taken by John Macdonald, William McMaster, Adam Hope, and numerous other merchants in this trade whose success would have been familiar to Timothy Eaton.

The premises rented at 8½ Front Street West from William Thomson and John Burns, the thriving hardware, china, and glass merchants at number eight, were situated on the north side of the street between Yonge and Bay streets, and had a twenty-six-foot frontage. The city's assessment for tax purposes of $5,000 for personal property (usually representing stock) suggests the seriousness with which the venture was undertaken. No mention was made of employees, but it seems unlikely that Timothy Eaton conducted the business single-handed. There may have been at least one young assistant. By contrast Thomson and Burns employed at least five clerks, and personal property was assessed at $25,000 with an additional $9,000 as taxable income. The extent of Thomson and Burns's success can be measured by their ownership of several other properties on this section of Front Street.[3]

This first Eaton business remained in operation for only a short time, and very little information exists relating to it. It was probably not successful, since Timothy Eaton's timing was unfortunate. Competition was extremely stiff for those entering the wholesale dry goods trade at this time. Of the eleven new firms that entered the industry in the 1860s, only two were still in business some ten years later.[4] Throughout 1869 constant references were made to the generally backward state of the dry goods trade. With imports of dry goods suffering noticeable declines from earlier inflated levels, merchants throughout the province were exercising great caution. Erastus Wiman attributed the trade's unsatisfactory condition to the enormously increased importation of dry goods, which, in his opinion, had escalated at a rate faster than the population could support. The situation was further aggravated by insolvency laws that allowed bankrupt traders to evade full payment of outstanding debts. Honest retailers were then compelled to operate in a market where ruinous price cutting resulted in disastrous competition for all.[5] There was little to prevent a merchant who had recently settled with his creditors for fifty cents in the dollar from immediately re-establishing himself in business with stocks received on consignment from yet another wholesaler. Robert Simpson is an interesting case. At a December 1870 meeting of creditors, Simpson, because of a lack of fire insurance coverage, was forced into assignment and compelled to settle for $37^{1}/_{2}$ cents on the dollar. Some three weeks later he was back in business, advertising 'a choice Stock of groceries and dry goods and boots and shoes.'[6]

One wholesale merchant, taking a more cautious stance, observed that with 'so many shaking the bankrupt law in our face we scarcely care to do business at all.' He therefore refused to sell to those who could not give a full account of their financial standing, for 'it is only throwing away our goods to sell them in any way just now.' Merchants such as J.D. Merrick, who thoroughly 'fleeced' his friends and 'betrayed those who trusted too much in his integrity,' were vigorously denounced, but, as the *Monetary Times* observed, 'some blame must be attached to those who gave countenance to this system of kite-flying for so long a period.'[7]

This unhealthy environment perhaps accounts for the concern expressed by Timothy Eaton that with so much opposition he might not be able to make a go of it in Toronto. The tight money situation combined with his out-of-the-way location undoubtedly presented problems that could not be immediately overcome. To further complicate matters, he suffered a grave financial loss when he entrusted a sum of money to a man travelling on a buying expedition to England, where both man and money vanished. A letter to James in February 1870 bears witness to these difficulties: 'If you look at my position with the past years Difficulties hanging over me and my money spread through the country – and every one hard up – how I am to attempt to carry on a business here in the face of everyone of the whole sale houses knowing all this ... it is altogether different with me now than If I was not involved in the Gilpin afair.'[8] His remark that 'My affairs being made public last Summer should any little thing happen now there would be trouble at once' may be an indication that the business on Front Street either came close to failure or did fail. But the move had been made and the outlook was not wholly black. Despite the temporary dullness in the Toronto market, the city at least had an abundance of well-paid and profitably employed labour, a factor of great importance to a shopkeeper.

The family, consisting of Timothy, Maggie, and the three children, had rented a three-storey frame house at 12 Gloucester Street.[9] With three children under the age of six years and another on the way, Maggie Eaton probably did not wish to contemplate a further move. Alternative business opportunities therefore had to be considered. Given the scope of Timothy Eaton's own background, several options existed, but decisions seemed slow in coming. Some time in November 1869 he wrote to James Matthewson, a large wholesale grocer in Montreal, requesting some information with regard to the grocery business:

Is it possible to do a profitable Grocery Business in Toronto (or any City you know of) Without — Licquors You will pardon the liberty I now take in addressing you. My reason for asking is this — I am about making arrangements to go into the Grocery business here 'retail for Cash' and everyone I have spoken to on the subject is of opinion I could not Succede Without keeping Licquors — I cannot myself see why it should be so — I have determined if Licquors is a necessary Appendix to have nothing to do with good or Bad.[10]

Even at this late point in the year Timothy Eaton was apparently still trying to locate a viable business. One can only assume that Matthewson's reply was sufficiently discouraging about 'Licquors' to make Timothy discard the idea of opening a grocery store. What is interesting is the fact that he intended this new business to be 'for Cash,' demonstrating some tenacity and continuity at least with regard to that concept.

Timothy Eaton then turned to a branch of merchandising with which he was familiar and, at the beginning of December 1869, paid $6,500 for the stock and goodwill of the dry goods retail business known as the Britannia House. This business, owned and operated by James Jennings and John Brandon, was located in rented property at 178 Yonge Street. James Jennings, like Timothy Eaton, was an ardent Methodist and in 1854 had been one of the original members of Elm Street Methodist Church, the church attended by the Eaton family until 1887. At a celebratory dinner after this purchase, Timothy was reported to have said to Jennings, 'I never talk business when eating. It affects digestion. Let's talk about church.'[11] As both Jennings and Brandon continued to operate as partners in a fairly large wholesale business at 38 Yonge Street, it is assumed that, like other merchants, they wished to dispense with the retail side of the business and to concentrate on the sector that offered the greatest profits.[12]

On Thursday, 9 December 1869, James Jennings publicly announced the sale of his business and urged all his old friends and customers to proffer their cordial and generous support to the new owner.[13] Since Jennings and Brandon had been in the dry goods business for nearly twenty years, the last sixteen of which they had been operating at the southwest corner of Yonge and Queen streets, the business appeared to offer some potential. In addition this intersection was a favoured location for retail outlets, and by the 1850s merchants were competing for the corner sites. By purchasing the stock of the Britannia House, Timothy Eaton had chosen both a location already accustomed to regular traffic and a well-established store of some long standing. The only fly in the ointment, about which Timothy would later complain bitterly to his brother, was the quality of the stock. 'Old stuff no use here – have 2 much already from Jennings – have been selling piles of dresses @ from 5 to 12 to 15¢ cost 10, 20 and 35¢ per yard and is going to mike [hawk] goods around.' He had the additional problem of unsold merchandise carried over from the Front Street venture: 'have been hamering away at my own stock piles of them we cannot move at any price.'[14]

Jennings's announcement in the *Globe* was followed by an advertisement stating that 'T. Eaton & Co.' would keep a 'well-assorted stock' of sound goods throughout the year. In the meantime it was proposed to offer special inducements on present stock 'by way of clearing it off rapidly.' Furthermore it was pointed out that 'We propose to sell our goods for CASH ONLY – In selling goods, to have only one price.'[15]

Much has been made of Timothy Eaton's introduction of the policies of cash and one fixed price, but it is clear that such policies were already in general use in many Canadian cities. Several other advertisements in the 9 December edition of the *Globe*, for example, specified similar terms. Given the unstable nature of the Canadian economy and Timothy Eaton's total unfamiliarity with an urban population many of whose members were still undecided as to their final destination, he would have been decidedly foolish to adopt the credit system. As W.N. Hancock pointed out in 1851, the adoption of the cash system in Great Britain had in part arisen from the simple fact that large shopkeepers were unable to acquaint themselves with the financial circumstances of their customers.[16] Timothy Eaton's determination to maintain the cash-only policy, therefore, was obviously prompted as much by necessity as by choice. But it is also evident from remarks made to James in February 1870 that this created as many problems as it solved:

You still have the old excuse which I have made use of many times with old adam [Hope] that we done so much credit and that we could not get our money unless we sued our customers. If he wished us 2 collect in that [way?] I could go home and do it – of course the reply alwyes was go home and do the best you can ... time and time again I used the above to the good old fellow & got about the same reply – with you should not give so much credit, etc., etc., of the above I cannot now say a word as I am selling only for cash.[17]

This problem would have been aggravated by the fact that small lots of merchandise picked up at local auctions had to be paid for with cash.[18] The earlier arrangement with both Adam Hope and the Buchanans had offered favourable credit terms and had not restricted business to any large degree. Timothy Eaton now had no such 'excuse' to offer to suppliers. He was further hampered by debts that still had to be met from St Marys. At the beginning of 1868 James and Timothy Eaton had acknowledged liabilities totalling $13,500, and a letter dated June 1872 refers to 'a grand sight the big pile of pd. up notes of the old B[uchanan] H[ope] & Co., I suppose it is what they never expected.'[19] Moreover it seems likely that Timothy Eaton had not received his full share of the business assets when he left St Marys. In a letter dated February 1870 he thanked James for the draft of $100, 'which I have placed to your Cr,' but it would appear that he had been expecting more, for in a somewhat sarcastic vein he continued: 'Your reasoning is all very good that money will be as needful three months from now as at present ... If I cannot get a Turn Out of the money this Spring to give a little confidence in me here, it will be a dull lookout. If you will make me share of the money in *May and June* ... but the trouble is unless you make up your mind to say *you will do it* – I cannot depend on it.' Timothy Eaton obviously needed the money immediately or at least the assurance that it would be coming at a definite date, for as he pointed out: 'I am selling only for cash &

I must have a little cash to pay part of my spring goods If I buy any to get a foothold here I must buy from good houses and If you can show me how I am to enter a good house in my present position without a little money I will be under a great compliment to you. Write me and let me know what you think I ought to do.'[20]

There is no way of knowing James's advice to Timothy with regard to this problem, but presumably the state of James Eaton's own finances allowed for greater flexibility, for some two months later Timothy wrote to James that: 'If everything goes right – I will sell you this place by the 1st June. If I do not get arranged by that time will keep it until December.' The possibility of his selling the business just five months after its opening is given further emphasis when he goes on to add: 'I have already given a promise to a party to give them the first offer of it, but his funds are in such a position that he could not get the cash before Winter.'[21] Since no further reference was made to the sale of the business, and since James Eaton opened a new store in London in the fall of 1870, it has to be assumed that Timothy Eaton either decided or was compelled to struggle on.

For the first few months the course of his business life was 'all uphill.' Having moved only recently from a rural general store to one in a large centre, Timothy Eaton was not completely familiar with the specific tastes of urban customers. This was knowledge that could be acquired only by trial and error but, where fancy goods were concerned, he was able to rely on the expertise of his experienced clerk, Hugh Robb.[22]

Following the early practice at St Marys, the business premises were rented, not purchased. The shop at 178 Yonge Street, for which he paid an annual rent of $1,040,[23] answered most of Timothy Eaton's business requirements for his first fourteen years in Toronto. The store initially occupied only the main floor. James Jennings, following the practice customary with many Yonge Street retailers, had lived in the upper portion of the building with his family until late in 1869. In 1871 a Mrs Anderson was listed as the upstairs tenant and as such was responsible for a portion of the tax assessment. For a brief period in the early 1870s several of Timothy Eaton's young male clerks occupied rooms on the third floor.[24]

Despite the complaints that fill many of Timothy's early letters, the store achieved a steady rate of growth almost from its inception. But perhaps when compared to sales volume at the St Marys store, these early figures were less than anticipated. A comparison of sales figures for the month of December 1869 and 1870 alone shows an increase of more than $1,700.00. Indeed sales for 1870 amounted to $24,415.66. Nevertheless, what little satisfaction Timothy Eaton derived from this increase was more than eclipsed by anxiety about his debt load. His notebook shows an overwhelming concern with interest payments due on merchandise purchased from John Macdonald. By January 1871 Timothy Eaton owed Macdonald $16,000.00 and by January 1872 this sum had risen to more than $31,000.00.[25]

Despite these problems, his occasional thoughts of selling out, and the rumours circulating within the trade about his possible failure, Timothy Eaton maintained his fixity of purpose: 'The past 2 years has been a hard tack – and it will yet take a long pull & a strong pull, but its all right – we are made 2 work – and as long as the Lord give me a continuation of health & energy – I am determined to work & work with a will.'[26] At no time does he seem to have contemplated discarding his sales policy of cash only, a concept that made very good commercial sense. Success would depend on his holding fast to the principles of cash sales and fixed prices that he had established in December 1869. The early Eaton advertisements emphasized the availability of cheap, good quality merchandise and drew constant attention to the concepts of cash terms and one price. As one contemporary observed, such innovations were an attempt to tighten up business methods and, by means of increased skill and quicker turnovers, to make the same amount of capital do a greater quantity of work than before, in much the same manner that an improvement in machinery decreased the cost of production.[27] Since the stress was on the stout quality demanded not only by the working class but also by the well-to-do, Timothy Eaton was not ashamed to make price a selling point. Commenting on the demands of Canadian consumers he noted that 'it takes a great deal of energy & matching to keep a head here – our goods must be the Newest & cheap,' although on

one occasion he stated that 'high prices or low prices does not make
so much differens with us here as nice goods.'[28]

Despite technological progress that allowed for the mass production of drapery and dry goods, retailers still had to have sufficient
expertise to be on their guard against substandard quality. Stan-
dardization of fabric had not yet reached high levels and, as Dorothy Davis points out, 'every consignment had to be expertly
inspected, valued and priced, both for buying and for selling again
in the shop.' Timothy Eaton, for example, professed himself surprised and delighted by the fact that two British suppliers had
dispatched such high quality goods to a small Canadian retailer.[29]

In the past, many staples were in no way subject to the vagaries
of fashion and maintained their value for several years. With the
general rise in the standard of living the old dependence on function
and practicality would gradually be replaced by a desire for fashionable merchandise. In order to achieve the goal of rapid stock turnover, goods were therefore purchased with an eye to the need to
balance 'nice goods' with those staples still in demand in most
Toronto homes.

Since the success or failure of a new Toronto merchant depended
upon the custom of social strangers and casual passing traffic,
Timothy Eaton tried to catch their attention by other means besides
the concepts of cash and fixed prices. He followed the common
practice of 'door dressing,' placing in front of the store or in
the doorway, articles of merchandise suitably priced to catch the
attention of passers-by. This method was less time-consuming than
the twice- or thrice-weekly formal dressing of windows. In addition, goods were advertised in such a way as to catch the eye of the
bargain hunter. On one occasion a huge sign drew attention to the
sale of '400 yards of cotton for 5 cents.' This naturally referred to
spool cotton or thread, but it was successful in drawing many
customers who were under the impression that the store was holding an exceptional sale on fabrics.[30]

A determined effort was made to dispose of the original stock
purchased from Jennings and Brandon by holding what amounted
to an almost continuous sale. From December 1869 to February
1870 advertisements appeared in the *Globe* several times a week.

Trade appears to have been reasonably brisk, as one advertisement also carried the statement, 'A respectable youth wanted.'[31] Advertising through occasional announcements in the daily papers and in the form of hand-delivered flyers was aimed primarily at those Torontonians in receipt of a weekly wage. As Timothy Eaton commented: 'As to our Sales we dont seem to have any Rush it seems to keep to steady all the time. Our customers seem to get their pay every week and spend as they get the next.'[32] The head clerk at the store at the time remembered that exact instructions were given as to the monthly distribution of 40,000 handbills, and these were always delivered to the working-class areas of Toronto. One employee later recalled that prior to the 1880s it was an unusual sight to see a carriage at the door of the store, and that the first one was beheld with a wonder not soon to be forgotten.[33]

By making a close study of daily sales and carefully observing customer demands and preferences, Timothy Eaton 'gradually formed his own ideas' and so conducted his 'business that this knowledge was turned to good value.' As Hugh Robb noted:

I have seen Mr. Eaton standing at the end of a counter watching a customer purchase a pair of stockings. When she had gone he would ask the girl whether the goods would go any more rapidly if he offered in groups of two or three pairs at a price reduced in the bulk – as, three pairs for 25 cent stockings at 60 cents. The plan was no sooner conceived, and approved by the selling end of the staff, than it was applied.[34]

In the early days the store carried the usual lines of dry goods, primarily yard goods for both personal use (such as silks, heavy cottons, and wool broadcloth) and domestic furnishings (bed and table linen, lace curtains, blankets and towelling). These were complemented by a variety of gloves and hosiery (the choice of colours for the latter in the early days being limited to black and white), woollen undershirts, fancy goods such as laces, ribbons, handkerchiefs, trimmings, and notions, and that ubiquitous garment necessary for all Victorian females beyond the age of puberty, the corset. One counter or more would have been set aside for mourning goods – widows accompanied by their whole household went into deep black for two years, and this included children down to the smallest babies.

Until the general introduction of sewing machines in the 1850s, every seam of a garment, whether made at home or professionally by a tailor or a dressmaker, was stitched by hand. With the gradual decline of the crinoline and hoop skirt, mantles and capes began to return to the fashion scene. These were among the first ready-made garments sold for women in the Eaton store. While the inventory of the 'Gentlemen's Furnishing' department included most smaller articles of male clothing from shirts and undershirts to ties, scarves, and kid gloves, it did not encompass the wide variety carried by the women's departments. Of the ten departments listed on one store flyer in 1877, only one offered men's goods for sale. It was taken for granted that women – or 'the ladies' as Timothy Eaton called them – comprised the largest proportion of the shopping public, for few women worked after marriage. Eaton's efforts, therefore, were directed almost totally to women's needs and desires.

By 1874 the increase in business called for an expansion of store space, and some time in the winter of 1874–5 a two-storey extension was built on at the back of the premises. The upper storeys of 178 Yonge Street were then utilized as showrooms for mantles and carpets and as a mantle workroom. With the addition of the millinery department in 1877, the entire second floor was taken over as selling space, and the workrooms were relocated to the third floor.

A flyer distributed in the fall of 1877 gives some indication of the changes to come in the small dry goods store. Merchandise was classified under ten separate headings – Mourning Department, Housekeeping Department, etc. Timothy Eaton, imitating many wholesalers in separating specific goods into different categories, merely refined the system used at St Marys of subdividing merchandise into the three categories of dry goods, hardware, and groceries. Given the size of the store, it seems likely that such departmentalization amounted to little more than providing separate counters and tables for some items. It does suggest, however, a degree of specialization that was probably necessary to compete with the emerging specialty stores.

Timothy Eaton carried specialization one step further, for merchandise was also broken down into separate categories from an accounting, or at least a stocktaking, point of view. In 1875 stock was divided into four separate groups – haberdashery, $10,135.63; mantles, etc., $7,243.44; dress department, $6,093.17, and staples, $4,817.45 – amounting to a total of $28,289.69. Some items, such as carpets, appeared only once in this period, suggesting perhaps that an odd lot had been purchased to test market demand. Boots and shoes were also added briefly to the stock carried in 1877. Gradually subdividing the earlier four categories, by 1880 year-end stock was listed as follows:

Domestics	*$16,011.57*
Men's Wear	*2,130.79*
Dress	*16,225.20*
Buttons	*4,998.67*
Hosiery	*2,372.24*
Gloves	*3,980.49*
Ribbons & Jewellery	*4,134.97*
Mantles & Millinery	*3,934.74*
	$53,788.67[35]

Despite the substantial increase in both sales and stock figures, the Eaton store continued to carry only those lines traditionally handled by a dry goods merchant.

Like many of his colleagues, Timothy Eaton occasionally exaggerated his trading capabilities. One such example is an 1870 advertisement stating: 'We import goods from Britain and foreign markets ... having every facility for buying cheap and getting the newest makes of goods as we buy direct from the manufacturers for cash.'[36] In fact by far the largest percentage of his stock was supplied in the first five or six years by John Macdonald on long-term credit, usually four months. This main supply was supplemented by bargain and auction lots from other Toronto wholesalers. Timothy once wrote to James, for example, that 'the goods to be sold at auction you will see description in The Mail and Globe. I propose having a lot today and tomorrow If I get them cheap.'[37] By 1873 his list of creditors included numerous Toronto wholesalers, but the amounts owing in many cases were very small and totalled only $3,000. By contrast, goods purchased from Macdonald amounted to $80,000.[38]

True to character, Timothy Eaton set plans in motion as early as May 1870 to arrange for a less expensive source of supply, for he had no intention of allowing this state of affairs to continue indefinitely. As he reasoned to James:

Suppose you Bought 7,000 Dol in England Could you pay for in 6 mos from date of Invoice. If you could shape your Business to do this it is quite as easy to buy in England as in Montreal. There are advantages buying at home that you know nothing of ... their 65 a/c is a mere sham – a pretence – there are trade lists & things of this kind which the wholesale keeps to themselves.[39]

Considering different supply arrangements worthy of investigation, Timothy Eaton sailed to England some time in the early part of July or August 1870, months that were customarily slow in the dry goods trade. A one-way ticket to Liverpool by Cunard steamship cost $14.00 and, provided the business could be left in safe hands for a period of time (on this occasion Timothy's nephew George Young Eaton sat in for his uncle while he was away), this investment could prove to be a lucrative one.[40] There is no way of knowing how much merchandise, if any, was purchased on this trip, but visits to Great Britain by either Timothy Eaton or one of his salesmen became an annual and sometimes semi-annual occurrence. James Holbrook, a close associate who boarded with the Eaton family for a short time, first travelled to England on store business in July 1871, where he appears to have exercised considerable initiative. 'Mr. Holbrook purchase jutted up to over $22,000, it was a little too much but I think it will be all right.' With sales for the six-month period from December 1870 to May 1871 'just Double what they were same months last spring' ($19,551.00 as opposed to $9,859.47), Timothy Eaton could undoubtedly afford to adopt a more optimistic attitude.[41] By January 1872 he reported: 'I am not extra anxious as I bought in England last Summer a lot of goods for Spring which will pay the 6 mos interest.' Purchases during 1871 exceeded over-the-counter sales by more than $12,000.00, but as Timothy Eaton noted to James, 'I expect to be even by 29 February.'[42]

Little can be discovered about the source of this merchandise, but in all likelihood the bulk was purchased from wholesalers or commission agents, either Canadian or British. John Macdonald, for example, had an office in Manchester, and perhaps this offered greater choice than his Toronto headquarters. Timothy Eaton's primary interest was on the savings that could be made on such goods. This in combination with his practice of reducing old stock before new merchandise was received and unpacked – 'Our stock is getting reduced down pretty low. I want it down 5 or 6,000 before the new goods come in'[43] – eventually provided the necessary basis for a more efficient cash flow.

A word should perhaps be added here with regard to the possible margin of profit expected by retailers. Timothy Eaton in a letter to James in May 1870 expressed the hope that 'The profits are in proportion to sales thus 7,000>25% – $1,750,'[44] which would certainly allow for considerable gain and would suggest that this was the expected profit. One presumes that this was the gross expected and that net profits, once overhead expenses such as rent, wages, heat, and light had been deducted, were somewhat less.

From a study made by David Alexander of gross profit margins in England before 1850, it is evident that for the majority of retail drapery outlets the gross margin of profit was considerably less than 25 per cent, ranging from 2.25 per cent for a small dry goods store in a small country town to 15 per cent and 16 per cent for medium-sized stores in Doncaster and London. Harold Barger has shown that retail margins in the United States gradually rose after mid-century and that by 1869 average margins for dry goods shops were 18.7 per cent. This figure compares favourably with a survey undertaken by the *Dry Goods Review* in the first decade of the twentieth century that found average gross profit margins ranging from 20 per cent to 30 per cent, as most merchants allowed from

7.5 per cent to 12.5 per cent for business and overhead expenses.[45] Timothy Eaton himself acknowledged that in 1873 his profits were in the region of $6,000.00 when the annual sales to year end 28 February 1874 had totalled $54,990.33. One assumes that he was referring to net profit here, since it results in a margin of about 11 per cent.[46]

Despite the fact that retail prices on merchandise continued to drop throughout the century as technological progress and productivity reduced manufacturers' expenses, competition remained brisk. The constant high rate of bankruptcies throughout the period attests to the continued 'floundering in ignorance' of many retailers at all levels of business. Sidney Pollard contends that many business men used only minimal accounting methods as a means of arriving at financial decisions.[47] For example, in 1870 Robert Simpson was accused of 'culpable carelessness' in the conduct of his business. Large sums of money received on deposit and as loans were never entered into any sort of account book and, as the *Monetary Times* observed, 'There was nothing to show that a balance of cash had ever been struck since March 1868.' But it also remarked that Simpson's books were 'in no worse condition than those of any other retail trader throughout that section of the country.'[48]

Based on his study of the Wedgwood archives, Neil McKendrick insists that innovative entrepreneurs who wished to remain in business were compelled during periods of financial crisis to undertake a full-scale investigation of costs and thereby avoid the fate of competitors who ended their careers in the bankruptcy court. Timothy Eaton was well aware of the dangers posed by possession of unsaleable stock purchased on long credit. His letters to James constantly make reference to 'smash-ups' or 'bust-ups' at both the wholesale and the retail level, suggesting that survival in the industry was far from certain.[49]

Considerable care therefore had to be exercised not only to ensure survival, but to guarantee that survival was accompanied by remunerative profits. To this end, despite statements to the contrary, Timothy Eaton was at all times fully aware of the financial state of his own affairs. Evidence in his notebook amply contradicts the statement made to James: 'I am not such an accurate bookeeper as you are – and when I want figures I am obliged to hunt them up ... I sometimes fear I shall be obliged to procure a bookeeper which I shrink from as long as I can ... I can get Through a lot of work in my own way – If reduced to a system – would take 2 men to follow it up.'[50]

At least until the early 1880s he personally looked after much of the bookkeeping and accounting side of the business, 'knowing as I do the multidenous little matters which go astray in the absence of The Head.' By 1877 his nephew Herby (W.H. Eaton) was employed full time in the office, but as Timothy pointed out to James: 'I am gradually letting The details rest on Herby – which as yet gives me a lot of trouble to watch & see he forgets nothing.'[51]

While his earlier statement to James may reflect his concern for financial privacy, Timothy Eaton's personal notebook contained full monthly sales figures for this period as well as information relating to stock, interest owing, and outstanding debts. This continuing concern with interest payments is but one indication of his desire to maintain his business on a sound footing. The ability to purchase merchandise at the lowest possible prices was also important. In Timothy Eaton's view a greater measure of success could be achieved by first contacting the best houses in England and then attaining a real degree of independence from the Canadian wholesalers. Writing to his brother James in the early summer of 1874, he set out his plans for the future:

I purpose to send an order to a few of the best houses I know and make a strike for liberty next summer ... perhaps you will be ready to accompany me & hold up my hand. My trade is now good for $4,000 to $5,000 per month cash eny day. I think I can step out quietly in another year If I am lucky ... McMaster has just called – we had a long chat – I think either you or I can buy goods quite as well as he can thro old man in London ... I think will be able to profit by some of his remarks at a future day.[52]

That it had long been his intention to try to bypass the Canadian wholesalers is evident from the comment made in 1871 that 'the privilege of the British Market is all I care for.' Never slow to take the plunge once the decision had been made, he divulged that:

I made my first step out this Summer. I ordered a case of Black Lustres from Bradford – from one of my old creditors – the invoice came in about 4 weeks and the goods one week Later a Splendid Value they never said a word, no more than If I had been buying from them regular. Of course I paid them up in full and had an offer from them that they desired to continue to sell to me as before.[53]

This 'first step out' is an indication that the purchase was made as an individual rather than through the auspices of a middleman, such as Macdonald. It was obviously a step Timothy Eaton had tried before, perhaps in St Marys. It should also be noted that by paying in full he gained financial credibility with an important British supplier, while holding Macdonald's accounts to full term, in much the same way that he had used Adam Hope to serve a similar purpose in St Marys. This habit would be put to further use as sales volume spiralled. Indeed Hugh Robb later asserted that,

Having secured a footing, Mr. Eaton was a large patron of the New York wholesale market. Case after case came through in bond, and the strange thing about it was that mention of his name was seldom heard among the New York shippers. He was known as 'Cash.' When asked why he did not use his proper name, he would reply 'You need not worry about my name, so long as I pay you cash.' In that way, he established a reputation not only in New York, but on the other side of the Atlantic as well.[54]

With the impetus of increased sales and the headway achieved regarding alternative sources of supply, Timothy Eaton gradually reduced his earlier dependence on Canadian wholesalers. By 1873 interest payments on the Macdonald account had decreased dramatically and by 1875 were almost non-existent. By the mid-1870s the improvement in Timothy Eaton's financial standing was bolstered by the addition of bank accommodation for short-term credit allowing even further flexibility in the purchase of merchandise. By 1878 amounts in pounds sterling began to appear in his notebook, although references had been made to British suppliers several years before this date, the names of Rylands and Sons, Stewart and MacDonald, and Leaf Sons appearing most frequently.[55] Timothy Eaton had apparently chosen suppliers with an eye to long-term gain, for both Rylands and Stewart and MacDonald were involved in manufacturing much of the merchandise sold in their wholesale houses.

It becomes obvious from later correspondence that the references to making a 'step-out' and 'going alone' and making 'a strike for liberty' related not merely to his intention of freeing himself from specific wholesalers, but to a long-held ambition to do what others had done and, by establishing himself as a wholesaler, make a bid for greater success. In a letter dated 1 July 1874, he stated:

Referring to my remarks in my last – I have been thinking over whether I ought to mention my intention to McD[onald] or waite until I am ready how much is St. Marys indebted to you now is the revenue you draw from it enough to induce you to hold on or are you trying to get out this winter ... I have set about reducing my stock and buying sparingly in the future not stintedly but buying often & small quantities. What effect would you think it would have on J. McD If I told him J. & T.E. was going to open a little whole sale place on Front Street. I have thought I ought to (like ask) [sic] his opinion. We have talked together so frequently again. I have held in least he might try to prevent me.

Timothy Eaton was obviously not prepared to jeopardize his present fruitful relationship, fully aware that A.G. Samson, Warring Kennedy, and Alexander Gemmel (although in a somewhat closer relationship, as employees of Macdonald) had, as he put it, 'split on that same rock.'[56] Although willing to make snap decisions when circumstances dictated, he never lost sight of his long-term goals. With this in mind he recognized, as he probably had not in 1868, that it was necessary first to initiate a solid working relationship with suppliers – either wholesalers, commission agents, or manufacturers – in Great Britain and Europe. By 1875 Timothy Eaton was receiving 'a case from Rylands every 2 or 3 weeks' along with regular packages from Stewart and MacDonald in Glasgow, a supplier in Manchester, '& 2 case of Black from R.T. & Co.' which, he commented, 'looks like importing on a small scale.' Indeed, he reported to James that they even seemed 'to be willing to credit us now – every mail brings circular or samples.' He therefore urged his brother to 'go to see old Ireland and ... your creditors in London, Glasgow, Bradford, Manchester, Leeds, Nottingham, etc.,'[57] a further indication that either one or both brothers were placing extensive orders with suppliers in Great Britain.

Although operating individual enterprises, the two Eaton brothers still drew strength from each other's reputation. In reporting an extension of credit from a Leicester supplier, Timothy Eaton remarked: 'Rainom T. & Co. (Leicester) has arrived   they also sent a great bunch of samples – nice goods. I sent them an order for a case to keep them in for Spring. The sample pss are magnificent. I think equally goods as they send you – therefore a good name or a good Brother's name must be a good thing. I sent for sample pss to see would they send them which they not only did but did it well.'[58] Orders from overseas suppliers initially only supplemented merchandise procured from Macdonald, but by 1877 had risen to quite large quantities. One letter refers to eighty-five packages of American goods and seventy-five imported from Great Britain, along with a lot of goods still on the way. While it is of course possible that some of this material had been ordered through Toronto wholesalers, evidence suggests that this was not the case. The amount owing to Macdonald by year end 1 March 1877, for example, totalled only $15,186.00, while sales figures for 1876 amounted to $78,105.09.[59]

Despite Timothy Eaton's stated intentions in 1874, his plans to establish a wholesale and importing house were held in abeyance, and some years were to pass before its actual inception. Several factors can be cited for this delay, but it is evident that he had no intention of embarking upon such a project until his own financial situation allowed for a successful outcome. Although the depression of the 1870s appears to have had little effect on the overall growth of the business (see Table 7), a letter to James in June 1875 bears witness to some financial problems: 'Draft for $432.53 ... just came in time ... not wanting to ask any more favours of the Bank for a bit.' Again in 1878 Timothy Eaton complained of being 'a heap scarcer of money,' having recently purchased a new house on Orde Street for his growing family. However, he seemed at all times to have maintained a cheerful attitude, counselling James on one occasion to 'plough deep while Sluggards sleep & you will have Corn to sell and to keep – These old puns are wonderfully true when you look at them.'[60]

The number of dry goods stores in Toronto remained high for much of the 1870s and 1880s. Indeed, when Robert Simpson opened his store at 184 Yonge Street, just a stone's throw from the Eaton store, in the fall of 1872, there were no fewer than thirteen other dry goods stores on Yonge Street in the four blocks between Adelaide and Albert streets, as well as nineteen more north and south of this area. These were supplemented by specialty outlets retailing merchandise ranging from ribbons, laces, baby clothes, and hoop skirts to men's haberdashery. Simpson's store resembled most of the others, measuring slightly more than twenty-two feet in frontage and only forty-five feet in depth and employing a staff of three. Much has been made of the competition between Timothy Eaton and Robert Simpson, but in all likelihood this amounted in the 1870s to little more than regular surveillance by respective salesmen of the goods and prices offered by competitors. One employee recalled, for example, that the price cards on printed goods would announce the relative attacks of each combatant and that 'door dressing' was the battlefield. These sometimes reached unheard-of cuts, but he claimed that Timothy Eaton always managed to go one better.[61] Such contests were probably a regular part of retail life, occupying the attention of most dry goods merchants.

Competition did not prevent real growth, and sales figures indicate that business was advancing at a fairly rapid rate (see Table 8). The small temporary decline from April 1875 to March 1876 reflects the very real tightness experienced by Toronto markets during 1875. Reports in the *Monetary Times* indicate that this monetary stringency affected all market sectors, causing both buyers and sellers of all manufactured and imported goods to exercise extreme caution.[62] Average monthly sales in 1870 totalled $2,117.97, but by 1875 these had increased to $5,350.38 and by 1880 to $12,914.84, resulting in annual totals of $25,415.66, $64,204.59, and $154,978.19, respectively. These figures demonstrate the extent to which the store had increased its number of daily customers, for as late as 1877 Timothy Eaton complained that the average sale per customer was less than one dollar, and that it took 'a lot of Customers These days to make a pile of money.'[63]

While his declaration (or at least the evaluation made to or by the city's assessors) with regard to personal property for this whole period ranged between $2,000 and $4,000, his own bookkeeping entries with regard to his evaluations of stock-on-hand show much higher figures. The personalty tax enacted on personal property by the Province of Ontario in the 1850s was a constant source of irritation for city merchants, as periods of economic depression and recession led to unusually inflated inventories, the holdings of which were taxable, at a time when merchants could ill afford the extra expense. To get around this problem, merchants either greatly underestimated their inventories for assessment purposes or else claimed the exemptions allowed on debts under the by-law. The former is certainly what Timothy Eaton appears to have done, for his stock-on-hand at year end ranged from $39,633.82 in 1872, to $28,289.69 in 1875, and $53,788.67 in 1880.[64] The drop in 1875 perhaps reflected the temporary decline in sales growth, the decision to seek the bulk of store merchandise directly from overseas agents, and possibly the tightness of funds mentioned earlier.

Despite the obvious rise in both stock and sales figures, Timothy Eaton does not seem to have considered it necessary to advertise this fact. The subject of the future of the Eaton store was, therefore, a matter for constant conjecture, both by the mercantile agency and by Timothy Eaton's own competitors. Although interested in the ratings given to James and himself, Timothy Eaton constantly refused to co-operate with Dun and Wiman's agents. Writing to his brother he reported:

I called on the Manager the other day and asked him if he thought it advanced the interests of his institution to report such nonsense,

*he replyed by saying as I would not give them any information they
had to report what was told them. You can see the force of story
he is very anxious I should give a correct report. I told him all the
other was correct – his reporting me with $2,000 was true my
profits in one year was over $6,000 ... I will give him more news
when I get ready.*[65]

His refusal to supply the Dun and Wiman agents with the information that would have enabled them to arrive at an accurate
rating was responsible for their negative evaluations of his business.
His ranking was extremely low – H3 – with his pecuniary strength
estimated at $2,000 to $5,000. This relegated him to the level of
only a fair credit risk. James Eaton, on the other hand, was considered a good risk and ranked F2$^{1}/_{2}$ – with an estimated worth of
$10,000 to $25,000. In July and November 1874, the agency
reported that Timothy Eaton 'was undoubtedly in Jno MacDonald
& Cos. hands though buying outside at times. "E" is a striving
active man, watches his bus. well & must turn over consigned stuff
in the year ... in the absence of anything definite, we can't recom'd
strongly for outside a/cs.'[66]

Needless to say Timothy Eaton fully agreed with John Macdonald in adjudging the credit agency's information 'not worth a snap,'
especially since in the winter of 1871–2 it had reported him close
to failure and had, as Macdonald put it, 'marked men good who
had not stood $^{1}/_{2}$ as well.' Convinced 'that every man [knew] his
own business best' and that keeping up 'with the times' was the
surest guarantee of success,[67] Timothy Eaton paid little attention
to such evaluations.

In maintaining this attitude his stance was wholly Victorian.
Sales flyers with somewhat misleading allusions to forced sales
only added to the confusion. The extraordinary sale advertised in
January 1878 when $50,000 worth was to be sold for about
$35,000 was obviously an attention-getting device: 'At Retail in
quantities to suit purchasers preferring to distribute among their
thousands of customers rather than let the Sheriff lay his fingers
upon them ... Ruinous as the above prices are, they prefer them to
letting the Sheriff touch them.' References to the sheriff's fingers

seem somewhat overstated when sales for 1877 totalled $112,657.00, up from $78,105.29 in 1876.[68]

The extent of his success undoubtedly afforded Timothy Eaton a certain measure of freedom. Since he continued to receive a constant supply of merchandise for the store, the rather negative tone of the agency's reports does not appear to have damaged his reputation with those suppliers he considered important. By 1876 the credit agency's evaluation regarding his dependence on John Macdonald was totally inaccurate, for he was in fact making heavy purchases elsewhere and by all accounts with a very large degree of financial credibility. By adopting the practice of meeting overseas liabilities promptly, he ensured that his financial rating with the suppliers who counted was maintained at a very high level. The comment made by one manufacturer that there were only seven houses in the United States and Canada that would pay promptly and Eaton's was one of these[69] proved that this tactic was effective. This is not to suggest that Timothy Eaton did not take advantage of any credit terms that might be offered. Discounts and interest charges continued to be regarded with great care. But his promptness in meeting some financial arrangements combined with the increasing size of the Eaton orders ultimately attracted suppliers on both sides of the Atlantic.

As owner-operator, Timothy Eaton continued to be closely involved with all aspects of the daily life of the store, remarking to James on more than one occasion, 'I have started to write you this time some 3 or 4 times & was called off.' By the late 1870s the crush of business was such that Timothy received complaints about poor service. On occasion emergencies at home took precedence over the affairs of commerce. The birth of a son in the summer of 1873 compelled Timothy to be, as he put it: 'Off Buss a little for the past 3 weeks – as usual the Girl we had ever since last fall left us the week before Baby was born & I have been changing Girls ever since After 5 changes we have got a Boss one now which just pleases me.'[70] This was important, as Timothy Eaton planned to sail for Great Britain the following week, and Mrs Eaton had only slowly recovered from the birth of Timothy Wilson some three weeks earlier.

With the birth of this baby, the third born to Timothy and Maggie Eaton in Toronto, they probably shared a common hope that their personal lives would not be marked by further tragedy. Their daughter Kathleen Herbison, born 10 September 1869, had died in August 1870, and her death was followed less than two years later in June 1872 by a stillbirth. As members of large extended families, both Timothy and Maggie could call on close relatives for support on such occasions. Timothy certainly made use of family connections, and from time to time several of his young nephews were employed as special assistants to their uncle. This does not always seem to have been a wholly satisfactory arrangement, probably because the store at this time was not very large. Placed in charge during their uncle's absence on buying trips, the nephews found it difficult to resume a lower ranking in the store on his return. Writing of his nephew Herby, Timothy Eaton on one occasion informed James that 'for the past 6 mos he has been selling – 3 mos in staples & 3 mos now in the Dress Dept. His being Bookkeeper first Then Boss after – now small boy makes his position very awkward & will be vy difficult for him to get his head up in the house ... When he was Boss, he used all the powers & more of his position and now he is being paid back in his own coin – You know how this is.'[71] One can begin to perceive the first allusions to the problems that would arise as the number of personnel within the Eaton store increased. Herby Eaton, writing to James in 1877 during one of Timothy's absences, complained: 'I looked around and saw them all idle. I thought if all the time would be like that it would not do very well.'[72]

By 1875 there were nineteen sales clerks and other workers in the actual store and six seamstresses in the mantle workroom. By 1881 these figures had risen to thirty-six and twelve respectively. Since the assessment rolls for the late 1870s list only four or five male clerks, it can be assumed that the majority of the staff were either adolescent youths or girls. As an employer, Timothy Eaton was not against putting women in positions of responsibility, and by the late 1870s a few women began to fill supervisory positions in some merchandise classifications. However, he later stated that while girls 'take hold more rapidly at first than boys,' the latter 'exert themselves more and aim at being something and rise higher.'[73]

The entrance of women into the dry goods business coincided in large part with the growth and expansion of retail outlets. The introduction of price ticketing and cash sales removed the need for a staff of skilled personnel and allowed dry goods stores to offer employment to unskilled young girls. Since women's wages were traditionally only half those paid to men, their employment represented a distinct economic gain to the shopkeepers, a factor of great importance in an era of severe competition.

The organized apprenticeship system, a practice continued in Great Britain beyond the turn of the century, was seldom resorted to in the retail dry goods trade of North America. Furthermore, the majority of North American store employees, unlike their counterparts elsewhere, were not compelled to 'live in'. This practice was a source of considerable contention in Great Britain, since employers frequently reduced overhead costs by housing their personnel in crowded, unhealthy quarters.

Little definite information exists regarding the wages paid by Timothy Eaton in the 1870s. What there is suggests that these ranged from $2.50 to $4.00 a week for beginners, rising to $6.00 to $12.00 for senior staff. Most young adolescents of both sexes began as cash girls or boys at $1.50 to $2.00 per week. It was their duty to scurry between sales counter, cashier, and parcel desk with sales book, money, and purchases. These rates were in line with those received elsewhere in Toronto. Comparative figures for New York for the same period indicate the same spread, with clerks at Macy's in the early 1870s averaging from $4.44 to $5.28 per week.[74]

'Spiffs' or bonuses supplemented the wages of those who were able to dispose of slow-moving merchandise, and these could on occasion increase an employee's wages by ten dollars a month. Timothy Eaton does not appear to have followed the custom of fining employees for either major or minor misdemeanours. This practice, common in many British and American dry goods stores, was imposed for such misconduct as cutting material so as to leave an unsaleable length or allowing a customer to leave without purchasing, even when the store did not have what the customer wanted.

Timothy Eaton's relationship with his employees followed the norm for the period, but unlike many of his contemporaries he welcomed and encouraged displays of initiative or individual endeavour. By allowing his employees a certain measure of freedom in the execution of their duties, he benefited from the introduction of new ideas that increased efficiency and productivity. The employee who instituted a more efficient method of taking stock in 1875 later recalled that Timothy Eaton's only concern was that the task had been accomplished; little attention was paid to its method of execution. The same employee also introduced the concept of invoice transfers, a method that allowed salesmen to remain in their own area rather than follow a customer through the entire store. With the implementation of the transfer system, it was then possible to keep a much closer eye on departmental sales, in a sense allowing each department to operate as a separate business. Both systems, initiated while Timothy Eaton was on a buying trip overseas, met with his complete approval upon his return. Indeed, he demonstrated his appreciation by presenting enterprising employees with cash bonuses. One salesman recalled the astonishment he felt on being presented with $150. As he explained: 'It meant something to me, and I know at that time, it meant something to him, but it showed that he appreciated a man's best effort.'[75]

Initially Timothy Eaton took responsibility for most of the buying and, as one employee put it, the 'bossing.' With the expansion of the store and its stock of goods, he gradually realized that his sales clerks were more familiar with consumer preferences and, by the end of the 1870s, allowed some senior employees to do much of their own departmental purchasing.

Working on the old-country adage that 'a job worth doing is worth doing well,' Timothy Eaton asked that his employees demonstrate the same interest in their work that he himself displayed. By following such a practice they would not only adhere to his convinced belief in the biblical injunction 'What thy hand findeth to do, do it with all thy might,' but would also ensure their own individual success.[76] In one sense a dilution of the Social Darwinist belief that ruthless competition was necessary for both progress and survival, this philosophy also accepted the concept promoted by Samuel Smiles that success was available to all who followed the biblical parable of the five talents. Older loyalties also had their place in his philosophy, however: one employee, William Elder, recalled that he had been hired because his mother had known Timothy at Portglenone. Hired by Timothy in January 1875 at the age of fourteen to drive the first delivery wagon, William Elder was also responsible for looking after the horse and equipage kept in the barn behind the store.[77]

Timothy Eaton, acknowledged by his contemporaries as a considerate employer, was a prompt and active supporter of the Early Closing Movement. In the mid-nineteenth century, retail stores maintained inordinately long business hours, from eight in the morning until nine or ten o'clock at night with Sunday the only free day of the week. Many employees, as a result of extreme fatigue and in some cases failing health, had no energy to attend to the proper observation of the Sabbath. For Timothy Eaton, a regular member of Elm Street Methodist Church, this was a grave failing. He took the words of the Ten Commandments and the four Gospels and the teachings of St Paul as a doctrine by which to live and was constantly on guard against tempting a brother to stumble. In this matter he held fast to the tradition of the old Irish puritans who believed that the sabbath day was holy and should be devoted to worship.[78]

The movement to shorten shop hours, begun in England in the 1840s, was part of a general movement limiting the hours of work for women and children and was also associated with the moral movement that sought the abolition of slavery and the enlightenment and education of the downtrodden of the world. Supporters drew attention to the complete lack of opportunity available to shop assistants not only for healthful recreation but also for personal educational activities. It was also suggested that exclusion 'from participation in that rapid diffusion of knowledge' that characterized the industrial era would produce a body of men 'unfit to mix with their equals in society.' Medical practitioners and linen drapers lent their weight to a movement that would allow 'a generally energetic and intelligent class' the same opportunities as those available to mechanics and labourers.[79]

The Early Closing Association, established in Toronto in 1853, met with limited success. Although it was widely recognized that long working hours and minimal recreational time could and did cut into regular church attendance, the several campaigns organized throughout the next two decades failed repeatedly to bring about an effective level of unanimity amongst the merchants of Toronto. Organized by merchants on both Yonge and King streets and by the Toronto Young Men's Early Closing Association, these campaigns were probably influenced by the ten-hour movement that was then making some headway in the city. In 1868 support was sufficiently strong that a public meeting in St Lawrence Hall was attended by the mayor, leading clergymen, and prominent citizens.[80] At Timothy's urging, a Methodist minister, the Reverend Dr Potts, preached a sermon advocating support for the Early Closing Movement – the text for the sermon being 'Blessed are the merciful, for they shall obtain mercy.'

Competition was the primary cause for the lack of co-operation among Toronto merchants. Many who initially signed agreements withdrew once it was realized that the movement lacked real meaning. Many of the smaller tradesmen, dependent on small turnovers, refused to co-operate. One young employee of a Toronto dry goods store claimed that one of his duties was to hang around the corner of Yonge and Queen streets until 9:15 p.m. every night and report to his employer if Eaton's admitted any customers after nine o'clock. The answer was always in the negative.[81]

It seems likely that the influx of women into the trade prompted greater concern and interest in the matter. One saleslady, in a letter to the Globe in May 1876, drew attention to the hardship suffered by standing from eight in the morning until late at night: 'As long as the ladies postpone their shopping until the evening, so long will the shops remain open. Our only hope depends on the ladies. If they would kindly take our case in hand, we should soon find that the merchants would not only be willing but be glad for their own sakes to close at a reasonable hour.'[82] Failing to achieve any unanimity over weekday closing hours, the movement's efforts were directed in the 1870s towards reducing business hours on Saturdays. At this time many stores, anxious to gain the custom of workers who were paid at the end of the week, remained open until ten, eleven, or even midnight on Saturdays. But with shopping fast becoming the preserve of the 'ladies' and the fact that most female workers left the work-force upon marriage, the question arose of whether it was really necessary for any dry goods store to remain open beyond early evening. Timothy Eaton had himself discovered that little was gained by remaining open late on Saturday evenings. He later confided to an employee that he got tired of people coming into the store in droves and not buying anything, doing nothing but pushing and shoving around the shop all night.[83]

In 1876, without waiting for official agreement from his fellow merchants, Timothy Eaton decided to close his store at seven o'clock on Saturday evenings; in 1877 this was changed to six o'clock. He was joined in this endeavour by only two other Toronto merchants, one of whom was Robert Simpson.[84]

Despite the rapid growth achieved during the first ten years in Toronto, it is apparent that demand had not yet reached the levels demonstrated in larger centres. Lyman Bloomingdale, who had opened his first store in New York in April 1872, had average monthly sales of close to $3,000 in his first year of operation. By 1877 his annual sales totalled $184,184, a figure not reached by Timothy Eaton until his eleventh year of business. Rowland Macy, who had commenced business in 1858, by 1870 had annual sales totalling well over $1 million.[85]

Nevertheless one would expect that Timothy Eaton's sales would have presented a more favourable picture than those of his brother James in London, Ontario. This does not seem to have been the case and may have been responsible for his complaints when he first started out in Toronto. Furthermore, James appeared to have a greater degree of flexibility where cash flow was concerned, and occasionally Timothy made use of this as a source of short-term financial accommodation. In 1877 he informed James that 'We have drawn on you yesterday for $300 @ 15 d/s.'[86]

Scattered references also indicate that Timothy Eaton achieved further savings by purchasing in bulk for the three family outlets –

his own, James's in London, and his nephew G.Y. Eaton's at St Marys. Merchandise was then traded between the stores, as with the seven cases of goods that Timothy berated James for taking in 1870. In a later comment, Timothy noted: 'I bought very little from him [G.Y. Eaton] this season, only 2,000 doll(ar)s ... I sent them 5 or 6 shawls nice ones cheap to sell for me or return.' By 1880 both Timothy and James Eaton had advanced a long way from the early beginnings in Kirkton. As Timothy stated, 'I was just musing about the time we used [to] buy over $2,000 from A. Hope & Co., and that you remember he then thought [that] was a big lick.'[87]

The end of the 1870s confronted both Timothy and James Eaton with the question of expansion. Both had achieved success in business, even though their personal lives had been touched with sadness. James Eaton had suffered the loss of his wife in 1877, leaving him with two small children to raise alone. Four children were born to Timothy and Maggie Eaton in their first seven years in Toronto, but of these only two survived: William Fletcher, born 12 May 1874, and John Craig born 28 April 1876. The deaths of Kathleen Herbison, on 13 August 1870 at the age of eleven months, and of Timothy Wilson, on 14 May 1874 at the age of ten months, brought great sadness to the family, but both Timothy and Maggie accepted the will of God and drew comfort from their belief in divine providence:

I have had an anxious and busy week quite different from last – we have had a birth on Tuesday morning as you already know. A suit at the County Court on a promisory note on Thursday as you would see in the Mail – the jury gave us a unainious [sic] Verdict – $400 Saved. After getting home at night Our little Timothy W. fell asleep in Jesus – after 3 days suffering with Cold Bronkitis took him off. We propose to bury him this p.m. at 3 o'c ... the Dr. recommended to keep the house quiet as possible – the cloud seems to hang heavily – We are endeavouring to trust in God. Ma & baby is well ...[88]

Timothy Eaton held to the conviction stated in a letter to James that hard times brought men nearer to God.[89] For Timothy Eaton,

God, through the saving grace of Jesus Christ, was a very real presence. While most of his letters to James are concerned with business and are thus somewhat brief and to the point, the few dealing with his other passion, his religion, are interesting for both their length and their detail, and convey more fully his feelings on this subject:

We are having a wonderful time this week in Shaftesbury Hall and indeed all through the Churches ... Mr. Varley ... talks about Jesus as plain & simple as ever you heard ... after an explanation of the night in Egypt when the Door posts & Lintels were sprinkled with the blood – he drew the picture of the safety of the children of Israel when the door was shut and the promise of the angle [sic] When I (the angle) see the blood *I will pass over – did the Lord keep his word – were they all safe ... he took a chair during his description sometimes sitting then rising up – his appeal to the people – are you inside – are you trusting – have you obeyed – are you believing – are you enjoying this feast with me.*

I am really afraid to make any attempt to describe his expressions – I can think on them I can feast on them *but when I attempt to describe them language fails ... he speaks plain he wishes to be understood it is not his Word but Jesus then he will sit down and read such a portion ... Jesus has said I will never leave you – right here with his finger on the verse – I will never leave you – does that mean* me – *does it mean* you *who does it mean – Doubting Christian do you ever feel cast down – has the suggestion ever been made to you to give up – give up what – give up Christ in the heart – give up? no never – Jesus has promised I will never leave you ...*

Timothy Eaton took great pleasure in the work done by such visiting preachers. Their efforts in 'the resurection business ... waking up all the old crochety & stiff dead members, private and official Talkative & mischievious'[90] could perhaps be compared to his own brand of salesmanship, but with a slightly different stock-in-trade.

5

The Move to
190 Yonge Street

'When all is said, the building is merely the shell of the
business.'
Daily News, 4 September 1886

'A tradesman ought to consider and measure well the
extent of his own strength, his stock of money and credit,
is properly his beginning, for credit is a stock as well as
money.'
Daniel Defoe, *The Complete English Tradesman*, 1745

The introduction of John A. Macdonald's National Policy in 1879
led to an expansion and extension of Canadian manufacturing and
ameliorated many of the problems caused by the depression of
the mid-1870s. Cotton mills and hardware, stove, and implement
manufacturers were swamped with orders. This growth gave rise
to an enormous increase in the number of industrial and wage-
earning employees and encouraged the development of a vigorous
trade union movement within the city, aided by those unions that
had been forced to suspend activities during the depression. Despite
the concern expressed by many members of the labour movement
regarding working conditions and rents in urban areas, there was a
general feeling that most employees were better off. The comments
made by a spectator of the Labour Day Parade in Montreal were
probably also true for Toronto. Remarking on the general well-

being of the marchers he noted that 'it looked as if all present not only were in the possession of money to spend but were accustomed to handle it freely.' By the time Toronto celebrated its fiftieth birthday in 1884, the city, according to one writer, was making great strides towards becoming the Chicago of the north. By 1890 the population had more than doubled, rising from 86,415 in 1881 to 181,215 in 1891.[1]

The volume of dry goods arriving at the port of Toronto demonstrated a healthy increase during the first quarter of 1881. Wholesalers reported not only that their efforts to introduce shorter credit terms were meeting with some success but also that an increasing number of buyers were prepared to pay cash.[2] Several merchants, no doubt expecting further growth, felt sufficiently optimistic to embark on large-scale building and expansion programs as the demand for dry goods continued unabated. James Eaton moved from London to Toronto and, in the spring or summer of 1882, opened a gentlemen's furnishings store at 86 Yonge Street. Petley and Petley of the Golden Griffin undertook considerable expansion of their selling space at 128–32 King Street East, while Robert Simpson enlarged and doubled his wholesale premises at 36–8 Colborne Street.[3]

For those merchants looking for larger premises, location was a concern of paramount importance. Both Timothy Eaton and Robert Simpson were pressed for space and needed larger retail premises, but both merchants wished to remain close to the intersection of Yonge and Queen streets in order to continue the connections already acquired. For Timothy Eaton further expansion was limited both by the size of his building and by difficulties arising from external factors. Expansion along Queen Street was rendered impossible by the presence of Knox Presbyterian Church, and the time had not yet arrived for the wholesale removal of churches and congregations to less central urban locations. By 1880 all three floors of the Eaton store at 178 Yonge Street as well as the two-storey extension along Queen Street erected in 1874 had been taken over for display and selling space. Timothy Eaton was forced to admit that 'being confined for room we cannot expect [sales] to increase by much more.'[4] An attempt was made to create an impression of greater size by giving the address on letterheads and in advertisements as 178 Yonge and 1, 3, 5, and 7 Queen streets.

In the winter of 1880–1, enquiries were made with regard to renting the adjacent store at 176 Yonge Street. Whether he and Robert Simpson were in competition for this store is not known, but Timothy was subsequently drawn into court for failing to fulfil the terms of an agreement. Appealing the case he reported to James: 'The house next door you speak of is let from 1st January to Simson The landlord did not feel so big when he found I did not want it, he lost 6 mos. rent @ $100.00 is $600.00 for his greed.' He expressed some relief at not taking the store 'as the two landlords would have been a nuisance.'[5]

Robert Simpson successfully solved his problem of space by relocating his retail business early in 1881, moving to the premises in question at 174–6 Yonge Street. In so doing he effectively blocked Timothy Eaton's expansion southward. Located immediately adjacent to the Eaton store, Simpson not only doubled the extent of his own store, but offered the challenge of size to his next-door neighbour.

Compelled to examine other possibilities, in the spring of 1881 Timothy Eaton leased property in the Rankin Block at 42 Scott Street, where he established a small wholesale business. This new venture (housed in a three-storey brick building with a twenty-seven-foot frontage), like the retail store, operated under the name of T. Eaton and Company and catered primarily to the needs of country merchants. When assessed in September 1882, the business owned only $4,000.00 worth of stock, and no mention was made of employees. By contrast, Samson, Kennedy and Gemmel, located next door, employed seventeen travelling salesmen and carried stock in excess of $40,000.00. Entries in Timothy Eaton's notebook indicate, however, that his actual stock at year end 1882 amounted to $38,382.56. By the following year this had risen to $41,145.00.[6]

The T. Eaton wholesale operation followed the traditional practice of wholesalers and allowed goods on credit. By year end 1882 book accounts totalled $7,951.68, and this figure rose to $13,900.00 for year end 1883.[7] Despite Timothy Eaton's remark to James on 6 October 1881, that 'Scott Street is creeping on nicely in a quiet way and dont interfere a single bit with our regular trade,' this long-anticipated move into wholesaling does not appear to have achieved any great degree of success. This was due in large measure to external economic circumstances.

The mild winters of 1879–80 and 1880 had caused a severe decline in the sale of woollen goods, leaving many retailers heavily burdened with unsold stocks of winter merchandise – and this in a market overloaded with manufactured domestic cottons from mills called into being by the National Policy. The effects of the decline were aggravated by the number of people entering the dry goods trade. Not only were shopkeepers compelled to operate on a lower margin of profits, but there were serious repercussions at the wholesale level. Along with the usual complaints about 'the too great cheapness of credit,' the *Monetary Times* drew its readers' attention to a slightly newer problem and one that had probably surfaced as more retail merchants adopted the cash-only policy: 'One complaint that our wholesale houses make is, and it is an odd one, that the cash buyer fights so hard nowadays for a heavy cash discount, and heavy discounts have been so freely given, that it is hard to get a good profit.'[8]

Robert Simpson's venture into the wholesale business, on the other hand, seems to have met with greater success. Simpson, in partnership with two other gentlemen, had opened a wholesale house in the winter of 1879 at 38 Colborne Street. In 1882 expansion was undertaken into adjacent property at 36 Colborne Street, and the business remained in existence until 1889–90.[9] The fact that three men were actively involved in the operation of this wholesale concern could account for its apparent success. With the management of the retail store in the hands of his brother-in-law and partner, Charles Botsford, Robert Simpson possibly concentrated the bulk of his efforts on increasing sales at the wholesale level. Certainly the opening of the wholesale house in 1879 had resulted in a steady stream of advertisements drawing attention to this new business, whereas few advertisements relating to the retail store at 184 Yonge had appeared in the local newspapers.

Despite the obvious shortcomings of his small store at 178 Yonge

Street, Timothy Eaton's retail business continued to expand and increase. Sales figures rose from a monthly average of $11,173.59 in 1879 to $17,224.92 in 1882, giving annual totals of $134,083.12 and $206,699.04 respectively. Stock, which had vastly increased by the end of the 1870s, now demonstrated a slower rate of growth rather than the enormous jumps it had exhibited in the past. Totalling $49,908.73 at year end 1879, it rose to $57,428.20 in 1882.[10] In addition the annual rate of turnover had increased from 2.69 in 1879 to 3.60 in 1882, although this was still far from the rates achieved by the large American stores. Both the Macy and Marshall Field stores were achieving turnovers of close to six times a year in the early 1870s.[11]

It seems likely that, guided by a strong sense of what was practically and profitably expedient, Timothy Eaton came to realize earlier than Robert Simpson that the retail trade offered far greater opportunities for increased profits than the wholesale trade. This same conclusion seems to have been forced upon Robert Simpson somewhat later. During the winter of 1887, Simpson attempted to sell his wholesale business, but even before that date he had directed its appeal to retail as well as wholesale customers.[12] Both shopkeepers recognized the gains to be made by 'pursuing the nimble sixpence.'

By bringing the wholesale business to a swift end in the spring of 1883, Timothy Eaton was able to immerse himself in plans for the future of the retail store. Time ultimately would prove that he had made the right decision, for as Alfred Chandler states, retailing after the 1880s would become more profitable than wholesaling.[13] The more enterprising merchants, those who demonstrated by their unconventional methods that their object was to reach as large a market as possible, were quick to realize, as many of their predecessors had earlier in the nineteenth century, that rapid turnover of stock resulted in enormously increased financial returns. Profits resulted from an increase in volume, not in mark-up. Timothy Eaton, like many of his successful contemporaries, demonstrated and expressed an early belief in this policy, although there would be several obstacles to overcome before he could put it into full effect.

Attention was therefore directed first to the problem of space, and early in 1883 Timothy Eaton took possession of property known as the Page Block on Yonge Street. By this time his financial circumstances were sufficiently fluid that plans were immediately set in motion to demolish the existing stores on the site and construct a large new store in this prime location. The Page Block consisted of five or six separate stores erected in 1856 by John Hillyard Cameron at a time when the retail business in Toronto was gradually beginning to move northwards from King Street. Charles Page, the British immigrant who owned the whole property, had established his dry goods business in part of the block in the late 1850s. By the late 1870s, contemplating retirement, Page attempted, without success, to sell his business.[14] Since Timothy Eaton was already operating a successful store, he was not interested in purchasing Page's business, but the acquisition of property in a good location was another matter. On 7 November 1882, Timothy Eaton paid Charles Page the sum of $41,000.00 for the stores located at 190 to 196 Yonge Street. Application was made to the Union Loan and Savings Company for a mortgage of $36,000.00, $32,268.84 of which was paid to Page on 30 June 1883.[15]

The new Eaton store would have a total frontage of just over 51 feet and a depth of 107 feet. Timothy Eaton's plan to demolish 'the finest block of retail stores in the city' was considered sheer folly by many Torontonians,[16] but by replacing the old structures with one large store, he could incorporate the upper floors fully into the store as a whole rather than as later additions and afterthoughts. Since the change involved the construction of a new building rather than minor alterations and renovations, it would be a matter of almost seven months before the new store was ready to receive its first customer.

Timothy Eaton used this time to good effect and extracted the greatest possible advertising mileage out of the expansion. All Toronto should be made aware of this planned growth. Early in January 1883 he launched into print with the announcement: 'Eaton preparing to move.' This general theme was repeated on an almost daily basis in various forms: 'Going North,' 'We Flit.'

Attention was continually drawn to activity on the site. The old building was 'pulled to pieces' some time in February 1883. Chatty, gossipy advertisements detailed the daily progress on the building site. Construction proceeded fairly rapidly, interrupted only by delays occasioned by adverse weather conditions. 'Men not working today, lumber stuck in a snow bank, frost interfering with bricklaying.' 'Bricks, mortar, dust, noise and confusion are having a high old time at the premises lately occupied by C. Page & Sons.' On occasion the advertisements were in bad verse:

> *Oh, the snow, the beautiful snow*
> *How we wish it would quickly go –*
> *It is seriously affecting work on our new*
> *Premises, and greatly retarding its progress.*[17]

Acting on the precept that 'It will be easier to move the cash than the stock,' a store-wide sale was held for the whole of July and the early part of August. At 4:00 p.m. on 21 August 1883, the doors at the old store were closed and locked for the last time, and at 9:00 a.m. the following morning, Wednesday, 22 August, the new store finally welcomed its first customers.[18]

Because the lease at 178 Yonge Street did not expire until 20 February 1884, Timothy Eaton deliberately kept the old store locked and vacant for more than six months. Robert Simpson – who had entered into an arrangement with the owner, Mrs Frances Doyle, in November 1883 to lease 178 Yonge Street – was thereby prevented from taking immediate possession. Timothy Eaton thus ensured that his customers would not mistakenly patronize the Simpson store. At some point during this period, Simpson, anxious to obtain measurements of the premises in order to facilitate expansion, broke into the locked building. Nevertheless, Timothy Eaton secured almost eight months in which to accustom shoppers to his new address, for it was not until 3 April 1884 that Robert Simpson was finally able to announce the opening of his new addition.[19] Despite the contiguity of numerous other dry goods merchants, by the 1880s Timothy Eaton regarded Robert Simpson as his one legitimate competitor. Indeed, Simpson is practically the only dry goods retail merchant mentioned by name in Eaton's correspondence.

By the mid-1880s Yonge Street was considered as aristocratic in appearance as King Street, and the new Eaton store was selected by one contemporary as an example of the splendid stores to be found there: 'Whoever would have predicted in 1847, when there was not a single dry goods store on Yonge Street, that such an establishment would be found in 1886, would certainly be the subject of ridicule.' The *Daily News* described the store as a mercantile palace and, as such, 'not surpassed in elegance by any in the city.' Featuring large plate-glass windows measuring sixteen feet square, separated by a sixteen-foot glassed entrance, the store's frontage was described as the widest in the city, although this may have been journalistic excess.[20].

The three-storey building contained many innovations in design and equipment. Architectural light wells topped by large sky-lights in the roof were spaced throughout the building and opened the interior of the store so that natural light could effectively penetrate all floors. This new feature could be found in department stores throughout England, Europe, and North America. Light wells had been called into existence as upper storeys were increasingly used for display and selling space, since in most cases it was cheaper to expand upwards than sideways.

The new Eaton building, comprising some 25,544 square feet of selling space on four floors, was served by two hydraulic elevators. A massive boiler located in the basement provided heat for the entire store, which was further illuminated throughout by electricity. The use of electricity was still something of a novelty in Toronto in the early 1880s. (The arc lights installed at the 1882 Industrial Exhibition to illuminate the grounds and buildings had provided a sight described with awe throughout Upper Canada.)[21] Edison's incandescent lamp, which first appeared on the market in 1879, had been readily accepted by many American merchants, for it had the advantage of providing a much safer and healthier environment than gas. It also allowed for the utilization of previously unused space; for example, in 1888 the basement of the Eaton store was taken over for the sale and display of bulky items, such as suitcases and trunks.

The introduction of electricity by shopkeepers in the form of lights and bells was an enormous attraction. True to form, Timothy Eaton took advantage of this to draw people to the store to view the new phenomenon. With Toronto thronged with visitors to the exhibition the store was kept open on the Tuesday and Thursday evenings of 18 and 20 September 1883. 'Positively no goods will be sold,' but 'all departments will be freely shown.' To provide suitable entertainment, a Grand Promenade Concert was given in the store on 20 September, and Timothy encouraged all his employees 'to vie with each other in showing every attention to visitors.' By the following year, Eaton advertisements urged visitors to the exhibition not to 'miss one of the best sights in the city ... The T. Eaton & Co'ys great cash store, where goods are all marked in plain figures and sold at one price to the rich or poor alike.'[22]

Other new services and facilities were gradually introduced, all designed to attract shoppers to the store. The provision of a 'Ladies Gallery and Waiting Room,' allowed ladies to wash off the dust of the train journey, meet a friend, or have a rest before continuing their search for bargains. The coffee room, opened in late April 1887, was later supplemented by a small restaurant, again following in the footsteps of the larger American stores. As the 1887–8 catalogue noted: 'Everything is looked to for your comfort in shopping, making it a pleasure rather than a drudgery. All modern conveniences known to establish your comfort ... have been adopted throughout the building.'[23]

The motive for much of the expansion and innovation developed from a more practical competitive rationale than 'the shopper's comfort' cited in public announcements. If, as Ralph Hower points out, the prices offered by individual stores were roughly equal, then something else had to be offered as a means of attracting custom to the store.[24] Services such as waiting rooms, parcel checks, coffee rooms, and restaurants all gradually made their appearance. Catering to the shopper who came to town for a day's outing and to the local residents, such services were an attempt to keep the customer in the store until all possible purchases had been obtained.

The hoopla and attention focused on the new store by means of advertisements and open house events undoubtedly attracted many out-of-town visitors and was probably partly responsible for the implementation of yet another service, a department dealing with mail orders. Introduced in 1884, this new service met with great success and, by actively supplementing the daily business of the store, compelled further rapid expansion. The information about the mail order department and the marketing both of store merchandise and of the Eaton name is sufficiently voluminous to require fairly detailed treatment and is therefore discussed more fully in chapter six.

During the 1880s the Eaton store underwent enormous expansion unhampered by external interference. Hostility to Timothy Eaton's aggressive merchandising techniques was slowly developing, but it had not yet reached the point of active protest. As the volume of business increased both from in-store sales and through mail orders, new departments retailing a wide variety of merchandise were gradually introduced and the question of space once more became a matter of concern.

Because expansion within the confines of 190–6 Yonge Street was not possible, during the early part of 1884, barely six months after the completion of the new store, Timothy Eaton considered purchasing additional properties on Queen Street. Difficulties with sitting tenants and incomplete title deeds prevented the fulfilment of this plan. Similar complications were encountered in 1885 with the properties acquired at 10 to 12$\frac{1}{2}$ Queen Street West, and it was not until 1889 that this sale was finally completed. Annual rents were therefore paid to the owners along with regular interest payments on an outstanding $4,000 mortgage.[25]

In 1887 other properties were purchased at 13, 15, 17, and 19 James Street, obviously with a view to future expansion, but these remained in the hands of the occupying tenants until the end of the decade. The Queen Street properties, on the other hand, received immediate attention, and the consumers of Toronto were once more regaled with almost daily items relating to the intended expansion.

We are extending our stores through to Queen Street. You didn't know it? No we know you didn't. The dust has been flying around for weeks, yet we haven't had a building sale, nor a must make room sale. The bricks and mortar have been whizzing skyward, yet no blare of trumpets has announced the fact. Now we've got to say something for the roof is on ... The new addition is one and one-fifth times larger than the present store. The two together will make a pleasant surprise for you.[26]

The construction of this new section more than doubled existing floor space and created a large L-shaped store accessible from either Yonge or Queen streets. Opened on 8 September 1886, the extension was incorporated into the same general plan as the Yonge Street section. With three floors and a basement, the light airy atmosphere was continued and maintained with the inclusion of several large light wells. C.C. Taylor declared that the store compared favourably with the finest stores in Great Britain and the United States. Despite Timothy Eaton's obvious pride and delight in his 'immense new store,' which allowed shoppers to 'picnic in our Mammoth Buildings,' he never overlooked its main function and purpose. 'But when all is said, the building is merely the shell of the business; the stock is the spirit of the place; the merchandise is greater than the store.'[27] Early photographs do much to reinforce this impression, for merchandise, whether in the form of household linens, notions, chinaware, or books, overwhelms all available departmental space and contrasts sharply with the rather plain furnishings provided for their display. This point was taken further in the 1887 catalogue. To counter comments that the new store would result in increased prices, the catalogue stated quite plainly that there was no fuss in the store – plain walnut counters, no elaborate carving, wooden seats, not upholstered in plush, which 'soon present[s] a faded soiled appearance.'[28] By providing a functional environment, Timothy Eaton could gradually broaden his appeal to embrace the whole range of Toronto's shoppers. Since the merchandise was greater than the store, slavish imitation of the luxurious decor found in some American stores was not necessary. Eaton customers from all walks of life could enjoy the benefits of shopping in a store that was conspicuously larger than the old shop at 178 Yonge Street.

Although the stock was, as Timothy put it, 'the spirit of the place,' it could not, in an era of personal service, move wholly of its own volition. In this matter Timothy Eaton to a very large degree was at the mercy of his sales staff. Because of the turmoil experienced during this period of rapid expansion, the service aspect of the business suffered some decline. The hiring of additional employees to staff the vastly enlarged store resulted in unforeseen problems and forced Timothy Eaton to delegate further responsibility for some of the administrative functions connected with this growing establishment.

Timothy Eaton's nephew John James Eaton, acting in a managerial capacity, was given responsibility for strengthening overall morale and loyalty. Drawing attention to the lack of harmony and agreement between departments and personnel, he described a situation where many members of the staff recognized no real delegation of authority or responsibility and operated completely independently. 'In January 1884 there was no management. Everyone doing as they liked – no head – no one responsible – no connection between one another and a constant disagreement and a constant quarrelling between departments and no harmony throughout ... Goods were bought indiscriminately whenever and where ever it pleased. No orders were placed ahead ... No authority was necessary as to quantity purchased.'[29]

The salesgirls, lacking proper supervision, had become 'lazy, saucy and impudent,' paying little attention to the proper hours of business, 'coming in and out at all hours, from 9 to 9.45 in the morning.' Possibly a more informal state of affairs had worked well in a smaller operation where discipline was easier to maintain and where senior personnel had constant access to the man at the top. Supervision of sales staff was, moreover, only part of a much larger problem of bringing the operation under managerial control.

According to Nasmith, the first year in the new store was something of a nightmare, and the problems were aggravated by the fact that everything Timothy Eaton owned had been invested in the new enterprise. Difficulties were encountered with stock taken over from Scott Street, which, intended for country merchants, was found to be totally unsuitable for city trade. This supplemented new merchandise, much of which had been far too hastily assembled from local wholesalers. By August 1884 the generally sluggish state of the economy provoked Timothy Eaton to remark that he had never found it so difficult to sell goods.[30] Sales for September and October 1884 for the first time showed a marked decline (see Table 8).

In one sense the year 1883 was unfortunate for the move to a new and larger store. As the *Monetary Times* pointed out, 'the backward spring and wet summer' along with other less definable causes had resulted in a less than buoyant feeling in dry goods circles. The prospect looked no brighter for the approaching winter, for 'the scarcity of money in the country' was plainly felt by both British and Canadian manufacturers, and there was a general feeling that 'too many merchants [were] dividing the trade.' Indeed, 1884 was difficult for both wholesalers and retailers. Advertisements appearing in the Toronto newspapers gave evidence of a widespread struggle to stay afloat. Although many stores, such as Petley and Petley, R. Walker and Company, and Philip Jamieson, tried to demonstrate that all was well with their own particular business, they declared that other 'old fogy houses and drowning traders clutching at straws' were having 'a hard struggle to hold their own.' Despite such optimistic language, Jamieson used several promotional gimmicks to attract people to his store, and in October 1884 offered to give every twelfth customer his or her purchase free, regardless of cost.[31]

The juxtaposition of several troublesome factors in a period when sales, although not seriously declining, were not demonstrating the leap anticipated by the opening of the new store probably led to an awareness of problems that might otherwise have gone undetected. While much has been written about the change to managerial control in the nineteenth century, it seems likely that this occurred in each individual instance only after an owner-operator became aware that the enterprise was becoming too large for him to handle alone. Timothy Eaton in large part followed the general pattern of appointing close relatives to executive positions, although in each case they were required to prove themselves by working their way up from the bottom in one of the three family stores. John James Eaton, the second son of Timothy's eldest brother, Robert, had earlier worked for some ten years in his father's store in St Marys. Timothy Eaton's eldest son, Edward Young Eaton, who was taken into formal partnership with his father on 1 February 1888, had begun his business career at 178 Yonge Street at the age of seventeen.[32] Both he and John James Eaton were responsible for many of the changes and innovations implemented in the years remaining before the turn of the century.

Timothy Eaton's method of allowing employees a certain amount of freedom and authority was obviously open to abuse by those whose work ethic was neither so personally well developed nor so single-mindedly directed towards the good of the company as his own. Yet in the long run, by adhering to this principle and dismissing those who did not rise to the occasion, he appears to have called forth responsibility and dedication to the business in enough good people to ensure its growth and continued existence. The tightening of management and control undertaken in 1884 by John James Eaton, at Timothy's behest, appears to have been entirely successful. Proper procedures were implemented for ordering stock, and fines were imposed on tardy workers. Legend has it that John James Eaton took exception to the fact that many of the employees were spending long breaks in the saloon across the street. He gave notice that such behaviour would no longer be tolerated and that those continuing the practice would be dismissed immediately. Holding to his promise, the following day, he dismissed some forty to fifty personnel.

By 1885 John James could point to a general overall improvement. Large discrepancies no longer appeared in the daily cash record, and the monthly sales figures once again began to soar. With great satisfaction John James remarked that 'The percent for selling alone [in 1884] was as much as in 1885 covers the selling, managing, delivering and all.'[33]

This concern with administrative costs separates the more personal style of management that had existed in the past from the style that would direct the future operations of the company. Although Timothy Eaton had demonstrated constant concern with regard to interest and discount charges, the evidence suggests that he paid little attention to the actual cost of running the business. For the small retailer employing only a limited staff and operating a strictly cash-based business, overhead expenses would have been few – a small monthly rent, wages, and small charges for such things as heat, light, and feed for the delivery horse. Tasks that had been handled by one bookkeeper (or even Timothy himself), one delivery man, and a small sales staff now required the attention of additional administrative personnel. As well, the enforced saving necessary to reduce and discharge recently acquired mortgages undoubtedly involved greater effort than that required by earlier rental payments. The increased financial costs arising from larger premises, a greater volume of stock, and the enlarged sales and administrative staff effected an enormous escalation of business expenses. Cost accounting thus became much more important.

During this rather shaky period of transition Timothy Eaton was also embroiled in a conflict with Stewart and MacDonald, one of his major overseas suppliers. Imports from Great Britain and the United States were reaching large proportions, and the amount purchased from John Macdonald had undergone further considerable reduction. By 1878 Macdonald supplied the Eaton store with only approximately one-sixth of the total stock, the remainder being supplied primarily by the Glasgow wholesale house of Stewart and MacDonald, supplemented by merchandise from a number of other British and North American companies. This pattern remained in effect for several years.

Timothy Eaton gradually increased his dependence on the Glasgow company, and by year end February 1882 he owed them close to $47,000. Since his method was to remit regular monthly sums of sterling, his total purchases for the year from Stewart and MacDonald were probably much greater than this figure. By the end of 1884, close to $2,500 a week was forwarded to Stewart and MacDonald through Molson's Bank in Toronto.[34] Assuming that such payments were processed on a regular basis, stock purchases could have amounted to about $130,000 annually at a time when sales figures were close to $250,000 a year.

According to one source, a disagreement early in 1883 over an order of print goods damaged in transit was responsible for souring this relationship. R.Y. Eaton, however, suggests that the problem arose from the introduction by Stewart and MacDonald of new management unfamiliar with Timothy Eaton's customary methods of payment. A letter from Stewart and MacDonald in January 1885 has a passage written in red ink that states quite clearly: 'In regard to any unpleasantness that may meet you, we certainly regret it but cannot take to ourselves any blame as it was your own doing and you had repeated warnings before we actually resorted to extreme measures.'[2] Never willing to submit to what he perceived as intimidation, Timothy Eaton gradually reduced the amount owing to Stewart and MacDonald (though perhaps at a slower rate than they wished), while increasing purchases from other British sources. These rose from approximately $1,400 in 1882 to nearly $25,000* in 1884.[35]

In December 1885 Stewart and MacDonald demanded immediate payment of outstanding balances amounting to $6,600. When taken in conjunction with their earlier refusal to renew several of Timothy Eaton's maturing bills, their actions placed the supply of both merchandise and credit in jeopardy.[36] Resentful of external pressure and interference and convinced of his rights in the matter, Eaton was determined not only to obtain restitution for the damaged goods but also to terminate his dependence on a supplier who appeared unwilling to give him a fair deal. He therefore journeyed to England first to finalize the whole unpleasant issue and then to institute alternative arrangements more favourable to a large retailer.

Given past practices, it seems that Stewart and MacDonald, like John Macdonald in Toronto, and Adam Hope and the Buchanans in London, were used as stepping stones to a yet more satisfactory

---

* For ease of comparison all pound sterling amounts have been converted to Canadian dollars using the contemporary exchange rate of £1.0s.0d. to C$4.92.

source of supply. Although the move in this case had been hastened by unforeseen circumstances, it was a successful one. Recognizing as he had in 1874 that the price lists offered by most wholesalers were a sham, Timothy Eaton had gradually and continually directed his attention to removing all unnecessary costs involved in the purchase of merchandise for the store.

With the increasing competition of the 1880s, manufacturers aggressively sought new markets for their expanding production. Many, following the example set by Crewdson Horrocks and Company, found that they could effectively reduce their own costs by retailing direct to the small shopkeepers. In this matter they were abetted by the growing number of steamship lines seeking to fill their holds with freight on their regular weekly Atlantic sailings. The gradual decline in the cost of freight rates also encouraged retailers to look to the United Kingdom and Europe for a greater proportion of their supplies. Feeling the pinch of competition, wholesalers did everything within their power to reduce this threat. Their survival depended on ensuring that their role as middleman between primary supplier and retailer continued unbroken.

Members of the Dry Goods Section of the Toronto Board of Trade conducted a vigorous campaign urging the continuation of reduced train fares for Ontario retailers travelling to Toronto wholesalers. As many as 2,300 Ontario retailers took advantage of these reductions in 1884. Some wholesalers – John Macdonald was one – encouraged retailers from places as distant as the Maritimes to travel to Toronto to inspect potential merchandise rather than making selections from small samples.[37] Attempts were also made to dissuade manufacturers from dealing directly with retailers, and in this matter the wholesalers achieved some success.

Timothy Eaton, unable to secure some of the merchandise he wanted from manufacturers, was compelled to establish a distinctly separate company for this purpose. Listing Edward Young Eaton as the sole proprietor of 'Wilson and Company,' the formal agreement stated: 'Whereas certain manufacturers refuse to sell their product direct to the T. Eaton Company Limited in their own name, and it is therefore desirable that [the] Company should have the use for purchasing purposes of the name of a Firm of Manufacturers quite distinct from the name of the Company ...' This agreement was not formally signed until May 1892, but it seems likely that the separate company was first established in the spring of 1889. Although the publicly registered partnership declaration relating to Wilson and Company completed by Edward Young Eaton formally stated that no person was associated with him in partnership, the formal agreement cited above, which was signed by Timothy Eaton, made it quite clear that, the different company name notwithstanding, 'the Business is the Business of the [Eaton] Company' and that the Eaton company was responsible for all profits and liabilities connected with this new venture. Furthermore it was pointed out that Wilson and Company would operate as a clothing manufacturer. This company remained in existence until the late 1890s. Large orders for Canadian-produced yard goods were made through Wilson and Company, which then used these supplies for the manufacture of shirts and whitewear for the Eaton store.[38]

Other sources were sought for woollen goods. Letters were sent to several large British textile manufacturers requesting information regarding volume purchases of woollen tweeds and broadcloth for boys and men's clothes.[39] The millinery workroom, which had been producing custom-made garments for some considerable time, was, in a sense, the early forerunner of this expansion into large-scale manufacturing. By responding to local demand and combining clothing production, albeit on a small scale, with his retail operations, Timothy Eaton avoided the problems initially encountered by other small manufacturers. John Northway, for example, operating in the early days from a very small capital base, had often been obliged to make too many garments in the same fabric, since most English manufacturers sold fabric only in bulk lots of sixty-five yards.[40]

Other items in strong demand, such as comforters, window shades, and men's shirts, were added to the production line. Window shades, a made-to-measure item, were first produced in limited quantities by a salesman in Eaton's home furnishing department. Men's shirts on the other hand had been produced on an out-work basis by providing seamstresses with the necessary cotton, linen, spool thread, and buttons for the fabrication of some two dozen shirts every two weeks.[41] Men's shirts at this time were not individually sized and, since they also did not feature an attached collar, their mass production presented no insuperable problems. Increased demand gradually necessitated the employment of other workers to keep pace with incoming orders.

With the installation in early 1889 of twelve sewing machines on the top floor of 198 Yonge Street, volume manufacturing of Eaton merchandise commenced in earnest. Later that year the whole operation was moved into larger quarters on Adelaide Street West, which allowed for the rapid expansion of manufacturing capacity to thirty-five sewing machines.[42] While the manufacture of merchandise had in the past catered to special orders and small lots, the emphasis for future output would be on the production of men's shirts and women's underwear in quantities suitable for both the store and the catalogue. Initial production seems to have been limited, for the 1890 catalogue carried a full-page advertisement extolling the quality of shirts produced by Williams, Greene and Rome, a Toronto manufacturer. But the endeavour produced the desired results – a reduction in primary costs. By 1893 Timothy Eaton noted proudly that the manufacturing department was turning out collarless shirts for thirty-five cents apiece. Collars for the shirts were then purchased from a Belfast supplier.[43]

In a sense Timothy Eaton resorted to methods adopted earlier by several Toronto wholesalers who had also turned to manufacturing in an attempt to reduce both supply and financial problems. In the 1860s Gordon McKay and John McMurrich had been involved in the manufacture of cotton and woollen textiles and by so doing had gained an advantage over other wholesalers. Wholesalers were among the first in the 1870s to attempt to secure cheaper domestic goods for imports, and by entering the manufacturing process to attempt to secure lower prices on domestically produced staples. But Timothy Eaton refused to follow the wholesalers' practice of retailing the cheaper North American calicos at exactly the same price as the better quality British goods.[44]

The implementation of the National Policy tariff in 1879 brought further turmoil to an already confused market. As the *Monetary Times* noted, the enthusiasm of Canadian manufacturers for taking orders was not always matched by their productive capacity. As competition increased, cotton production soon exceeded consumption, and the collapse of prices in late 1882 created something of a crisis for this industry.[45] Timothy Eaton seldom expressed opinions with regard to national or even local politics, but in April 1883, in line with his belief that the industrious efficient businessman could not help but succeed, he questioned the validity of taxing the Canadian working man for the sake of small Canadian producers: 'Eaton's Query to Sir John. Dear Sir John Is it right that Sir Leonard ... should impose upon the working classes of Canada, and the great North West a duty of $7^{1}/_{2}$ cents upon cotton goods in order to support one small firm near Montreal.'[46] Despite this expressed concern for the 'working classes of Canada,' Timothy Eaton probably strongly resented a tax that affected the large volume of his merchandise imported from Great Britain and elsewhere. He deplored the idea of government intervention in business matters and resented the introduction of the tariff, which not only drastically increased the taxes on dry goods but also necessitated endless hours at the Customs House. The precept inscribed in his notebook, 'If almost Starved depend upon yourself and not upon others,' testifies to his refusal to depend upon anyone or anything for support. The establishment of his own wholesale business in 1881 was an attempt to free himself of obligations and mark-ups imposed by others for their own benefit, a practice he believed they indulged in whenever an opportunity arose. His entrance into manufacturing was yet another attempt to reduce costs by further vertical integration.

The constant attention to such matters is evident from a study of sales figures. These rose from $154,978.19 in 1880 to $334,165.56 in 1885. By far the largest increase came in the last seven months of 1885, suggesting that the quirks and problems encountered in the new store had been satisfactorily dealt with. It is also possible that the volume of mail orders was on the increase. Unfortunately no further sales figures exist for the 1880s, but the amount paid in customs duties gives some indication of continued growth. In 1888, $66,653.00 was paid, and this figure rose to $103,473.00 in 1889.[47] If the rate averaged one-tenth the retail value of the goods, then sales for 1889 could have totalled more than $1 million.

By the mid-1880s Timothy Eaton's personal financial position had recovered from the problems suffered at the time of expansion. His notebook meticulously details the assets and liabilities of this period. As evidence of this improved position, annual sums were placed to an ongoing deposit that was built up over a period of sixteen years with amounts ranging from $1,600.00 in 1872 to $26,191.43 in 1887. By 1887, $126,594.89 had been accumulated. This money was presumably kept in an account separate from that pertaining to store finances and probably served as a rainy-day fund.[48]

The Eaton catalogue for 1887 remarked that 'the signs of the times point to an era of general prosperity.' This prosperity was reflected in further physical expansion of the Eaton store and its facilities. Properties purchased at 13, 15, 17, and 19 James Street from the Cathcart estate and from John Enoch Thompson for $13,500 came under the wrecker's hammer in the early part of 1889, with the erection of a new three-storey building to be fully integrated with the Yonge and Queen store. The addition of these extra properties increased floor space from 50,688 square feet to 120,304 square feet (a gain of more than 120 per cent), to create one of the largest retail establishments in Toronto. The Eaton catalogue felt fully justified in repeating the comment made by one Toronto newspaper that signposts should be erected in the store so that customers would not get lost.[49]

The constant increase in physical space necessitated changes in the maintenance, operation, and physical plant of the store. A telephone was first installed in 1885, and in 1887, at the urging of his son Edward, Timothy Eaton installed a system of overhead cash carriers throughout the store. Dispensing with 'the noise and bustle of cash boys ... the automatic conveyors ... do the work of conveying packages and cash in the same basket noiselessly and effectively.' This ingenious system was introduced in the early 1880s by an American company and within a decade could be found in progressive stores throughout North America and Great Britain. Hydraulic elevators operating independently of the external water supply were installed some time in the late 1880s. Timothy Eaton had no intention of subjecting his operations to the whims of the Toronto Waterworks. Writing to a fellow merchant he stated:

when it suited them they would give us power, and when it did not suit them we could get none until they were ready. When a storm came on ... they gave us a good supply of sand, which was very expensive when it got into the cylinders; and the last straw that broke the camel's back was they made up their minds that a retail house to them was no object on Saturday for power, and they decided to close down on Saturday, and that was the day we required it. We set about putting in our own plant.[50]

For very much the same reason a full Daisy generator was installed in the basement of the store in the fall of 1889, thus ensuring a continuous supply of electricity. To celebrate its successful installation a grand promenade concert was given in the store by the band of the Queen's Own Rifles.[51]

With the constant rapid expansion and mechanization of store facilities, the number of employees increased and a measure of specialization was introduced. For example, a superintendent and full maintenance crew were hired to take responsibility for the operation of all mechanical and electrical devices.

By 1886 the total staff had risen to 150, and this figure would rise again by 1887 to between 250 and 300. As in the past the staff was headed by experienced supervisory personnel who received their training on the job, either at the Eaton store or in junior capacities in other retail or wholesale dry goods houses. These were assisted by adolescent youths or young adult males and females who had entered the business world at the age of fourteen or even younger. The Education Act of 1874 applied only to children between the ages of seven and twelve, and recommendations by the 1889 Royal Commission on the Relations of Capital and Labour forbidding the employment of children under the age of fourteen were often ignored. As Timothy Eaton testified before the commission in 1887, he did not think he had any girls under twelve years of age working in the store, but there were occasions when destitute mothers, whose home lives had been upset by accident or death in the family, urgently requested employment for their children. Some young boys and girls, therefore, began working in the store at the age of eleven or twelve either as messengers or cash and parcel assistants at a weekly rate of $1.50 to $2.00. Samuel Wilson, for example, who later became a director of the company, first began as a cash boy at the Eaton store at the age of eleven.[52]

Like many of his peers, Timothy Eaton considered on-the-job training (even for his own sons and nephews) an essential preparation for those wishing to rise in the retail industry. As he pointed out in 1887, no specific period of time was allotted for the training of new employees, since this depended entirely on individual ability. Many of the later managers began at an early age in lowly positions; one director had begun as a parcel boy in knee pants in 1885.[53]

For employees demonstrating special interest and aptitude, advancement was both rapid and encouraging; wage increases four and five times within a year were not uncommon. Harry McGee, who in 1883 at age twenty-five had begun his Eaton career prepared to sell goods and sweep floors, spent his first day at the new job on an express wagon moving furniture and stock from 178 to 190 Yonge Street. He started at six dollars a week, and some two weeks later this was raised to seven dollars. Seven months later, as manager of the carpet section, he was receiving eight dollars a week plus a regular commission. The fact that just three years later he was considered one of the oldest employees suggests the extent to which the Eaton company was plagued by high staff mobility and transiency. Sales clerks moved constantly from one store to another seeking promotion. Offering rewards for effort was probably the only way to retain competent employees, and to this end Timothy Eaton implemented profit-sharing in the form of annual premiums, over and above regular commissions, for certain valuable employees.[54]

By 1885 responsibility for the hiring of sales personnel had been delegated to a senior employee, but it seems likely that departmental managers also exercised a measure of control in making the final selection of those considered most suitable. Additional temporary employees were frequently hired to staff the counters during the busy seasons, to be let go once the rush was over.

Given the state of the Toronto job market, positions in the store were in high demand. Brothers, sisters, and even cousins of employees continually applied for jobs and were frequently hired unseen to fill vacant positions. Advertisements for both male and female staff were placed in the local help-wanted columns; while some advertisements stated that experience was necessary, others merely asked that the applicant be 'smart' or 'quick with figures.' Clerking was considered one of the few respectable jobs open to young women, and there were numerous applications from girls in domestic service. By 1882, in an article entitled 'Woman's Sphere of Labour,' a writer noted the increasing demand for saleswomen in places other than dry goods stores. Citing women's neatness and adaptability as reasons for their popularity, he also mentioned a factor of prime importance to employers, namely cost. 'To the plea that they should be paid equally well with men for the same work, the employer has the answer ready – and it is probably a true one – that they are not physically equal to the same strain of continuous work.'[55] The comment ignores the fact that sales clerks, whether female or male, all worked the same inordinately long hours.

One female clerk, hired in 1885, later recalled her gratitude at being able to obtain a job that paid a weekly wage during the training period. Beginning at the age of sixteen she had received $2.50 a week; once she had proved herself, she was promoted to the position of junior clerk and her pay was raised to $3.00. When she resigned her position prior to her marriage some five or six years later, she was earning $4.50 per week. This was in striking contrast to the wage of $1.00 offered by one Yonge Street store to a nineteen-year-old female and cited by Sara Jeannette Duncan in a *Globe* article of 1886.[56] The weekly wage of $6.00 to $8.00 quoted by Timothy Eaton in his evidence to the royal commission applied only to very senior female clerks. The majority, due largely to the brevity of their work lives, received much less than this. Since most girls worked only for the few years before marriage, the store experienced some difficulty in securing qualified females. Timothy

Eaton considered this state of affairs unfortunate, for he had found that in retailing certain classes of goods, women were equally as valuable as men. As one Toronto merchant reported:

A girl who is wise enough not to get married can earn $800 a year if she sticks to the business ... have to be pretty brainy girls. I have one I would not lose for $800 a year ... A girl who will keep attentively working at the business and leave men alone is as valuable as a man is ... Up to a certain extent they are more valuable, but when they get valuable they generally get married. That is the trouble with female labour in our business.[57]

Since details with regard to managerial personnel are almost non-existent, it is not known how many women achieved the rank of manager or buyer at the Eaton store. That some did, however, is clear from from a few examples mentioned in company correspondence.[58] Several women filled positions as assistant managers and acted in that capacity when the departmental manager was absent on buying trips.

The problem of staff discipline occasionally reared its head. At one point a mild system of fines was introduced for those who regularly returned late from lunch breaks. Several cautions were given before fines were imposed, but as Timothy Eaton informed the royal commission, a reasonable excuse could erase the offence. Serious misdemeanours, however, resulted in instant dismissal with little opportunity for explanation. The application forms for employment carried the notation that termination of employment by either side could be effected immediately without notice and upon payment of accrued salary to date. This was common practice in retailing. Given the general overall improvement in working conditions, Eaton employees on the whole fared better than their counterparts in the smaller stores of Toronto. By the end of the decade provision was made for an employees' lunch-room and separate sitting-room, as well as for separate toilet facilities. In recognition of services rendered by the whole work-force during a period of great competition, funds amounting to $2,000 were distributed in February 1887 to all those who had been with the firm for a year. In this respect Timothy Eaton was more liberal than Rowland Macy, who had no intention of sharing more of his income with his staff than was absolutely necessary.[59] It was also during this period that the Eaton company established the practice of taking special note of those employees who had served their country during times of crisis and war. Of the one hundred male employees in the store in 1885, six of their number volunteered for active service during the North-West Rebellion of 1885. Upon their return their jobs were still waiting for them.

While the introduction of electricity had gone a long way to improving conditions for employees, the introduction of shorter hours begun in the 1870s constituted a greater benefit. By the mid-1880s, ignoring general Toronto practice and following the example set earlier by several New York stores, the Eaton store closed its doors during the week at 6:00 p.m. In the summer of 1886 Timothy Eaton went farther and introduced the practice of closing at 2:00 p.m. on Saturdays during the months of July and August. This was a significant innovation at a time when many stores continued to remain open extremely late on Saturday evenings to accommodate those who received their pay at the termination of the week's work; but as the Eaton advertisements pointed out, 'mechanics do not work Saturday afternoon.'[60]

Timothy Eaton recognized that the customer had to be recruited in this move for shorter hours, since he neither wished nor could afford to lose patronage. As Sarah Smith Malino points out, since success in retailing is so closely linked to public confidence, most merchants were very anxious to cultivate a reputation as a benevolent employer, especially at a time when large numbers of women were entering the work-force. The matter was therefore presented to Torontonians as one of moral and social concern: 'Early Closing – "to be" or "not to be" is the question. It is in your hand – you are most concerned in the matter. Can you do all your shopping before 6 p.m. on Saturdays? Ladies, take up the agitation ... We have adopted a ballot box system which will be found inside our door. Vote early. Vote often for early closing.' Customers were encouraged to choose either two o'clock or six o'clock closing, an indication that the store normally remained open until a later hour on Saturday evenings. It is possible that the demonstration of public sympathy for the workers involved in the Toronto streetcar strike in the early spring of 1886 convinced Timothy Eaton that the move to Saturday half-holidays would meet with similar support.

Despite a ballot of 1,500 to 1,190 in favour of six o'clock closing, Timothy Eaton held fast to the earlier hour and was supported in this endeavour by thirty-nine other retailers. Stores that chose to remain open on Saturday afternoons did so because they felt it would be 'unfair to the working people of Toronto to deprive them of the only convenient day on which they can make their purchases.' One dry goods salesman, however, repudiated this statement and reported that he found many more people of wealth shopping after hours than labouring classes.[61]

Concern for the worker was not the only consideration. Competition and lack of unanimity continued to prevail as it had in the 1870s. Robert Simpson's decision to adhere to normal Saturday hours because of 'the unsatisfactory working of the early closing movement on Yonge Street' prompted Timothy Eaton to observe that 'all but a few have more preference for Dollars than Principle.' Where his own principles were concerned, however, Timothy Eaton left himself open to attack when, during the months of July, August, and September, the weekday hours at the Eaton store were extended to ten o'clock each evening.[62] Customers were thus more than adequately compensated for the Saturday half-holiday, with the result that Eaton employees were obliged to work longer hours during these summer months.

The idea of a half-holiday was sufficiently popular for some twenty-one other stores on Yonge Street (including that of Timothy's brother James) to opt instead for a Wednesday half-holiday during the months of July and August. Such stores continued to remain open late on Saturday evenings, but in 1888, as a concession to his employees, James Eaton closed his store for the supper hour and then remained open until 10:00 p.m.[63]

The Early Closing Movement, which had first gained widespread support in the 1870s, probably benefited in the early part of the 1880s from the high visibility achieved by labour organizations, most notably the Knights of Labour. Indeed employers of large numbers of workers could not ignore the threat posed by these organizations nor the public sympathy accorded to striking workers at the Massey plant and the Toronto Street Railway in 1886. By the late 1880s the question of hours of work reached the attention of the provincial government, and the Ontario Factories Act of 1887 was aimed specifically at the hours worked by women and children in the factories and workrooms of Ontario. The passage of the Ontario Shops Regulation Act of 1888, which allowed for the optional regulation of shop hours by municipalities receiving the support of a sufficiently large majority of local stores, was quickly taken up by Toronto City Council. As with much of the legislation of this period, it merely rationalized customary practice. The clauses relating to the hours of employment for boys under fourteen and girls under sixteen were considerably in excess of the sixty hours per week specified for women and children under the Factories Act of 1887. Store owners could still require a young person to work for seventy-four hours a week, or fourteen hours (including mealtimes) on Saturday and twelve hours during any other day. Stores could therefore remain open from 8:00 a.m. to 8:00 p.m. during the week and from 8:00 a.m. to 10:00 p.m. on Saturdays. This contrasted sharply with the hours worked by females in Toronto factories; in 1888 these ranged from forty-four to an average of fifty-five per week.[64]

To ensure a greater measure of success for the Saturday half-holiday, Timothy Eaton promoted the idea of 'Friday Bargain Day.' Continued sporadically through the remainder of 1886, this new feature did not become a regular weekly attraction until some time later. Further attempts to reduce shop hours on Saturdays throughout the year proved unsuccessful, and annual calls for customer co-operation continued down to the end of the decade.

As Timothy Eaton's business grew and expanded, his reputation within the commercial community experienced a similar increase, particularly in the esteem of those connected with the Methodist church. Elm Street Methodist Church, which had earlier served as a centre for Methodists living in the downtown core, by the mid-1880s was beginning to feel the pressure of a larger congregation, as Toronto began to expand north of Bloor Street. Since no church existed nearer than Broadway Tabernacle on one side and Bathurst Street Methodist on the other, a specific rallying place was needed to serve the Bloor-Yonge area. A committee of officials from several Methodist churches was thus convened to discuss the establishment of a new church, to be known as Western Methodist. Timothy Eaton and W.J. Gage representing Elm Street Methodist joined C.R.S. Dinnick of Queen Street Methodist and Benjamin Westwood, Sr, of Broadway Tabernacle, to investigate this undertaking. After due consideration, property was purchased on Bloor Street West between Major and Robert streets, and Timothy Eaton, along with the three other members of the committee, took responsibility for the necessary mortgage and financing.

A congregation of six hundred attended the opening services held in a large tent at the site on 12 June 1887. Timothy Eaton was actively involved in all aspects of the life of this new church, presiding over regular meetings of the initial committee and the early building committee, accepting responsibility for the acquisition of the property itself, and purchasing collection plates for the opening services. Several members of the Eaton family later became active leaders and members of both the Sunday school and the weekly prayer meetings. In 1889 the five adult members of the family – Mr and Mrs Eaton, Edward Young, Josie, and Maggie – were formally received into this new church as full members.[65]

In 1888 Timothy Eaton moved his family from 4 Orde Street to a large newly erected house at the northwest corner of Spadina and Lowther, within easy walking distance of the new church.

Another son, George J. Eaton, had been born to Timothy and Maggie in August 1882, but his life had been brought to a swift end by an unfortunate accident before he reached his second birthday. Receiving this sad news while away on a business trip, Timothy Eaton lamented: 'Weeping yet rejoicing, he has gone to the arms of his Father in Heaven'. As in the past, Timothy and Maggie Eaton continued to draw strength from their religious faith. Among the many texts copied in his notebook, Timothy included verses of comfort and consolation: 'he that dwelleth in the secret place of the most high shall abide under the Shadow of The Almighty. I will say of the Lord he is my refuge & my fortress my God in him thereto I trust.'[66]

6

'Trial Is the Surest Test'

'The Store's advertising ... is the autobiography of the
business ... the drift of what is going on day by day in
the store.'
Globe, 26 September 1889

'Tell your story to public what you have and what you
propose to sell ... that every article will be found just
what it is guaranteed to be.'
Timothy Eaton, *c.* 1890

During the middle decades of the nineteenth century most well-
established Canadian merchants and tradesmen purchased space
in newspapers to inform the public of their various wares and
services. Most advertisements conformed in both space and style
to the limited dimensions of newspapers that frequently consisted
of only four to six pages. Although the mid-1870s saw the appearance of larger and in some cases more flamboyant advertisements,
many merchants continued to follow traditional practices. Thus a
small two-inch-square notice was usually deemed sufficient, and
Timothy Eaton was not alone in relying on such brief insertions.
Advances in printing technology aided by increased circulation
allowed for a gradual expansion of both news content and advertising material, and by the 1880s large urban newspapers regularly
comprised ten to fourteen pages, with larger editions on Saturdays.
Newspaper proprietors actively encouraged this trend. Edmund E.

Sheppard, the proprietor of the *Daily News*, in an announcement covering two complete columns of a large page, informed his readers that 'Judicious advertising is the keystone of success. Merchants cannot build up a business without it.'[1]

During the 1880s there was a definite shift from the modest, dignified twice-weekly insertions to larger and more eye-catching daily entries. Dry goods and men's clothing stores tended to be in the forefront of this change, and many of these advertisements were neither refined nor polished in their presentation. Where the earlier low-key advertisements frequently ran from April through to October with no change in content, the new style of advertising undoubtedly catered to a public able to patronize stores on a weekly or even daily basis. Informing contemporary readers of bargains and novelties, the advertising of this period also affords later observers some insight into a frame of mind shaped to a large degree by self-interest, competition, and the ardent desire for survival. Through the medium of his advertising material, a merchant projected a definite image of his store and his business. This was true not only for his merchandise but also for the principles by which his business was directed and controlled.

Although Timothy Eaton's advertisements changed in both format and style over the years as the company attempted to keep ahead of the competition, the image projected remained constant. Determined that the Eaton name would be identified with service, quality, and honesty, Timothy Eaton urged his managers to 'Tell your story to public what you have and what you propose to sell. Promise them not only Bargains but that every article will be found just what it is guaranteed to be. Whether you sell a first rate or a third rate article, the customer will get what they bargain for ... Use no deception in the smallest degree – no nothing you cannot defend before God or man.'[2] By the end of the 1870s Timothy Eaton had delegated responsibility for advertising to a member of his office staff, but he continued to ensure that it projected his own publicly expressed principles. Like everything else in the Eaton store, the advertisements were expected to produce effective returns. For this reason monthly journals were considered neither appropriate nor productive. Special values had to be announced in the daily press.

Beginning in March 1886 the Eaton advertisements underwent a major change. Instead of regularly informing readers of the prices of goods, the new column extolled the virtues of the store. Moreover, it resembled an ordinary newspaper article, except that it was printed in a larger, twelve-point Caslon type. This approach was first introduced by John Wanamaker in the Philadelphia papers in May 1880, on the advice of his advertising counsel, John E. Powers, and the effective contrast of both type and style was widely imitated.[3] In the past the stress had been on quality and low cost at a fixed price and for cash only and had concentrated on bringing the name of T. Eaton and Company to the attention of Toronto shoppers. The new style was more relaxed and co-opted the consumer into an active and ongoing partnership. As one Eaton advertisement stated: 'It used to be a different thing. The glory of it was keeping one's name up in conspicuous lettering – the blacker and bigger the lettering the more enterprising the advertiser. Now we are content with the easiest types for the eyes, with a mere formal heading and signature. So familiar that it's taken for granted.'[4] The Eaton store, having achieved wide renown among Toronto residents, could now adopt a more democratic approach and address its appeal to the whole population and not simply to those interested in the price of staples. With the store's increase in physical size and variety of merchandise it became important to secure the patronage of all levels of society. It was about this time that the first reference was made to carriages waiting before the door.

While competition undoubtedly compelled a constant change of pace to ensure that one's name was always well to the fore, the attempt to broaden the store's appeal also indicates a certain confidence in the reputation the owner had taken such pains to develop. The statement made in the early 1880s that 'the best way to further our own interests is to study the interests of the customers' was reiterated and expanded upon throughout the decade. In referring to the large cash business, it was pointed out that 'It's not money we're after. It's to invest our capital so that it will pay you to invest your money in our business.' The concept that 'our-Your store' had grown to greatness by its principle of service allowed the company to appeal to the ladies of Toronto in considering the matter of early closing on Saturdays during the summer months. As a partner in this endeavour, the company pointed out that 'we feel bound to promote in any way possible any movement for the good of those who toil.'[5]

The formal introduction in 1884 of a mail order catalogue allowed for a fuller expression of Timothy Eaton's ideas of honesty, quality, and service. This service constituted an advance over earlier methods practised by many stores in both Great Britain and Europe. A rural English customer ordering a riding habit from a London tailor, for example, had asked him to 'chuse the cloth, good, stout and dark blue ... send the habit by the Mail [coach] to Hereford.' The Paris store Petit Saint Thomas published a catalogue in the 1840s for its out-of-town customers.[6] It seems likely, however, that such services were offered only to valued customers who were part of a known and recognized clientele, rather than on a universal basis.

The Eaton catalogue was not the first such publication to be issued in North America, but it was one of the first in Canada to be distributed by a retail store. The small single-sheet flyer issued by Aron Montgomery Ward in 1872 had inaugurated a totally new company dedicated solely to 'furnishing farmers and mechanics throughout the Northwest with all kinds of merchandise at whole-sale prices.' His subsequent official endorsement by the National Grange movement was responsible for much of Montgomery Ward's success, since he was able to use the movement's member-ship to develop a market. Other mail order services developed as an outgrowth of something already in existence, albeit on a more limited and informal scale. Enterprising merchants recognized the existence of a different type of customer – one who was not able to visit the store itself but who still needed both good-quality practical merchandise and, on occasion, the latest fashionable nov-elties. Such customers, in utilising a service not offered by competi-tors, could become a source of regular income. Rowland Macy stimulated his sales in 1861 by soliciting mail orders for any merchandise that could go through the post. By 1874 he had established a special mail order department. John Wanamaker's mail order service inaugurated in 1876 was, by the early 1880s, receiving more than one thousand letters a day. Several Toronto merchants were also reported to be doing a 'large letter order trade.'[7]

The introduction by the Eaton store of an official service simply formalized a practice that was already in existence, for by the end of the 1870s Timothy Eaton's delivery system included a special delivery to convey goods to the train station. While this was no doubt for the benefit of rural shoppers in town for a day's shopping, it is likely that those unable to make the journey to town could avail themselves of the same service. Old customers who had moved to Manitoba and even Saskatchewan wrote to the store that had served them so well in the past. One in Rivers, Manitoba, recalled making purchases at the Eaton store in St Marys, and another in Grandview, Manitoba, called to mind an order of dress goods he had bought for his wife in the early 1870s.[8] Settlers such as these took with them the knowledge that certain stores in central Canada could be relied upon to deal both honestly and fairly even with customers located miles from the store.

'The immense increase in our mail order department' cited in the first catalogue provided the impetus for devising a more effective method of catering to this growing market. Little risk was involved, since the initial overhead expenses were low, but in gaining a march on commercial travellers and drummers, the service could act as a force in establishing a new clientele. Timothy Eaton would later refer to this catalogue as the cheapest possible traveller and one that could be placed in the field by the thousands.[9]

The first catalogue, a small thirty-two-page publication, was distributed to out-of-town visitors to the annual Industrial Exhibition in the fall of 1884, possibly on the nights when the store itself was open for public inspection. The following spring a six-page flyer, approximately six by eighteen inches in size, was circulated by mail to advertise the opening of the Timothy Eaton Mail Order Department. A young female employee was transferred from the hosiery department to the mail order office to address the envelopes for these flyers. Unfortunately no information exists with regard to that early address list, so it can only be assumed that the flyers were sent to already known customers as well as local postmasters for distribution.[10] Flyers were sent as far as Manitoba, a territory then attracting many settlers from eastern Canada.

As many recipients of these early catalogues were not familiar with the company, each issue carried chatty comments regarding the store's background and history. One such edition pointed out that the store had been 'Established some Fourteen years ago upon the healthy Cash System – no bad debts, no interest bills, no loss on runaway debtors; but on the contrary, cash prices, small profits, a pleased people, and consequently an ever increasing Business.'[11] The physical size of the store was emphasized along with its many facilities, including passenger elevators and electric lights that allowed everything to be done on 'broad daylight principles' in all senses of the word. For out-of-town customers who could make an occasional visit to Toronto, the catalogue gave detailed instructions on how to get from the various railway stations to the store. The prime focus of the catalogue, however, was to draw attention to the enormous variety of merchandise available for, as one advertisement stated, 'the stock is the spirit of the place; the merchandise is greater than the store.'[12]

The catalogue carried information about each of the thirty-five departments, but it also noted that the merchandise listed was but a sample, 'since it did not give a correct idea of the immense varieties and extensive stock carried in the store.' Furthermore, it stressed that 'any order of goods wanted, which are not in the Catalogue, will be executed to our best judgement.'[13]

At first glance the concept of thirty-five departments is quite impressive, but a further study indicates that although the stock had been widened to include trunks, valises, and iron bedsteads, the store continued to carry predominantly dry goods merchandise. With access to greater space in the new store, such notions as ribbons, buttons, laces, and dress trimmings now sported a department of their own, attesting to the importance of these items at a time when most articles of feminine clothing were still made at home. In some cases the 'department' may have amounted to little more than a counter, but it indicated a desire to offer the widest variety available and to suggest the expertise that comes with specialization. The silk department, for example, was managed by a skilled professional to ensure complete customer satisfaction.

The enormous range and variety of merchandise was much in evidence. Ladies' gloves were offered in fifty-one different types and styles in fifteen different colours at prices ranging from twenty cents to a dollar seventy-five a pair. The hosiery department carried a similarly huge selection. When buying lace curtains, a customer could choose from three hundred patterns. The same variety was available in nearly every department, but as the 1884 catalogue pointed out:

Our trade is so enormous that the most desirable goods remain in stock but a short time, hence the advisability of making an early selection after receiving samples; and in order to meet the possibility of your selection being sold, it is advisable to make a second choice. Occasionally goods ordered are closed out of stock, and are not procurable, in consequence of which, please state whether we shall use our own judgement in making the selection.[14]

This suggests that the actual stock of an article might be quite limited. It is also an indication that Timothy Eaton, rather than receiving several large deliveries a year, was now receiving goods on a weekly or almost daily basis. This gave the store the benefit of a constant supply of fresh stock, alleviated storage problems, and facilitated cash flow.

The inclusion in the 1884 catalogue of mantles and dolmans at prices ranging up to seventy-five dollars belies the earlier stress on cheapness and suggests that attempts were being made to widen the store's appeal. Contemporary commentators remarked upon the general improvement in public tastes that was accompanied by a desire for a better class of merchandise. As a keen observer of customer preference, Timothy Eaton was quick to take advantage of any change in consumer demand. The increase in the number of white-collar workers in Toronto was probably partly responsible for this change. Studies by several historians reveal that many of the larger dry goods stores rose to greatness by catering primarily to the middle class – of which the white-collar worker was an important component. By contrast, the Eaton store catered to the diversity so evident in the Canadian population. Although men's outerwear was not carried by the store until towards the end of the 1880s, items needed by those employed in heavy outdoor manual labour were stocked: heavy underwear and shirts and stout boots at prices ranging from ninety cents to two dollars a pair. By the early 1890s overalls, with or without a bib, and smocks could be purchased for as little as forty or fifty cents. As one advertisement noted: 'We treat ... the most humble customer as we serve the lordly patron. We remember that the poor man's dollar goes as far as the rich man's, and treat them all alike.'[15]

Following the example of most newspaper advertisements in merely listing items and articles, the early editions of the catalogue contained no illustrations. Towards the end of the 1880s occasional illustrations depicting boys' suits and silverwear were produced by John L. Jones, a wood engraver. The first fashion illustrations drawn in pen and ink appeared in the 1890s and were reproduced using the boxwood method.[16] As with the sale of store merchandise, all mail order sales were for cash only, and no goods could be sent on approval. Goods found unsuitable or not as represented were cheerfully exchanged or the money refunded.

Since the merchandise for mail order customers was identical to that offered in the store, the procedure for dealing with these orders was simple. Miss Arnold, the clerk in charge of this department, merely opened the letters, put the cash in the cash box, and took care of each order. After the daily mail was opened, clerks acting as surrogate shoppers would progress through the store obtaining the articles listed in each letter. In this manner the store was able to provide distant purchasers with the 'benefit of a thorough knowledge of the most advanced fashions.' 'Wholly independent of the regular selling force,' these mail order clerks were 'carefully selected for their painstaking dispositions and excellent judgements in matters of dress.' Compelled on occasion to rely entirely on their own judgement, they sometimes had to determine from tracings of a foot or a shoe whether the item was for an adult or a child.[17]

The Canadian population at this time was largely rural. Once these potential customers were reached and convinced of the guarantee promised by the store, the mail order market provided an almost unlimited clientele. By 1887 the catalogue attested to

the daily increasing list of new names coming to us ... from all parts of Canada and the Provinces. Dwellers in sections which a few years ago could be found only on the most accurate maps now order merchandise through our Mail Order with the same facility as though present in person ... This catalogue is destined to go wherever the maple leaf grows, throughout the vast Dominion. We have the facilities for filling mail orders satisfactorily, no matter how far the letter has to come and the goods have to go.[18]

The personal care and concern demonstrated in the filling of orders was actively perceived and appreciated. Many customers took the time to write letters of thanks; others sent baskets of fruit and eggs to the Eaton family. Such responses attest to both the skill and the interest of the buying clerks, many of whom were barely out of their teens. One customer requested that Mrs Eaton or one of her family try out a piece of sheet music before shipping it, observing that if they liked it, the order would be successful. As one lady in Selkirk, Manitoba, recalled, 'her comfortable little home' had been completely furnished by the T. Eaton Company. Since they had always treated her right, she added, she saw no reason to deal with any other store.[19]

By 1890 the store had supplemented its enormous range of dry goods merchandise with such items as toys, novelties ranging from manicure boxes and cuff boxes to writing desks, silverware, brass goods including bedsteads, stationery, toilet articles, sewing machines, books, oil paintings, and wallpaper. Even with the addition of all these items, the store's appeal was still largely directed to the female shopper. Possibly in an attempt to widen its scope, one 1890 advertisement noted that, in selling men's shirts for fifty cents, 'There's little in them for us, but it brings the men in here and helps them to get over the idea that this is only a woman's store.' Two years later another advertisement declared that the store considered 'the interests of men and boys on a par with women and girls.'[20] Even in the mid-1880s, men's wear – or gentlemen's furnishings, to give it its correct departmental name – had been located on the main floor immediately inside the Queen Street entrance. This strategy was followed by most large store owners, for it was hoped that making this department easy to find would overcome the reluctance sometimes felt by male shoppers to enter a department store.

Whether each new item or category of merchandise was added in anticipation of customer demand or because of specific customer requests is uncertain, but the catalogue constantly assured customers that 'efforts will be constant and unwearied in searching the markets for all the latest productions and inventions which can be desired throughout each department and which [the customers] can rely upon getting at extremely low prices.'[21]

Competition among the numerous stores in urban centres meant that customer patronage could be fickle. In Toronto the number of dry goods stores remained constant. These were supplemented by numerous specialty shops retailing merchandise similar to that offered in the Eaton store. To maintain an edge each merchant tried to ensure that his goods were the newest and most attractive. The constant search for novelty may have prompted the introduction of some new departments, such as Japanese goods; but Timothy Eaton, like William Whiteley, probably added items as customers raised enquiries about their availability and supply. Mail order customers undoubtedly took the catalogue at its word and sent for quotations and samples of items not previously carried, thereby instigating the birth of further new departments.

New merchandise for which Timothy Eaton or his managers discerned a demand would at first be allotted a small space or display table and, as demand increased, extra space would be provided. Books, for example, which first appeared in the 1887 catalogue, were initially presented on a table adjacent to the stationery department and ultimately acquired a complete area of their own. By 1888 books had expanded to fill four full pages of the catalogue. A wide selection of classical and popular novelists and poets in both cloth and paper covers was offered. These ranged in price from ten cents to sixty-five cents and undercut publishers' prices in some cases by nearly 300 per cent. Prayer books, hymnals, and Bibles were offered in Presbyterian, Catholic, Methodist, Episcopal, and Ancient and Modern versions.[22]

The expansion of the millinery department provides a measure of Timothy Eaton's appeal to the ladies of Toronto. For men and women, young and old alike, hats or head coverings of some kind were regarded as a necessary article of clothing and an indicator of social respectability. Stores that offered millinery at dry goods prices could be said to have facilitated the spread of respectability to every class of society. The Eaton millinery department first underwent expansion in 1886 and again two years later to meet increased demand. By 1888 it had more than quadrupled its earlier size and occupied more than nine thousand square feet of floor space. A well-staffed millinery workroom ensured that orders could be trimmed while the customer waited. Mail orders were executed and mailed the day the order was received. In the case of sudden bereavement, the largest family order could be handled on 'four hours' notice for owing to our large business we employ special crape workers.' Two years later this offer was reduced to two hours. Those suffering familial loss also received assurances that Eaton's did not take advantage of the bereaved, as some retailers did, by piling on 100 per cent profit.[23]

Evidence from both sides of the Atlantic attests to the cutthroat nature of this branch of the dry goods trade. David Lewis of Liverpool was severely criticized in 1886 by the British Hat and Cap Traders Association for selling hats to the public at half the normal retail price. Gene Allen, in his study of wholesalers in the 1880s, refers to the aggressive marketing of millinery goods. The Toronto firm of D. McCall and Company, for example, offered to pay the return fares of all intending buyers journeying to the city. The Eaton store, in competing for patronage, frequently offered millinery goods as 'loss leaders.' One advertisement in the *Daily News* in August 1886 referred to 'running off our Children's and Ladies' Dress Hats at 10 cents.' But it seems likely that such sales did not always produce profitable results, for in the year ending February 1887 the millinery department suffered a loss of

$1,079.67. A further loss of $2,581.85 was sustained on mantles and clothing also produced by the millinery workroom. This department continued to experience problems down to the end of the decade, suggesting that costing needed some attention. It seems likely that rapid expansion of this department had effected a reduction in its sales per square foot. Slower expansion might have resulted, if not in a profit, at least in a markedly reduced loss. This was probably an example of the difficulties involved in trying to reconcile customer demand and the consequent increased traffic with the problems posed by cutthroat competition. In an attempt to overcome this in 1890 Timothy Eaton wrote to a large millinery firm in New York requesting assistance in locating an experienced superintendent for this department.[24]

As the store grew and acquired more space, opportunities presented themselves for further and more diverse growth. Most newspapers by this period carried a large selection of advertisements pushing a full line of ready-to-wear clothing for men and boys. By 1879 Petley and Petley and Jamiesons were offering men's and boys' ready-made coats and suits at prices ranging from $2.50 to $13.00. Meanwhile, until the mid-1880s, the gentlemen's furnishing department in the Eaton store continued to carry only such things as underwear, shirts, and ties. Ready-made clothing for boys was not introduced into the store until 1886, when it was quickly followed by a full line of men's outerwear, suits, jackets, and overcoats. Since the catalogue gave full instructions with regard to the measurements to be supplied when ordering men's suits and coats, and since no sizes were specified in the catalogue,[25] it is possible that such garments were in fact either made up or finished on the premises.

Women's ready-to-wear clothing, on the other hand, did not reach a high level of production until later in the 1890s. The boning common in women's garments was the prime reason for this. Although Timothy Eaton had achieved some success with a line of women's costumes in the spring and summer of 1873 and 1874, it is not known whether these were wholly ready-to-wear or simply sold half-finished, as many women's garments then were. No indication was given, for example, about the range of sizes available.

The introduction in the late 1880s of the shirtwaist, a type of blouse free of boning, to be worn with a gored skirt, ensured the success of ready-made clothes for women, for both could be made up in various sizes.[26]

The Eaton store, like many other dry goods stores in Toronto, had always carried such loose garments as mantles, capes, and dolman jackets that did not require a close individual fit. The ready-made print dresses, wrappers, and tea gowns listed in the catalogue for 1887–8 carry no indication as to available sizes. The fact that customers were requested to send bust measure and dress length from front of neck to bottom skirt suggests that some degree of alteration and finishing was in order for each garment. Alan Wilson points out that this was common practice at John Northway's establishment. Ready-made garments were acquired in bulk from a large supplier and then alterations were made for each article ordered by the customer.[27] The logical next step for most larger merchants was to move directly into the manufacture of such garments, as both John Northway and Timothy Eaton did in the 1890s.

Some historians credit the success of the emerging department stores to the steady influx of ready-to-wear clothes for both men and women. Hrant Pasdermadjian, however, points out that the growth of this business developed at the expense of piece-goods sales and ultimately became an important factor making for increased expenses – yet another reason encouraging Timothy Eaton to venture into the mass production of ready-to-wear. With the growth of ready-to-wear, a new type of outlet, the specialty clothing store (such as Stollery's and Tip Top Tailors in Toronto) emerged to compete with department stores. These often posed a greater threat than piece-goods stores.[28]

The emerging department stores of North America were, however, able to draw strength from the fact that brand names were not yet fully established or accepted by the public for most dry goods. There were some exceptions – for example, the cottons manufactured by Horrockses in England. The dresses designed and produced by Canadian dressmakers, such as O'Brien and William Stitt, had some following among the upper classes of Toronto, but in general the field of dry goods merchandise, and in particular ready-to-wear clothing, was ripe for commercial development and exploitation. As Porter and Livesay point out, before the onset of national brand advertising customers relied very largely on the retailer to give them good products.[29] This would account for the statement in the 1884 catalogue that 'No department in the business requires as much attention as this department ... We find from experience that ladies in buying silk, besides using their own judgement, have got to depend a good deal on the seller.'

Thus merchants already established in business and recognized as purveyors of good-quality merchandise were ahead of their competitors when ready-to-wear garments were first introduced and produced in large volume. Timothy Eaton had constantly stressed the virtue and value of a good name – 'Virtue of a name, a good name is better to be chosen than riches.' Drawn as most of his guidelines for life were from the Bible, this precept was echoed in the catalogues' declaration that 'Our Name is a Warrant.' 'Our goods have made for us a name. Our standing in the community is a guarantee for the quality of our merchandise. We cannot afford to misrepresent. How well we have carried out the spirit of these principles in dealing with our customers, we prefer that they should say. We refer to all that have dealt with us.' Advertisements indicate that manufacturers such as Hollis Shorey and Company of Montreal, makers of children's, boys', and youths' clothes, also recognized the value of such a warrant and wanted their products associated with the Eaton store.[30]

Timothy Eaton was determined that his customers would always associate the Eaton name with the idea of quality and value and would recognize that anything purchased at the Eaton store was backed by a solid guarantee. He was determined that no one, be it family or friend, should encroach upon this preserve. In 1883 Timothy Eaton's brother James opened a men's clothing store at 86 Yonge Street. Timothy had no intention of allowing his brother to take advantage of his own hard-earned reputation. Shoppers should immediately identify the Eaton name only with the store at 190 Yonge Street. An advertisement in the *Daily News* similar in style to his own and headed 'Eaton's London Branch – 86 Yonge

Street' prompted Timothy to remove his own advertisements from that newspaper for some considerable time. James Eaton's attempts to pass his store off as a branch of Timothy's store was firmly repudiated in the 1888 catalogue: 'But first of all let us remind you, that we HAVEN'T GOT or DON'T RUN any branch stores. All our energy and all our experience is centred at 190 Yonge Street ... Don't be influenced by any so called branch stores. If you are told this is "Eaton's," yes! this is a branch of "Eaton's," see if it is 190 Yonge Street.'[31]

Some of James's later advertisements removed the offending words 'Eaton's London Branch,'' while others pointed out that this London Branch had only one store on Yonge Street. Nevertheless another stated: 'We emphasize 86 Yonge Street because we don't want to deceive you. You can't find these bargains anywhere but 86 Yonge Street ... It's the Eaton of 86 Yonge Street thats a'talking to you now. Don't go to other stores thinking you are at James Eaton & Company's, 86 Yonge Street.'[32] This must have irritated Timothy. While it is possible that he and James were in collusion in an attempt to boost business for both stores, this seems unlikely in view of the fact that in the mid-1890s Timothy Eaton was reputed to have taken James's son John Weldon Eaton to court for similar, albeit more blatant, behaviour. After having worked together for many years, the Eaton brothers had gone their separate ways.

Despite constant public references to the ideals of honesty, quality, and value, it seems likely that Timothy Eaton's principles were not cast in stone. While exhorting his staff always to tell the truth with regard to the advertising of merchandise, he once stated: 'If you humbug do it right – let it be genuin that no one but yourself will see through and that they will conjecture – use no deception in the smallest degree – no nothing you cannot defend before God or man.' This memorandum appears to contradict publicly stated beliefs in honesty and plain speech – 'our advertisements can always be relied upon as being literally true.' 'The best foundation of business is confidence: and the best way to get it is to earn it.' 'Honesty is the best policy for a merchant who means to be great. So is liberality. You can deceive some of the people all the time, or all the people some of the time, but you can't deceive all the people all the time.'[33]

Whether Timothy Eaton's definition of 'humbug' referred to the possibility of deliberate deception or was meant to refer to the inclusion of nonsensical jargon in advertising material is difficult to discover. It seems unlikely that he would have remained long in business if he had constantly deceived the buying public. As the 1888 catalogue stated: 'You've seen us grow from a little store to a big one. You've been right with us all that time. If we have been crooked and mean, you know all about it; so we needn't make any confessions. If we've been upright and generous, you know all about that too.'[34]

Although most advertisements complied with his demand for plain speech, one in the *Telegram* in 1883 was something of an anomaly. It used strange one-word headings to introduce merchandise, and the advertising copy was unnecessarily verbose:

MINNIE
The sun was lifting its radiant head above the fleecy clouds of the morning when Minnie more radiant than Diana walked into Eaton's and purchased some of their washing lace.[35]

Perhaps this was the type of 'humbug' Timothy Eaton was referring to. Insofar as other kinds of 'humbug' were concerned, these involved suggestions that the business was larger and more diverse than was actually the case. Constant reference was made, for example, to the fact that the company purchased only for cash at a time when much of the supply was purchased on long- or short-term credit. Indeed, Timothy Eaton had on occasion been taken to task by suppliers for exceeding the stated credit period. As well, statements in the early catalogues imply that certain articles of merchandise, such as gloves and hosiery, were obtained directly from the manufacturers when it is clear that these were still being obtained from wholesalers.[36]

Mild deception can be found in suggestions that the Eaton company itself manufactured shirts and underwear:

We are one of the largest distributors of white dress shirts for strictly retail purposes in the country, and every shirt offered is of our own manufacture. As a consequence when you buy of us, you stand almost face to face with the producer ... We have completed a system in the manufacture of our Cotton underwear, whereby the stitching is very fine, we give you 15 stitches to the inch, where formerly you only got 11. Steam power and every modern appliance conducive to the economy is utilized in the manufacture of this important branch of ladies wear, consequently we produce garments at prices which make it impossible for us to be undersold by any other house in the same quality of goods.[37]

Like similar Macy advertisements in the 1850s, these were no doubt written to create the impression that the retailer not only operated a store of recognized financial credibility but was also determined to supply the best-quality bargains for his customers. In a sense Timothy Eaton projected what he hoped and planned to bring about. The inclusion of some forty to fifty advertisements of companies and manufacturers supplying merchandise to the Eaton store in the 1890 catalogue was perhaps another method of demonstrating to the customers the enormous range of suppliers with whom he dealt. Such appeals to his customers thus conjured up an establishment or organization that left no stone unturned in the service of its clientele, from the preparation of the raw material to the delivery of the finished product.

The demand for dry goods continued to rise as more of the population joined the ranks of regular salary and wage earners; at the same time, retailers had to take greater care to ensure that goods were of the latest fashion and design. The unwearying search for the new and the different was a constant theme, for 'Novelty is the order of the day.'[38]

The decline in sales experienced in 1884, was, according to various reports, largely due to the fact that old stock from the Scott Street operation had been incorporated with stock at the new store. Retailers had little, if any, control over the fact that, by increasing the variety and scope of their merchandise to attract a wider clientele, they allowed and encouraged that clientele to assume a role in the moulding of popular tastes. On occasion this could have disastrous consequences, not only for retailers, but also for manufacturers who chose to produce goods no longer in demand. As the *Monetary Times* observed in 1881, the constant questions of moment to fashionable females were 'What is being worn?' and 'What is going to be worn?' The demand at the end of the 1870s for lighter and softer French woollen goods, for example, had been such as to 'press heavily upon the Bradford [textile] plants' whose works were half idle.[39] As the available income of more and more shoppers allowed for the acquisition of what had once been considered luxuries, so the appeal to the multitudes underwent a marked change.

During this period of expansion some store executives were convinced that they merely had to fill the store with attractive goods and advertise widely, and the sales people would have nothing to do but place those goods in the customers' hands. No selling techniques or skills would be required. The Macy store in New York, for example, in the decade 1877 to 1887, became both conservative and complacent, with the result that it began to lose ground to others. The concept of a fixed price had, in a sense, reduced the customer to a passive role of either accepting or rejecting the merchandise. Stores that wished to expand would have not only to stimulate demand but to create it. According to both contemporary and later observers, this is what the most successful set out to do. The big 'pushing' shops, as they were commonly regarded, attracted new clients but did not get all their trade at the expense of their smaller rivals.[40]

Increased volumes were stimulated by various new tactics – special sales and advertising that captured the imagination and demanded attention. In the past sales had been used to dispose of goods damaged by fire and water, or bankrupt stocks; now sales were used to move every item in the store. 'While the rule at Eaton's is to sell cheap all the time, yet there are periods in the year when it becomes necessary to sell cheaper than other times, in order to convert surplus stock into ready cash and hence the origin of Eaton's Big Clearing Sale.'[41]

Department stores drew customers to their large, attractive, modern establishments by means of advertisements. Catalogues actively promoted the idea of shopping as a pleasure in a deliberate policy of temptation: 'Everything is looked to for your comfort in shopping, making it a pleasure rather than a drudgery.' In a world of mass consumption, as Rosalind Williams astutely observed, 'the needs of the imagination play as large a role as those of the body. Both are exploited by commerce, ... [invited] into a fantasy world of pleasure, comfort and amusement.' She further contended that the growth of technology, while making possible an 'equalization of enjoyments,' did so without a corresponding 'equalization of incomes.'[42] Encouraged by advertising to browse through all departments in the store, shoppers were educated into wanting a higher standard of living. Where in the past stout quality and long wear had been considered the requisite virtues with regard to articles of personal wear, the developing department stores became the first preachers of the creed that goods could be replaced when outdated rather than outworn. Thus customs and practices that in the past had been associated only with the upper classes would now gradually come to be adopted by a much larger section of the population.

The effort to bring more people into contact with the consumer ethos made the presentation, advertising, and display of material increasingly important. In the considered opinion of Nathaniel C. Fowler, a Boston newspaper reporter who in the 1880s began writing books of guidance with regard to advertising: 'Half of the customers in any community do not know all they want until somebody tells them.' As one contemporary shopper observed, 'It is not that we need so much more, or that our requirements are so increased, but we are not able to stand against the overwhelming temptations to buy which besiege us at every turn.'[43] Examples of this type of merchandising in the Eaton catalogue point out that 'at our prices you are able to have 2 hats otherwise you could only buy one,' and suggest that sometimes more than money can be saved: 'with the present perfection of machinery, home work on underwear is a loss of time, the garments are sold for about the ordinary price of the materials.'[44] The latter example questioned the logic of the custom of sewing all articles of personal underwear by hand at home, even after the introduction and wide distribution of personal sewing machines. The Eaton store, however, did not resort to the tactics adopted by the Bon Marché in Paris, which widely separated the departments for women's coats and dresses, compelling customers to traverse almost the whole length of the store to reach one or the other and thus to be exposed to the full array of saleable merchandise.

Although the decade of the 1880s was marked by setbacks of one kind or another, along with the usual unsubstantiated rumours of failure circulated by competitors, it was on the whole a decade of enormous growth for the Eaton enterprise. In 1880 the store had been located in cramped quarters at 178 Yonge Street, but by 1890 Timothy Eaton operated a mammoth emporium fronting on three main downtown streets. Such success more than vindicated his faith in simple maxims.

7

Private Incorporation and Public Expansion

'Business, dear friends, is a severe conglomeration of
dollars and cents ... the reliable sixpence [is] vastly better
than the slow shilling.'
Eaton's Catalogue, 1892–3

The steady growth experienced by the Eaton store during the early part of the 1880s and the subsequent more rapid expansion towards the end of that decade continued into the 1890s with what amounted to an explosion of activity as enormous advances were made by the company in all areas of its operations. External momentum was provided by the rapid extension of urbanization and industrialization in the city of Toronto, a change that affected all sectors of the community. By 1890 the population had risen to more than 180,000, as the annexed areas of Yorkville, Brockton, Riverside, Parkdale, Seaton Village, and Deer Park were added to the city. By 1900 the population, a large percentage of which was under the age of thirty, totalled well over 200,000. This growth provided a constant pool of young workers for Toronto's growing industrial and commercial sectors. The number of industrial wage earners rose from 12,700 in 1881 to 25,250 in 1891, and this figure had nearly doubled again by 1902. Similar growth was experienced in the construction industry as the city embarked on numerous large construction projects – Massey Hall, City Hall, Union Station, the Ontario Parliament buildings – as well as a host of new buildings for local institutions. From January 1890 to December 1894 more than $13 million was injected in this manner into the local economy. The growth of financial institutions, banks, and trust and insurance companies kept pace with this expansion. The number of white-collar workers within the city rose from 3,864 in 1881 to 36,463 in 1911.[1] Similar growth, while not so rapid in all areas of Canada, was duplicated throughout Ontario and the Dominion at large and provided Canadian retailers with an ever-expanding market.

In 1891 Timothy Eaton officially incorporated his business. Although growing companies frequently undertook incorporation in this decade to raise the capital for proposed programs of expansion and rebuilding, the transition from private to public ownership did not always follow automatically. The Eaton company – unlike Harrods in England, which became a limited liability company in 1889 – continued to operate as a private company. As contemporary advertisements pointed out, the name change to the T. Eaton Company Limited in no way interfered with the usual management of the store.[2] Undoubtedly implemented to ensure continuity of the business and to place the concern on a secure legal footing, incorporation also allowed its owner to provide potential suppliers with financial information regarding the extent of company capitalization.

Incorporation was effected under the provisions of the Ontario Joint Stock Companies Letters Patent Act on 21 April 1891, and the new company began with a capitalization of $500,000 divided into 5,000 shares of $100 each. At the time of incorporation 2,485 shares were taken up by Timothy Eaton and four members of his immediate family. Timothy, as president, held 2,310, Edward, as vice-president, 145. The remaining 30 were equally divided among Mrs Eaton and their two daughters, Margaret Beattie Burden and Josephine Smith Eaton. Slowly at first and then more rapidly as the decade progressed, both the number of paid-up shares and the list of shareholders increased. However, Timothy Eaton and his family at all times held well over 80 per cent of the shares. The number of shareholders expanded from thirteen in December 1896 to some fifty-eight by 190 (holding 4,483 shares), as senior personnel from the store were invited to share in the company's growing success.[3]

Although the majority of those listed held only minimal amounts, several senior employees owned quite large blocks, a matter that after the turn of the century offered the potential for conflict.

The company does not appear to have extracted any material gain from these transactions; to assist them in the acquisition of stock, employees received dividends of 6 per cent on the shares set aside for their ownership. These funds were then placed against the purchase price of the shares. No formal arrangements existed with regard to the purchase of stock, and the opportunity was offered to only a select few.

Timothy Eaton's personal holding dropped from 2,310 shares in 1891 to a low of 1,574 in 1896 and rose again to 2,670 in 1900. The number of shares held by Edward Young Eaton grew from 145 in 1895 to 652 in 1896, but dropped to zero in the following year. Listed as director and vice-president from 1891 to 1897, Edward then disappeared from the brief list of office holders until 1899, when he once again held a large block of shares (440). In 1900 he returned as vice-president. By the mid-1890s, Edward was already suffering from Bright's disease, which was to take his life in October 1900 at the age of thirty-seven. His place as director for the two-year period 1898–9 was taken by a senior member of the staff, and it was not until 1898 that his younger brother, John Craig Eaton, was appointed first a director and later, in October 1900, vice-president.

The full 5,000 shares were not completely taken up until the turn of the century. Capitalization was increased to $1 million in April 1905.[4]

Formal incorporation of the company in 1891 had little effect on the actual operation of the business. Its size and complexity, however, necessitated a greater delegation of both authority and responsibility. This required the introduction of further new methods and concepts by senior personnel who obviously regarded themselves as active participants in a highly successful venture. The added incentive of personal gain suggested in the acquisition of company shares was matched by Timothy Eaton's willingness to allow for the implementation of changes beneficial to the business as a whole.

In addition the store benefited from the active participation of Edward Young Eaton. Despite poor health, he set in motion a new cashier system and streamlined the delivery process to remove the possibility of error and to increase profitability. Buyers visiting large department stores on both sides of the Atlantic were instructed by him to take careful note of practices that could be used to advantage in the Eaton store. The ensuing suggestion book provides a fascinating glimpse of the many facets involved in operating a late-nineteenth-century department store. Proposals for change encompassed subjects as wide-ranging as the display of goods, the interior decoration of different departments, a speedier method of distributing wages, and the calibre and skill of the sales help.[5]

This concern for more efficient operation was necessary for a company whose overhead expenses rose with the expansion of the store. The cost of doing any kind of business, as Ralph Hower demonstrated, was rising well before the turn of the century.[6] The new procedures that were instituted recognized that minute deviations in cost could make or break an enterprise. Full and careful records were therefore kept of each expense. A separate account was maintained in the general ledger not only of each interest payment made on loans, but also of minor expenses such as carfares for messengers and postage stamps. A complete record of all expenses involved in the running of a large dry goods store allowed those in charge to arrive at a wholly accurate appraisal not only of the business as a whole, but of each department. The careful summary included with the financial papers at the time of incorporation indicates that this method was already securely entrenched by the late 1880s.

Each department was expected to operate as a profitable entity and was therefore charged for all services required in the running of its business. Costs included rent, light, heat, water, salaries, wages, and stationery, as well as a proportionate share of the delivery system, mail order, advertising, and general store management expenses. In this way a very close check was maintained on even the most trivial expenses. In the mid-1890s, for instance, by calculating to the tenth of a cent the operating costs of the check office, both before and after the introduction of adding machines, John James Eaton ultimately effected a savings of $3.09 per week. This concern with cost was common among Eaton employees. The manager of the London office reported a decline in freight charges for 1895 resulting from the regular use of secondhand cases to forward new goods.[7] A similar careful check was maintained on all expenses, from the major item of salaries and wages to the more trivial one of the wrapping paper and string used in the parcelling of goods. This constant attention to the whole range of company expenditure ensured that, as the store grew in size, the operation would not become bogged down in conservative complacency and extravagant waste.

Throughout the 1890s the physical expansion of the store advanced at an accelerated pace as the company acquired property on all four frontages of the block bounded by Queen, Yonge, James, and Albert streets, to house retail, manufacturing, mail order, and delivery facilities. Property was also acquired on Louisa and Orde streets for stable facilities and on the north side of Albert Street for a mail order annex building.[8] Timothy Eaton also owned one hundred acres of farm land in Georgetown and two hundred acres in Islington. These farm properties, which remained in his personal holding for some time, provided the store with dairy products for its restaurants as well as hay and oats for the delivery horses.[9]

Where possible, property was purchased at the time of acquisition, but in some cases, as with 202–10 Yonge Street, 14–20 Queen Street, and much of the property on James Street, the locations were leased initially and purchased later as circumstances and finances allowed. By 1896 the addition of these buildings had resulted in the creation of a store of mammoth proportions all under one roof and with entrances on Yonge, Queen, James, and Albert streets. Store space then totalled 293,538 square feet, more than double the 1890 figure of 137,504 square feet. In November 1897 a further 33,000 square feet was added with the purchase of additional property on Yonge Street. On each occasion the most up-to-date machinery was installed in all the buildings: elevators, pneumatic tubes for transporting cash from the customers to the central cashier desk in the basement, electric generators to allow complete independence from the municipal supply, and a full Grinnell sprinkler system. By 1899 the estimated cost of these buildings, exclusive of land, plant, and fixtures, amounted to $367,069.[10]

This constant expansion also generated several rumours throughout the 1890s about the opening of branch stores and factories in places as distant as Ottawa, Niagara Falls, Montreal, and Sydney, Nova Scotia.[11] Several Toronto citizens, no doubt attracted by the prospects of profits from increased land values, were prompted to offer to sell property in the vicinity of the store, but these offers were largely ignored.[12] Timothy Eaton preferred to make full use of property already in his control, and in 1896 he approached Toronto City Council for permission to use the areas under the sidewalks of James, Queen, and Albert streets. Later in 1898–9 he gained permission to excavate tunnels under Albert Street to allow for easier movement between company buildings.[13]

Cash was and would continue to be Timothy Eaton's preferred method of purchase, but he was not averse to obtaining adequate financial accommodation as and when circumstances required. At the time of incorporation he had a mortgage of $50,000 from the Canada Life Assurance Company on the Yonge Street building and further mortgages amounting to $41,000 on Queen Street property. As well, liabilities due to the Bank of British North America and numerous suppliers amounted to some $387,000. Offset against this debt load and his obvious willingness to take on further liabilities were his assets of real estate, buildings, plant, fixtures, and stock at 190–6 Yonge Street, 10–12 Queen Street, 13–19 James Street, the Orde Street stables, and some $4,000 cash in hand. He had obviously travelled quite a distance from the day when he startled John Macdonald by declaring that his assets were a wife, five children, and seven dollars.[14]

Although the full extent of his loans during this decade is not known, mortgages were raised to finance some of the early expansion. It is evident, however, that decisions regarding expansion were neither conceived nor undertaken in haste, and that the terms of any financial agreement had at all times to meet certain stringent requirements. Timothy Eaton refused on one occasion to accept a six-month demand option on a proposed loan. In doing so he pointed out that the nature of his business precluded such a possibility since the length of time between placing orders for merchandise and the final cash sale sometimes amounted to six or eight months.[15] Horses could not be changed at mid-stream. This was especially true when arranging for the opening of a new department or when enlarging smaller departments. For this reason he would accept only mortgages that placed no such restrictions on his financial arrangements.

Despite the apparent success of the business, life was not all plain sailing. The attempt to obtain financial accommodation in February 1891 met with rejection when the British broker refused to accept Timothy Eaton's appraisal on the Queen Street store, regarding it as not worth the $130,000 quoted by its owner. When the property was formally appraised in February of the following year at $141,872 it was pointed out that while the property value was likely to increase, few individuals could afford either to rent or buy it *en bloc*. This in effect considerably reduced its actual market value. In 1894 Timothy Eaton obtained a mortgage of approximately $91,000 on the store from the North British and Mercantile Insurance Company. In line with his earlier practice, this debt was fully discharged nearly two years before maturity.[16]

It is at times difficult to know which came first, the expansion of physical space or the new departments, for expansion was continuous. Timothy Eaton's willingness to venture into constant rapid and extensive expansion set him apart from all his Toronto competitors in this period. Acting on the old premise of 'nothing ventured, nothing gained,' he continued to stretch his resources to their uttermost limits. As he informed one mortgage source, 'I want a building for the purpose of merchandising goods, to be made capable of holding all the goods that could be packed into it.'[17] Advertisements declaring 'this store is big, but not big enough' and stating that plans for another addition were 'made necessary by perpetual trade increase' indicate his determination to meet those demands and to respond to the needs of the ordinary consumer. At times the increase in trade appears to have surprised both Timothy Eaton and his managers. The millinery department, for instance, needed continual expansion, and by September 1896 covered 12,500 square feet of space. The sales of toilet goods, candies, and patent medicines also increased at a rapid rate. As one advertisement pointed out: 'The remarkable growth of this department has been surprising even to ourselves. Possibly no other department in the store has such a large number of patrons ... The growth has been so rapid that new quarters were necessary.'[18]

Thorough investigation preceded any venture into new areas of merchandise or a wider variety of current stock. As Timothy Eaton wrote to one of his managers: 'have it wrought out, thought out, threshed out and be ready for action when I see you. Then we will be able to put into motion a Department where you can discharge your duties to your own, and to our satisfaction.'[19]

As the store grew, so too did the services offered to the customer. By the mid-1890s the Eaton shopper could browse through the largest selection of merchandise in the city, enjoy cool drinks and ice cream in the summer and hot meals all year round, have shoes repaired, obtain magazine subscriptions, and take advantage of the free bus service offered by the store to certain boats and trains. The latter ensured that customers would not be tempted even to enter the establishments operated by competitors. Although most of these additional services paid for themselves, some, such as waiting rooms, parcel and coat checks, and the bus services, were absorbed in the interests of good customer relations.

The profit test facilitated quick decision making. Writing to the Butterick Publishing Company Limited in December 1889, Timothy Eaton noted: 'What we want is to test the matter, and see whether there is any money in it. If there is we want to buckle right in and push it for all it is worth. If there is not any money in it for us we do not want to touch it.'[20] The expansion into manufacturing (to be dealt with more fully in chapter eight) was yet another undertaking aimed at increasing both sales volumes and profits. Manufacturing initially accounted for only a small percentage of store merchandise; by far the largest portion was acquired from a host of other sources. New suppliers were constantly added. By 1891 the list encompassed wholesalers and manufacturers on both sides of the Atlantic and included, as a portent of things to come, a wholesaler or commission agent in Yokohama, Japan.

At the time of incorporation the record of outstanding accounts lists more than 213 companies in North America, 123 of these in Toronto, with 54 in other Canadian centres, and 36 in the United States. An additional 88 companies were listed for Europe, most in Great Britain and just 10 in continental Europe. Since these accounts cover a period from July to December 1891, it can be assumed that they represent a more or less complete list of Eaton suppliers at that time. The sum outstanding for current accounts and for goods ordered amounted to nearly $230,000.00, roughly 40 per cent of which represented merchandise purchased in North America. One indication of the great change that had occurred in the Toronto dry goods industry is the fact that purchases from local suppliers amounted to only 20 per cent of the total. The company of the late John Macdonald still appeared on this list, but the figure of just under $5,000.00 suggests the distance both companies had travelled. Many of the individual accounts represented quite small sums, such as the $10.15 owing to the Port Elgin Brush Company. The list did include some fairly large accounts. Among the Canadian suppliers, H.H. Woolf and Company, A. Bradshaw and Son, G. Goulding, and Williams, Greene and Rome had provided the Eaton store with goods amounting to $27,730.07. Although Timothy Eaton was still purchasing fairly large quantities of merchandise from some Toronto wholesalers, he preferred to deal directly, where possible, with primary suppliers. In this way he was assured of purchasing only the newest and most up-to-date stock and could avoid merchandise the wholesaler was finding difficult to move. By the mid-1890s city goods were ordered only when they were required for immediate sales to replace goods in high demand. In order to prevent the acquisition of unsaleable merchandise, a very close eye was maintained on all wholesale houses. In 1892 Timothy Eaton warned the manager of his London office that one large London house was falling behind and had too many held-over stocks. Care should thus be taken to ensure that only the buyers dealt with this supplier.[21]

The liabilities to mainly British and some European accounts by contrast amounted to more than $130,000, or some 60 per cent of the total debt. Of this total nearly a third of the merchandise was supplied by three large wholesale houses in London (Rylands and Sons, Cook Sons and Company, Pawson and Company) that Timothy Eaton had patronized since the mid-1880s. Customs duties on Eaton imports rose from $103,473 in 1889 to $137,491 for the first nine months of 1891, suggesting that the volumes of imports from overseas were continually on the increase.[22]

Although trade journals provided information relating to the special manufacturing areas of Europe, Timothy Eaton appears to have relied on personal introductions to gain access to new sources of supply. A mutual business acquaintance and local commission agent, Feodor Boas, arranged for the introduction to George Merz, a commission agent with R.D. Warburg and Company in Berlin. By 1891 Merz not only organized appointments for Eaton buyers with manufacturers in Berlin and Saxony, but also arranged for the subsequent shipping of Eaton merchandise from Hamburg to Montreal.[23] The Eaton company was thus able to establish relationships quickly with suppliers throughout much of western Europe. Once the initial contact had been achieved, the resulting large orders worked their own magic. By the mid-1890s the Eaton reputation had become sufficiently well established in North America for manufacturers themselves to approach the store directly. By the turn of the century the Paris office was besieged by the salesmen of European manufacturers, the doorman on occasion being offered bribes to admit salesmen to see the buyers. One silk salesman lamenting a lost order complained that the commission alone would have paid his salary for eight months.[24]

The net was spread far and wide in the search for desirable goods. Care was taken, however, to ensure that the store did not become unduly dependent on any one supplier. Individual items were obtained from a number of different manufacturers. Boots and shoes were purchased from five or six different suppliers in Toronto, Quebec City, and Rochester, New York; hosiery and gloves came from numerous suppliers in both Great Britain and Germany. Visits to expositions and trade fairs, such as the World's Fair in Chicago in 1893, were part of the endless quest for novelties and quality goods and provided buyers with valuable information from both American and European suppliers. On occasion these

Timothy Eaton, *c.* 1863

Timothy Eaton's birthplace, Clogher, near Ballymena,
Ulster, Northern Ireland

The store at Portglenone, Ulster,
where Timothy Eaton served his apprenticeship.
The picture was taken before 1854.

Margaret Wilson Beattie Eaton, *c.* 1870

The Page Block at 190 Yonge Street, Toronto, in 1870,
which was bought by Timothy Eaton in 1882
to allow for the erection of his new store in 1883

178 Yonge Street, Toronto, in 1892,
looking east on Queen Street.
The store was at that time operated by Robert Simpson
but the building remained largely unchanged
from Timothy Eaton's time.

Above left: Yonge Street, Toronto, *c.* 1900, looking south. The Eaton store is on the right with the Robert Simpson store in the background.

Below left: Cover of the 1897–8 Fall and Winter Catalogue showing the extent of mail order coverage across Canada and the spread of company property in Toronto. It also carries two of the slogans most commonly used during the 1890s.

Below: Exterior of Eaton store, Toronto, *c.* 1905, showing crowds waiting to enter the store for the Friday bargain day

Eaton employees' volunteer fire brigade, 1897.
John Craig Eaton is third from the right in
the back row.

Timothy Eaton and John Craig Eaton
in the Private Office, 1899

Interior views of the store

Above left: Whitewear and bedding department, *c.* 1900,
with stools for customer's use in front of the counter

Below left: Dress goods department, *c.* 1903,
showing balcony and light well

Below: Hatpins and handkerchiefs, *c.* 1904. The number of
assistants testify to the high demand for such goods.

Manufacturing areas

Above left: Eaton's shirtwaist factory, *c.* 1906

Below left: Tailoring department, *c.* 1904

Below: Harness-making department, *c.* 1907

Head cashier's office (old counting room), *c.* 1904.
This was the collecting centre
for all cash and invoices.

Central cash office
located in the basement of the main store, *c.* 1904,
which received payments made in all departments
by means of a pneumatic system.
The change was then returned to customers
by the same system.

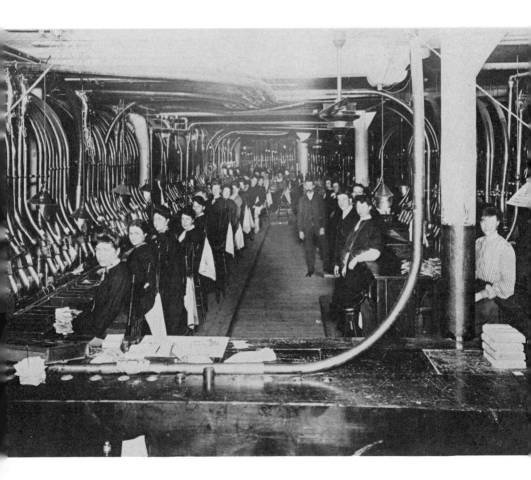

Employees arriving at staff entrance, Louisa Street,
Toronto, 4 July 1911

Loaded horse-drawn wagons
for a special shipment to China, *c.* 1906

Packing and shipping department,
mail order building, Toronto, 1908

Santa Claus in Toyland in the Eaton store, Toronto, 1906

The Eaton Santa Claus Parade, Toronto, 1906

The Eaton store in Winnipeg, 17 July 1905

Special Easter display
in the central well of the Toronto store, 1907,
in memory of Timothy Eaton

forays took strange paths. In 1891 a Methodist missionary in Japan was asked to obtain information from Japanese manufacturers and suppliers.[25] Perhaps it was hoped that his contacts would be more direct than those acquired through the commission agent in Yokohama.

The vastly increased productive capacity of large industrial concerns, not to mention their greater capital investment, compelled manufacturers to secure guaranteed markets for their output. Placing their own agents in the field, they bypassed the older methods of supply and assumed the functions undertaken earlier by wholesalers and jobbers. Edward Gurney, in an address to the Toronto Board of Trade in 1896, acknowledged that manufacturers' agents from Europe and the United States were frequently in the city.[26] An increasing number of retailers were only too happy to take advantage of this new trend. By the 1890s many stores were prepared and willing to purchase a manufacturer's entire stock for the season. W.A. Murray in Toronto boasted of securing more than ten thousand ladies' shirtwaists, almost the entire production of three American manufacturers.[27] This closer relationship not only provided manufacturers with a guaranteed market, but also allowed them to respond more quickly to changes in consumer demand.

The alacrity with which this new practice was adopted damaged a system that had been in existence for well over a century and was in large measure responsible for a decline in the wholesale sector of the industry. In Toronto the wholesaling of dry goods had peaked in the 1880s, and the 1890s saw the failure of several of the older and larger businesses. McMaster and Company, established in 1837, failed in 1897, as did one of Timothy Eaton's earliest suppliers, Adam Hope.[28]

The spectacular failure in 1895 of Samson, Kennedy and Gemmel offered a prime example of the hazards facing Toronto wholesalers. In an attempt to ward off disaster, goods had been offered for sale at sacrifice prices. The *Monetary Times* severely censured attempts to gain business by marketing domestic goods at prices that other wholesalers could not rival.[29] One unnamed retailer suggested that wholesalers were the authors of their own downfall:

Yes ... I am an importer and a sincere believer in the system of direct importation for retail merchants. The wholesale jobbers are compelled to handle domestic goods upon inadequate profits and often at a loss. They naturally try to make it up on the goods bought abroad, and unless successful in securing large profits upon imported stuffs, their trade is a loss. In consequence the retail trade have themselves undertaken the task of importation.[30]

Timothy Eaton had always rejected the widely accepted attitude that competition 'as the life of the trade [was] no longer considered good logic' and held firmly to the idea that with the strangulation of competition 'in nearly all lines of business ... the independent retailer need[ed] to be sharp-witted to keep abreast of combinations.' One Eaton advertisement stated this belief quite plainly:

We accept the responsibility of doing better than anyone else. We want you to expect better value and better service here than in any other store. Is that plain enough? ... There's a movement on foot to prevent our buying to as good advantage – to make us pay more for goods in order to give the wholesalers a chance. Just to show how much we think of it we crowd prices down a notch lower and give that sort of competition something to think about.[31]

Although the material in both newspaper advertisements and the catalogues suggested that both sales and purchases were made entirely on the cash principle, this was not the case. Timothy Eaton, as in the past, continued to utilize each financial association to its fullest potential. Once convinced of a reasonably sure market for specific items of merchandise, he placed large orders for which payment was made in the form of bank acceptances dated, on occasion, two, three, and four months ahead. Timothy Eaton thus took advantage of the best aspects of both systems, the older credit system for his own purchases, and the newer one of cash for selling the merchandise.

The German commission agent George Merz complained that this practice placed the Warburg business on a very insecure footing. Merz then went on to add that, if Timothy wished the relationship to continue, he must adhere to the initial agreement of paying each monthly statement as it came due, rather than accumulating two or three months' invoices and then sending acceptance notes, post-dated three or four months in the future. As he pointed out:

You must make up your mind gentlemen to accomodate [sic] your-selves to our terms, viz. 3 ms. acceptance in London, England, every first of the month for all invoices of the foregoing month ... You are profiting of all advantages by buying through us, directly from the manufacturers, but the capital invested in your account is too important and the time until settlement reaches us so extended that the business begins to be unsatisfactory to us.[32]

Timothy Eaton replied that the situation had arisen from comments made by a mutual business friend who had informed him that the house of Warburg 'was immensely wealthy and not particular about day or month' of payment. It seems likely that each case was dealt with on an individual basis; the buyers' notebooks, for example, regularly listed different terms for each supplier. Buyers suggested either immediate or delayed payment of each account.

In proffering his apology to Merz, Timothy Eaton then went on to state: 'The only thing we will require of you is to do your best to see that our orders are placed in the proper hands and at the best prices, looking well to all discounts.'[33] Best prices, meaning those at rock-bottom level, and discounts were matters that constantly engaged the attention of Eaton buyers. The buyers themselves were wholly responsible for securing merchandise at suitable prices, arranging terms, and setting the final selling price. As one stated: 'In regard to buying I endeavour to buy at the cheapest markets and get bottom prices, and then try to sell lower than anyone else.' It seems clear that where volume purchases were concerned, buyers established acceptable rates before they even left Toronto. In this sense it could perhaps be said that 'the visible hand of management,' at least where Eaton buyers were concerned, replaced the 'invisible hand of market mechanisms.' Gone were the days when a pair of cotton hose could fluctuate from 8s.0d. in 1811, to 1s.6d. in 1831 and up again to 3s.4d. in 1840, depending on the vagaries of the market-place, rather than on the manufacturer's cost. Eaton's buyers would therefore endeavour to persuade manufacturers to meet their prices rather than the other way around. In this respect they not only had the power of volume, but as one executive pointed out in 1898, with the security of certain cash at the back of them, they could reasonably expect to obtain any price they desired.

Timothy Eaton also continued to hold the view that 'if buyers choose stuff, it is their responsibility and they have to sell it.' Eaton buyers thus of necessity became experts in discovering the best markets for every item of merchandise in the store. Jewellery could be purchased at greater savings in New York; chinaware from German manufacturers, whose labour costs were extremely low.[34] The savings that accrued from such purchases were further enhanced by the practice of securing the most satisfactory discounts. As the manager of the general office pointed out to his colleagues at a meeting of senior employees early in 1894, they should try to get better discounts:

We could do the same amount of business we have been in the habit of doing with a less amount of stock ... The amount of money that is lying on these shelves is due to Discounts not being anxiously looked after ... The other day I noticed an Invoice going through at 2$^{1}/_{2}$–10. It was an American Invoice and it took all of ten days to get these goods passed and delivered into the Department. I asked the Head of the Department if he could not get these terms extended and he informed me the next day that he had got 2$^{1}/_{2}$–60. This was a gain of 50 days ... It is the little items that count, either on the right or the wrong side at the end of six months.[35]

He was elaborating on ideas put forward by Timothy Eaton, who constantly encouraged the practice of frequent handling of small quantities, compelling the manufacturers to assume storage costs while ensuring a steady supply of fresh goods on his own shelves.[36] As the century drew to a close, the practice of seeking a more rapid turnover increased. By 1892, although a complete inventory of stock was taken every six months, the turnovers of many of the departments were much more frequent. Bi-weekly shipments were received from overseas as individual manufacturers forwarded goods at regularly requested intervals. The stock once received was placed immediately on the sales floor. The staff could then see at a glance which items were popular and which were not. In this respect Timothy Eaton was ahead of his Toronto competitors. Both Robert Simpson and W.A. Murray were accused of leaving arrivals of new goods on the sidewalks outside their respective stores for several days until room could be made for them in the various departments.[37] This is also an indication of the extent to which Timothy Eaton had progressed beyond his close competitors in buying frequently and also limiting the stock to amounts that the store could handle comfortably. From the few figures available, it appears that stock at the Eaton store was turned over on an average of four times a year. In departments such as millinery the rate might have approached six or seven times a year. This compares well with the Macy store average of five times a year in the 1890s.[38]

The dedication of staff and resources to this primary activity of securing merchandise for the store was enormous. In the early 1890s Timothy Eaton acknowledged that he was no longer conversant with contemporary values and withdrew completely from this aspect of the business.[39] His skill in selecting men and women who excelled in their field was matched by the energy and enthusiasm with which they tackled their demanding jobs. Success in this field was dependent not upon age, gender, or seniority but on a thriving record of sales profitability and increased volume. J.A.C. Poole, the buyer of china and glassware, was first sent overseas at the age of nineteen; in the course of his very successful career, he made forty-five such trips to Europe as well as several to the Far East.[40] At Timothy Eaton's urging, buyers constantly sought out the new goods and novelties the public demanded, and the expansion of store merchandise into new departments followed closely on the heels of their expanding travels. A huge volume of dolls, toys, gloves, china, glassware, jewellery, and cutlery came from Europe, silk and rattan-ware from the Far East, bicycles and jewellery from the United States, and a continually expanding supply of textiles, hosiery, and assorted fancy goods from Great Britain.

Buying trips of two to three months were the rule rather than the exception as buyers visited manufacturers and suppliers on both sides of the Atlantic at a time when all land travel was accomplished by train. Armed with explicit instructions on where to go, whom to call on, where to stay, how much to tip, how to behave with suppliers, and when and how to order the actual goods, the buyers followed a recognized procedure. Samples had first to be obtained to allow for comparison shopping. When it came time to order, as one buyer recorded in his notebook, 'Place your order personally ... you might squeeze a better price when you return back personally.' No goods were to be purchased 'after daylight or on Sunday under any consideration.' The former instruction was of supreme importance when selecting textiles, and the latter was in line with Timothy Eaton's religious practices. The notebooks carried by each buyer were venerated as Holy Writ, since they were filled with comprehensive information regarding manufacturers, suppliers, prices, and discounts. By 1899 the notebook of one such salesman contained details relating to nearly 250 separate suppliers in Great Britain and Europe for toys, glassware, and crockery. For this reason it was suggested that the book be kept closely guarded in an inside vest pocket, since 'money is nothing without this book.'[41] Buyers could exceed their spending limits if they felt the addition of extra items was justified. If the opposite proved to be the case, excessive purchases could bring dismissal. The credit agency report in January 1894 criticized Timothy Eaton's buying system largely because too much licence was given to his buyers with the consequence that the store sometimes got 'overloaded with certain lines at prices which must of necessity cause a loss to the Company.'[42]

To facilitate the selection, purchase, and shipping of this growing volume of merchandise, the company opened buying offices in London in 1892 and in Paris in 1898. The advantages gained by having someone on the spot to seek out new items and expedite the regular shipment of goods ultimately outweighed the problems encountered by the inexperienced staff. Located in the City of London, the Eaton office was close to the headquarters and warehouses of many large wholesalers and manufacturers, and thus within easy access of local salesmen. Timothy Eaton had to warn the young Canadian office manager to 'keep those London fellows out of your office' and confine himself only to those lines selected by Eaton buyers. As the London staff acquired experience, samples of goods were secured and appointments arranged with potential suppliers before the buyers arrived in England. Having a central office for the acquisition of both British and European supplies removed much of the worry and anxiety from the financial side of the business, since all primary invoices were first scrutinized and checked in London before being forwarded to Canada for payment. As in the past the company extracted every ounce of usefulness from the new location, assuring customers that 'there's nothing local about this business,' and urging customers travelling to England to 'use the facilities of our London office at Warwick Lane.'[43]

With the exception of the manager sent from the Toronto store to open the London office, the staff was hired locally, and several ultimately rose to positions of prominence within the company. In this initial period, however, Timothy Eaton complained that lack of qualified personnel prevented the company from opening further European offices.[44]

The volume of sales at the Eaton store continued to accelerate at an awesome rate throughout the 1890s. The monthly average rose from $27,847.21 in 1885 to $108,966.00 in 1890 and $243,689.00 in 1895. At first no attempt appears to have been made to discover just what percentage of these sales totals represented mail order sales. The fact that mail orders continued to be filled from regular departmental stock probably made independent assessment difficult. In 1895, however, as part of an extensive study undertaken by John James Eaton to discover the actual detailed costs of this operation, attention was focused on mail order sales. It seems that this was done with the intention of bringing the mail order department into line with the overall store policy that held each department responsible for its own expenses and its own profitability. John James Eaton's figures show that by far the greatest proportion of the increase in sales was in the store, with mail order sales accounting for only 18 per cent to 21 per cent of the total. Amounting to only $533,607.00 in 1895 out of an overall figure of nearly $3 million, this figure appears to have given the management some cause for concern. As one manager stated in 1894, 'We cannot make a success of the Mail Order unless we have the assistance of the heads of the departments and their associates.'[45]

It is not known precisely what efforts were made to improve the performance of the mail order department, but the visit made by Frank Beecroft, the mail order manager, to the Montgomery Ward mail order house in 1896 was probably more than just a coincidence. By 1896 the proportion of mail order sales to total company sales had risen to 21 per cent and, from the sparse figures available, it appears that by January 1897 this proportion had risen to just over 25 per cent.[46]

By 1890 the mail order department had more than one hundred clerks filling orders. Complaints from departmental managers resulted in efforts being made to discover a less confusing method of completing this part of the operation. Secure in the knowledge that Timothy Eaton was not averse to implementing methods proven successful in other retail establishments, Frank Beecroft adopted the system used by Montgomery Ward. Orders were analysed as they arrived and then a purchase slip, rather than a mail order clerk, was sent to each department. The gradual introduction of order numbers for many of the catalogue items, beginning in 1893, took much of the guesswork out of the filling of orders and eventually removed many of the difficulties associated with the personal selection of individual items of merchandise. The growing utilization of detailed drawings or engravings and later actual photographs, along with a fuller explanatory text for each item, also provided customers with a much clearer idea of the goods available. Customers were required to cite order and page numbers of goods requested on specially printed order forms along with information relating to size, colour, price, and quantity. The problems of filling some orders, however, continued to exist. As late as

1900 the confusion caused by the throng of mail order clerks mingling with city customers both in the store and on the elevators as they obtained requested merchandise posed a severe problem for store management.[47]

The catalogue was produced in massive quantities at an average cost of eight cents each. In the spring of 1893 it was expanded into two editions a year, Spring-Summer and Fall-Winter. In 1895, the number of copies printed for the Spring-Summer edition was increased to 75,000 copies from 37,000 in 1894.[48] These two major editions were supplemented by smaller runs of other minor catalogues for such items as groceries, bicycles, and Christmas goods, as well as by the 'Monthly Store News' circular produced for several years in the 1890s.

By the end of the decade the catalogue had acquired an extremely professional appearance. Printed on heavy quality paper, in contrast to the earlier newsprint, the 250-page catalogue of 1899 contained numerous fashion plates, which supplemented the black-and-white illustrations found on almost every page. Gone were the opening pages of gossipy small talk; the merchandise alone now spoke for the excellence of the store. As an advertising tool delivered free to homes across Canada, it informed both infrequent shoppers as well as old customers newly located in western Canada of the increasing variety of stock as new goods and departments were added to the burgeoning store. Once accepted into a household, whether in Toronto or in western Canada, the catalogue became an ongoing mouthpiece acquainting fashion-conscious Canadian women with the latest styles and designs from Europe and the United States. In an attempt to reach potential new customers, gifts were offered to those who supplied new addresses for the mail order list. In 1896, for example, the wife of a missionary farmer in northern British Columbia received a winter coat for providing the store with a list of neighbouring families.[49]

Although volume buying resulted in considerable savings for the customer, Timothy Eaton acknowledged the various obstacles that had to be overcome in drawing customers to the store: 'People often get in a rut which, once out of they wouldn't go back to. We refer to shopping exclusively in the small towns and villages where two prices are asked for most everything you buy.'[50] Nellie McClung, in recalling the purchase of her own first set of dishes from a prairie general store, suggests the uniquely, highly personalized attraction of these rural stores: 'We bargained a bit at first, according to custom, but on my third visit he wrote the price on a piece of paper shading it with his hand, as he would a match on a windy night, and let me see the magic figures. I had a feeling that this was a special price to me only, and for this moment only, and that was surely good salesmanship.'[51]

Stories abound in Canadian literature about the uses found for Eaton catalogues in rural areas, from decorating backhouses to serving as goalie pads. Largely because of the illustrations, they achieved a popularity far beyond their original intention. Known as the 'prairie Bible' or 'want book' they provided entertainment, education, and reading material for long winter evenings for many homesick and lonely new settlers. One early settler recalled that many new Canadians spoke 'Eaton's-catalogue English.'[52] Perhaps it could be said that the catalogue acted as a socializing force and assisted in the process of familiarizing many new Canadians with an alien culture.

Many catalogues were also delivered to households in Toronto and its surrounding area. The exhortation to 'make Friday your visiting day to the city' could hardly have been made to customers in Manitoba or further afield. Perusal of the catalogue educated even the city shopper to an awareness of the enormous variety of goods carried by the store, and the figures for store sales continued to outpace those for the mail order department by a wide margin.

By 1896 the number of parcels dispatched by the mail order department amounted to 135,000 by parcel post and nearly 74,000 by express. The average order amounted to approximately $3.92. The quality of service ranked with that offered in the store. Each order was acknowledged by return post with information regarding possible delays or substitutions of stock and the proposed method of transit. Since orders were filled solely on a cash basis, the card or letter notified the customer of discrepancies in funds, no matter how small, and requested remittance of the necessary sum. In the case of overpayment, again no matter how small the amount, printed refund checks in denominations from $0.01 to $5.00 were forwarded, to be either applied to future purchases or exchanged for cash at the store. Orders ranged from requests for a single item to lengthy lists for annual supplies from settlers in remote regions of the west.[53]

Despite the economic problems of the 1890s, the Eaton store had continued to grow and had become a national retailing institution. At the end of the century it still lagged behind such giant enterprises as Macy's, the Bon Marché, and Whiteley's, both in size and sales figures (see Table 12), but it compared favourably with stores such as Harrods of London and Bloomingdale's of New York, especially when one considers the comparatively smaller size of the Toronto-area market. In some ways Timothy Eaton's success was much greater than that achieved by retailers in other large urban centres. Certainly by comparison with his closest competitor, Robert Simpson, he had achieved enormous success. By 1898 sales at the Simpson store amounted to only $1,250,000, barely a quarter of those for the Eaton store.[54] Based on the figures that are available, Timothy Eaton's sales in 1898 amounted to around $5,000,000, an indication that the Eaton store had gained an inordinately large share of the Toronto market.

The operation of the store absorbed by far the largest part of Timothy Eaton's life. Unlike many of his contemporaries he had no desire to shine on the public platform or to strive after positions of importance. For him the store was platform enough, and his only interest lay in ensuring that it remained at the head of the field. Consequently, the expressed behaviour and perceived attitudes of the store itself are the chief source of clues to his character and personality.

He found some time, however, to perform his regular church duties, although over the years these appeared to decline. For a time he continued to be closely involved with the activities of Trinity Church (earlier known as Western Methodist) in both its administrative and religious aspects, serving as a steward on the Quarterly Official Board and attending the regular Tuesday evening religious studies class.[55]

Aside from this association there is little evidence that he involved himself closely in any other outside activities. Always careful with his money, he was similarly cautious and prudent about investing in the stock market. This caution extended even to family affairs. He refused to invest in anything that did not promise a favourable return, and family members had no option but to respect this view. As he pointed out to his nephew Herby Eaton, when refusing his request for a loan of $3,000:

I would like very much to help you, but do not see my way clear through what you purpose doing. It would be an unwise thing for you to borrow money from one person and assume the responsibility of it to give to another set of persons ... Don't forget this one point, that when money is borrowed it doesn't make you any better off as it has to be paid, and doesn't decrease in any way your indebtedness.[56]

In one instance Timothy Eaton seems to have overcome his caution, for in 1899 he was actively involved with a group of Toronto businessmen in financing the takeover of the *Toronto Daily Star*. The prime objective of this operation was to create another Toronto paper openly committed to Sir Wilfrid Laurier and the Liberal party. Although never clearly identified as a Liberal, Timothy Eaton was said to have been a great admirer of Sir Wilfrid. His contribution of $10,000 was offset by the ownership of one hundred shares in the Star Printing and Publishing Company but, according to Ross Harkness, none of the investors expected to receive a return on this investment, regarding it rather as a donation to the Laurier cause. In spite of this marked support, Timothy Eaton refused to resume advertising in the *Star*, a practice he had discontinued when circulation began to drop in the mid-1890s. He did, however, inform Joseph Atkinson that if he could provide a red banner headline similar to that used by John Wanamaker in the Philadelphia *North American*, he might reconsider this decision. This goal was achieved in the summer of 1900.[57]

Because of his growing reputation as a wealthy man, Timothy Eaton was frequently approached by individuals and institutions for charitable donations, and many of them had reason to be grateful for his generosity. A large supply of tents, for example, was forwarded to house those rendered homeless by a fire near Ottawa in the fall of 1897. A new church in Arthur, Ontario, received fifty dollars, and a kitchen table was given to the Elizabeth Street School so that senior girls there could receive cookery lessons. Donations amounting to several thousand dollars were made to various Christian organizations with the stated intention of reducing their debt loads.[58] But Timothy Eaton was also aware that charity was open to abuse. When asked by a member of the Salvation Army to distribute soup and bread tickets to those in distress, his reply was both honest and revealing:

I wanted to thank you for the Soup tickets and also to say that I am not exactly in sympathy with so much Soup and Bread as is being slushed around, and so much racket being made under the garb of pious popular politicians. Please find enclosed my cheque for $25.00 but not to be used for Soup. I would prefer that it be used for your Shelter in the taking care of unfortunates. In my judgement, you will fill your bill to better advantage by keeping out of the Soup business and attending to your own special department. Persons who fall under your control in the Shelter are surrounded by Christian people and you get acquainted with them, obtain an influence over them, and ultimately lead them to Christ in this way; not so by distributing promiscuously to 'Dead-beats' and 'tramps' on the Street. Reports come to me of Grocers in out-lying districts claiming free bread and taking it home and selling it. I like best to deal personally man to man; know your man and help him all you can.[59]

His concern with the spiritual aspect of man was responsible for many of his charitable donations. In 1892 he had offered the sum of $5,000 to Victoria College, 'to place a man of the Moody stamp to teach young business men and women how to study the English Bible with a view to spread them over our Protestant Sunday Schools ... My offer was held over – not refused, but not accepted.' Two years later he stated that 'the money is still waiting.' The offer indicates a profound impatience with those centres of secular learning, for as he complained to Dwight Moody, 'Our city is full of Colleges and our people are hungry for Christian knowledge.'[60]

By the turn of the century, Timothy Eaton had acquired the appearance of a typical Victorian businessman, complete with beard and watch-chain. He is said to have remarked to a friend that, as he grew older, he had come to the conclusion that he could not judge other men by his own standards.[61] That may well have been the case, but this did not prevent him from trying to exert his influence in those realms, both spiritual and commercial, where he wielded considerable power.

8

A Department Store

'This store takes its part in the pulse beat of the trade.'
Eaton's Catalogue, 1892–3

Despite a period of acute recession beginning in 1893 that caused considerable hardship for many and gave rise to several reports of industrial exploitation, sufficient funds were generated during this decade to allow more people to purchase goods that had earlier been out of the reach of most consumers. Increased consumption was reflected in the greater adornment of both home and person and in the acquisition of novelty items, bicycles, musical instruments, and sports equipment. Numerous observers drew attention to the growing acquisitiveness and materialism visible in Canadian society, as urban inhabitants of every class attempted to create a display of individual affluence. As one contemporary observed just after the turn of the century:

Anybody who perambulates on one of the fashionable thorough-fares of any of our large cities of an afternoon and observes the well made dresses, hats and footwear of the young people of both sexes can scarcely help considering what a vast amount of money it takes to pay for it all ... Every novelty in extravagance finds people eager to possess. The bicycle of a few years ago – which everybody old enough to ride must have ... all tend to show what an extravagant age we live in.[1]

Other historians have pointed out that given the long hours of work and the decrepit housing in which many workers were compelled to live, clothing at least 'afforded the illusion of stepping out of one's circumstances ... it represented a transcendent escape.' The abundance of cheap, ready-to-wear clothing, one of the first acquisitions of the urban poor, 'was one of the few areas in which the promises of industrial plenty could at least superficially be met.'[2] Mass fashion was often procured before more necessary but less visible goods, for it provided the means by which poor people could develop an outward appearance of upward mobility. Eaton's and stores like it catered to this demand by enlarging their variety of merchandise to include all those items now considered so necessary for everyday life.

The extent of company growth and its advance into areas not connected with dry goods merchandise had by the early 1890s transformed the earlier dry goods store into what was coming to be known, often disparagingly by its many competitors, as a departmental store. Similar in one sense to the older bazaars and general stores, departmental stores differed from them in several important characteristics, though there is still some lack of agreement on this matter. By late-twentieth-century standards many large stores are recognized as department stores, largely one suspects because the older appellation, dry goods store, sounds antiquated, and yet clothing store does not fully cover their complete line of merchandise. Defining characteristics cited by some historians – a central location, aggressive specialized advertising and promotion, a large volume of business, the organized disposal of old stock and special purchases through bargain sales, and the reliance on cash for both selling and buying – could have applied to any number of aggressive retailers of the late nineteenth century who carried only one line of merchandise. Philip Jamieson at the corner of Yonge and Queen streets, for instance, exhibited many of the above traits, yet retailed only men's clothing. Similarly, many successful Canadian businesses at the end of the nineteenth century sold for cash with a low mark-up and one price to all. For some historians the introduction of specific lines of merchandise, such as home furnishings, is seen as a determining factor. If one accepts this definition, then the Eaton store had already reached department-store status by at least the early 1870s. Brass bedsteads, blankets, curtains, and oilcloth had long formed part of Timothy Eaton's merchandise. Such items classified under the general heading of 'House Furnishings' supplemented the many dry goods staples. Ralph Hower, on the other hand, contends that the introduction of a fancy goods department in the fall of 1860 launched Rowland Macy's store on the road to department-store status.[3]

Hrant Pasdermadjian suggests that this new entity differed from the former general merchandise stores or bazaars by the visible locational segregation of the different lines of merchandise. Each type of merchandise had not only a distinct location in the store but also its own buyer and sales force.[4] Such segregation allowed a merchant to ensure that each department bore responsibility for its own profitability. With this as the criterion, it could again be said that Timothy Eaton as early as 1875 was operating a primitive department store since, from a stocktaking and accounting point of view, he listed goods by specific lines. Present in a primitive form in the Kirkton and St Marys stores in the late 1850s and 1860s, this method conformed to that used not only by his supplying wholesaler but also by many of the larger Toronto wholesalers. Timothy Eaton merely refined this practice further as more lines of dry goods were introduced and the volume of each gradually expanded. Nevertheless, the Eaton store down to the end of the 1880s was predominantly an outlet for a wide variety of dry goods.

Ralph Hower goes further and identifies a combination of other features that characterize a full-fledged department store. These include the selling of a wide range of merchandise, centralization of such functions as accounting, delivery, and administration, the offer of many free services, and the direct purchase of goods from the manufacturers in large quantities.[5] A more precise definition is cited by W. Tonning from the Standard Industrial Classification Manual used by Dun and Bradstreet:

Retail stores carrying a general line of apparel, such as suits, coats, dresses and furnishings; home furnishings such as furniture, floor covering, curtains, draperies, linens, major household appliances and housewares, such as table and kitchen appliances, dishes and utensils. These and other merchandise lines are normally arranged in separate sections or departments with the accounting on a departmentalized basis. The departments and functions are integrated under a single management. Establishments in this industry normally employ 25 or more persons.[6]

By the measure of these two definitions, the Eaton store reached and exceeded department store status in the early 1890s with the introduction of furniture, china, silver, jewellery, bicycles, drugs, housewares, groceries, and utensils. Brenda Newell's argument that the addition of ready-to-wear clothing to the older stocks of dry goods was responsible for the rise of department stores thus seems much overstated.[7] The stores that added clothing and ready-made garments to their stock-in-trade in most cases were also the stores offering groceries, patent medicines, furniture, and an increasingly wide range of leisure and agricultural merchandise.

Although the catalogue of 1886 referred to 'these immense stores' and that of 1892 stated that 'to call this a dry goods store wouldn't be comprehensive enough,' Timothy Eaton vehemently insisted that his store was merely 'a bigger general store,' not a department store. Freely acknowledging the 'half a hundred different departments under one roof' he drew attention to the fact that 'dry goods lead in interest at all times.'[8]

Since few stores had ever sold such a wide variety of merchandise, it was often not clear just how to integrate or segregate the different categories. In some cases classification was simple – for example, dress patterns and dress goods clearly belonged together. In other cases, merchandise defied easy integration. Buyers travelling outside Toronto studied the various ways departmental segregation was achieved in other large urban stores. The Bon Marché in Paris, it was noted, placed baby carriages in the same department with trunks and valises; counterpanes, pillows, and bedding went with sample stock displayed on actual bedsteads and mattresses. (In the latter department the buyer observed that the bedding so displayed showed to greater advantage than at Eaton's, where it was placed on the best packing cases found in the receiving room.) Lewis's of Manchester, England, another buyer noted, combined trunks, valises, parasols, umbrellas, rugs, blankets, and harness under one head. Macy's made use of floor space in the basement for the sale of crockery, tin goods, and bird cages.[9]

Many new lines of merchandise were introduced into the Eaton store in existing departments. Bicycles, for example, were probably first displayed in the basement along with trunks, toys, and doll carriages; drugs and watches were in the fancy goods department; saddlery was next to sporting goods. Customer response to some new items led to the provision of greater floor space, not only for the original line of merchandise, but also for subsequent offshoots. Profitability would also have played an important role when decisions were made regarding the allocation of floor space, since rent was probably one of the larger expenses charged to each department.

In the early days, when textile goods formed the bulk of the stock, silks, prints, cottons, linens, and flannels all required and were allotted sections of their own. The household furnishings category then acted as a catch-all for all manner of household goods. Ultimately this area became a spawning ground for numerous new departments.

It is sometimes difficult to establish just when a new department acquired independent status. Furniture, for example, like most other departments in the store, developed from merchandise offered in the house furnishings section almost from the store's inception. Curtains, shades, draperies, oilcloth, and carpets, a small selection of mattresses, pillows, blankets, comforters, and a few enamel bedsteads had all been offered at 178 Yonge Street in the 1870s and early 1880s. Folding armchairs, first offered in 1886, were swiftly followed by other larger pieces. In January 1890 suites of furniture made their first appearance. Possibly at this stage furniture was still lumped together with household furnishings and not set apart as a separate department. With the opening of new extensions to the Queen and Albert streets sections of the store, space was made available for a greater segregation of merchandise. An advertisement in October 1892 speaks of a new furniture department and its 'most gratifying success.' The service of uphol-

stering was also added at this time. The 1893–4 Fall-Winter catalogue contained nearly thirty illustrated pages of fine furniture and
allowed customers to 'furnish a house from top to bottom in
any desired style.' Stressing quality, style, price, and variety, the
company reaffirmed its ability to meet a genuine public need, since
it condensed profits and was 'on the whole ... less greedy for gain.'[10]

Wallpaper was first introduced as a new feature at the Eaton
store in 1889. Timothy Eaton's ability to purchase large quantities
at the lowest possible prices was important to the success of this
line, as with most other goods. By 1893 the catalogue devoted two
or three pages to hints and advice on how to measure a room,
prepare the walls, mix the paste, and finally hang the paper. As one
newspaper advertisement asserted: 'We're not amateurs in this
business however much others may so represent us.'[11] In logical
progression, paint and paint brushes were soon added to the stock.

By the 1890s the Eaton store had not only achieved a momentum
of its own but had also introduced some lines several years ahead
of comparable American stores. Macy's, for instance, did not open
a full furniture department until 1896, and it was not until several
years later that wallpaper, oilcloth, and linoleum were carried at
the New York store.[12] Each new line of stock introduced into the
store developed from the earlier successful sale of related items.
Just as blankets, bedding, and bedsteads led to the introduction of
a full furniture department, so the sale of tea ultimately led to the
opening of a grocery department.

Early in 1890, when Timothy Eaton was travelling in the United
States, he noticed that several large American stores were successfully retailing packaged British tea. Following enquiries regarding
its sale in Canada, a satisfactory arrangement was concluded with
Tetley and Company whereby the Eaton store received the agency
for wholesale and retail sales for Toronto and all of Ontario west
of the city. The Toronto market was duly notified:

*By steamship Oregon there comes to us the first consignment of
Tetley & Cos. celebrated India and Ceylon tea. Although practically unknown in Canada, its merits are being successfully pushed
by the leading retail dry goods houses in the States. We'll be the*

first to introduce it here ... Tea retailed by such leading firms as John Wanamaker, Philadelphia, Jordan Marsh & Company, Boston, Wechsler & Abraham, Brooklyn.

An area was set aside in the store manned by a 'nice old lady,' who dispensed fresh-brewed samples to interested shoppers.[13]

Some success was achieved with this new product, but resistance was encountered with regard to price. Shoppers accustomed to purchasing tea in bulk at twenty-five cents a pound or even less considered the packaged tea's price of fifty and seventy cents a pound very expensive, especially since the customary free gift offered by most Toronto grocers was not included. Timothy Eaton offered to refund money on opened packages if shoppers found the tea not to their liking. Following a trial period of two months it was found necessary to introduce a cheaper Tetley tea under a different brand name. Thus the reputation for quality of both the Tetley company and, by implication, the Eaton store could be maintained. This merchandise was vigorously promoted both in the daily press and through the catalogue, and limited funds were secured from the British producer to cover some of this cost. This is the only instance when Timothy Eaton appeared to receive any external help in offering merchandise for sale. The promotion still failed, for customer demand compelled the Eaton store to introduce still cheaper teas, breaking the exclusive arrangement with Tetley and Company.[14]

Despite these problems, tea sales were sufficiently encouraging to suggest the addition of several other foodstuffs. In the spring of 1890 a wide range of candies was displayed near the tea counter. Despite an announcement stating that no future expansion in this direction was planned – 'Candies and tea, sounds a good deal like a grocery shop, but it isn't. We stop there' – nuts and candied fruits made their appearance in the fall of 1891. The following year, coffee, cocoa, and canned milk were added to the stock, and by the summer of 1894 the store carried a full line of groceries, ranging from tea, coffee, spices, canned goods, jams, sauces, and jellies to packaged merchandise such as oats, starch, and baking powder. By 1899 the Eaton catalogue was offering pork and hams from

Eaton's own farms. Fortune hunters travelling to the gold fields of the Yukon could obtain a year's supply of food along with all the necessary camping and gold-panning equipment.[15]

Whether this new department was in response to, or ahead of, customer demand is uncertain. What is known is that some time in the late summer of 1893 an Eaton buyer paid a visit to the Siegel Cooper store in Chicago. There he discovered a grocery department with a reputed turnover of $200,000 a year supplemented by a very profitable butcher's shop. Although Whiteley's in London opened a grocery department in 1875, such a department was something of a departure for American stores. The grocery department that opened in the Macy store in the spring of 1892, for instance, was later considered to be without parallel in America. During the 1890s, however, many of the larger Toronto stores added a line of groceries to their stock-in-trade. By 1896 Robert Simpson's catalogue offered some twelve pages of grocery items, all at prices comparable with Eaton's.[16]

The Eaton catalogues provide an almost encyclopaedic record of the merchandise carried by the store from the early 1880s. The fancy goods and small wares department, as Ralph Hower observed at the Macy store, also acted as an incubator for a host of new departments. Toilet goods was one such line of merchandise offered initially in the fancy goods department; by 1888 they warranted a department of their own. The addition in the fall or winter of 1891 of a large selection of patent medicines led to a departmental name change, and the catalogue for the following year listed numerous brands of patent medicines showing the difference between Eaton's prices and those in regular drug stores. The retailing of patent medicines led to the introduction in 1895 of a full line of drug preparations. Entries in the suggestion book for September 1893, which noted that Siegel Cooper's put up first-class prescription drugs at popular prices, suggest that the addition had been under consideration for sometime. The first prescription was filled on 30 May 1895. By the winter of 1895 the catalogue contained four closely printed pages of drugs available for home preparation in small or large quantities. As well, this catalogue listed nearly a full page of veterinary supplies for the treatment of farm animals.[17]

As with patent medicines and drugs, the popularity of other items originally carried in the fancy goods department eventually prompted the creation of separate departments for toys, china, glassware, silver, jewellery, and kitchen equipment. Several new lines first appeared under the general heading of the holiday goods or Christmas department in the late 1880s. The china heads of many of the dolls, for instance, led to their being included in the catalogue with china vases, shaving jugs, and cups and saucers. Merchandise introduced gradually at times of peak sales, such as Christmas, Easter, or Thanksgiving (the latter celebrated in late November at that time), allowed the company to test demand. Both glass and chinaware, for example, rated only nineteen lines of text in the 1890 catalogue of 175 pages; but by 1892 these had expanded to fill four pages, and by the winter of 1893 one could purchase a complete dinner service for twelve.[18]

In 1886, the small jewellery department, another offshoot from fancy goods, was located just inside the main door on Yonge Street and carried only a narrow selection of brooches, earrings, and hat and scarf pins. The space in the catalogue and the store was at first quite limited, and in the catalogue for 1887 jewellery rated only twenty lines of space. This was only very gradually expanded, and it was not until 1893 that watches were offered for sale.[19]

The pace of innovation was relentless. The safety bicycle, first introduced into Canada in the late 1880s, appeared in the Eaton catalogue in the fall of 1892. While noting that 'It is not quite orthodox to sell bicycles in a dry goods store,' the catalogue observed that 'whatever the public calls for, the same we endeavour to supply.' When one considers that wages for skilled men averaged between $10 and $12 per week, the prices for these early 'wheels' were very expensive at $110 to $135. By 1893 sales more than justified expectations, for young men were only too ready and willing to pay cash. The consumer's willingness to purchase expensive novelties initially allowed the retailer the benefit of a fairly substantial mark-up. By 1897 the bicycle was no longer a luxury but a necessity, and the price for a popular 'wheel' dropped to $50. Bicycling, with its air of unconventionality, called for less formal attire. Cheap tweed suits, sweaters, and cloth caps therefore began to make an appearance, as well as a wide range of other accessories for both bicycle and rider, all of which could be found in the Eaton store or the catalogue.[20]

Increased leisure time was probably an important factor in the growth of the sporting goods department. In 1889 the store had carried only lacrosse sticks and baseball bats, but by 1893 a full range of A.G. Spaulding and Brothers baseball equipment was available, along with gear for hockey, boxing, football, and croquet. The inclusion of buggy whips, curry combs, and horse clippers in the 1893 catalogue presaged the introduction in the spring of 1895 of a full department for harness and saddlery 'at dry goods prices.' Much of this merchandise was ultimately manufactured in the company's own factory. One western Canadian pioneer later stated that the local blacksmith only fixed harnesses since he could not compete with the new merchandise produced by 'old Timothy's factory.'[21]

These advances, most made concurrently, all occurred within a comparatively short space of time. The whole process, as Ralph Hower said of Macy's, was one of slow growth and a series of small logical changes rather than one of distinct innovation. Unlike Rowland Macy, Timothy Eaton placed his own reputation on the line in introducing new lines of merchandise. Silverware, china, and shoes were first introduced into the Macy store by leasing the departments to experts in the trade, a strategy that considerably reduced Macy's own risk. Such goods were placed on consignment in allotted areas in the New York store. Hower asserts, moreover, that the silverware and china departments leased to the Straus brothers during the 1880s acted as the driving force of the Macy store, which was then undergoing a period of conservative management and some decline. Leasing of store space was a fairly common practice in many American stores, and the Strauses had similar arrangements with John Wanamaker in Philadelphia and four other stores in Boston, Washington, Chicago, and New York.[22] Timothy Eaton, on the other hand, always acted wholly independently, never leased space, and yet kept pace with the larger American stores in the inauguration of his departments.

The actual space occupied by some departments may have been

comparatively limited when compared to millinery, carpets, or house furnishings. Ribbons and jewellery, embroideries, and silks and velvets – merchandise that required little space – probably needed only one counter each to display a wide selection of merchandise. The fact that each of these departments was listed separately indicates that a high demand existed for such products. Their successful marketing and subsequent profitability could not be left to chance, and individual managers were appointed to secure the desired results.

The net for suppliers and manufacturers, flung far and wide, was undoubtedly a factor contributing to the Eaton store's expansion, as was the company's financial standing in foreign markets. Eaton buyers regularly travelled to the manufacturing areas of Great Britain, Europe, and the United States and continued the search begun in the past for novelties that would appeal to the ordinary shopper. In 1892, for example, Timothy Eaton urged the London office to 'Search the periodicals in London and find the advertisements with electrotypes or lithographs of lamps. Write to the Factory and get quotes ... I understand the German Provinces are the places where Incandescent Lamps are sold that is the best kind at the lowest prices ... the London periodicals will give you the important points.'[23]

The introduction of Butterick's dress patterns in 1890, another novelty of growing appeal, also provided an example of the increasing democratization of the consuming public. First produced by Ebenezer Butterick in the 1860s, these dress patterns offered a reliable and fashionable product that could easily be utilized by most home sewers. (Earlier patterns had required the services of a professional seamstress to ensure good results.) By 1871 the Butterick Publishing Company in New York was producing more than six million patterns a year. Butterick had achieved this volume by enlisting the services of reputable local firms and had established thousands of branches and agencies throughout North America in this manner.[24]

Recognizing the opportunities inherent in the promotion and sale of such an item, Timothy Eaton in 1890 acquired sole Canadian distribution rights. The Butterick company benefited in securing a much wider visibility for its products than it had attained through the one or two smaller agencies established earlier in the city.[25] The Eaton store took steps to ensure its monopoly on sales in Toronto: on at least two occasions, for example, Mrs Fieroe on King Street was asked to remove Butterick signs from her store.[26] As company advertisements stated: 'We're now the exclusive agents for these patterns in Toronto and it's a foregone conclusion that they'll soon be more generally used in Canada than ever before.' To ensure maximum coverage the patterns were also offered through the catalogue and through subsidiary agents in other centres across Canada.[27]

By the spring of 1892 the sales of patterns, priced at fifteen to twenty-five cents apiece, amounted to an average of $90 or about 500 patterns a day.[28] The purchase of a pattern was usually followed by the selection of the necessary material, notions, and trimmings for its fabrication, all located conveniently next to the patterns.

The patterns, however, comprised only one element in what was, from a promotional point of view, a thoroughly comprehensive and highly productive package. Two monthly magazines published by the Butterick company, the *Delineator* and the *Metropolitan Fashion Sheet*, encouraged the use of the primary product. Although different in character, each magazine carried news, information, and advice regarding current styles, as well as illustrations of the latest Butterick patterns. The *Delineator*, printed on coated stock and priced at one dollar a year, was aimed at the top end of the market. The *Metropolitan Fashion Sheet*, on the other hand, was produced on regular newsprint, cost only twelve cents a year, and resembled a store flyer. To secure free transmission of these publications through the Canadian mails, Timothy Eaton established a separate company, the Delineator Publishing Company of Toronto Limited. The Toronto company assumed all responsibilities connected with the printing, production, and publication of both the fashion sheets and the actual paper patterns. Royalties on all publications were forwarded to the Butterick company in New York.[29]

Demand ultimately compelled the Eaton store to carry patterns put out by other companies, but for a period of ten years the relationship with the Butterick company proved highly remunerative. The circulation of the two monthly journals familiarized even more people with the services of the Eaton store. Available to individual subscribers, the *Delineator* was also sent in bulk lots from Toronto to dry goods stores across the country. Henry Morgan in Montreal, took 5,000 copies a month, for instance. By May 1892, 25,000 copies of this magazine were shipped to numerous cities across Canada, from Saint John to Victoria. Robert Simpson, not to be outdone, carried Standard patterns throughout the 1890s, but it is not known precisely when these were introduced into his Toronto store.[30]

During this decade one line of merchandise – ready-to-wear clothing – gained dominance. It was a category that would ultimately represent a large percentage of modern-day inventories. In the fall of 1892 the manufacturing operations were transferred from the Truth Building on Adelaide Street to the first floor of the new building on James Street. As Timothy Eaton pointed out: 'The first floor is to be occupied by Mr. Dean who is now running 35 sewing machines ... This room will give him capacity for 80 machines which if he had today he could keep them running.'[31] The manufacture of men's neckties and women's clothing was now added to the production of ladies' underwear, men's shirts, and boys' pants. It was hoped that increasing the work-force and expanding output would make this money-losing area of operations profitable. The manufacturing manager later observed that, when he had first taken charge of the operation, the output had been 'too small to guarantee expenses.' But with the employment of more workers and increased output this situation was reversed. The manager also complained that the sales departments' insistence on underpricing a large percentage of company manufactured goods made profit margins almost negligible. In his opinion, 2 per cent on cost was totally insufficient. Yet another problem was that of obtaining sufficient orders from the store to keep the department going.[32] It is not clear whether this problem was caused by the

unwillingness of Eaton's own buyers to purchase company manufactured goods or reluctance on the part of the consumer to purchase ready-made garments.

Although the catalogue carried a fairly wide range of ladies'
cloaks, tea gowns, and skirts, a large majority of women continued
either to make their own clothes or to have them made by a local
milliner or dressmaker. The style of many dresses and costumes
still demanded close attention where fitting was concerned. Sales
of dress goods, trimmings, patterns, etc., for the six-month period
January to July 1891 amounted to $191,188, while those of cloth-
ing, mantles, jerseys, and costumes totalled only $73,190, or less
than 40 per cent of that spent on dress goods. As late as 1896 the
Canadian Journal of Fabrics remarked that the great majority of
Canadians continued to wear custom-made clothing. Promotional
attempts were made to rectify this problem:

*Isn't it a comfort to have the dresses and wrappers and tea gowns
ready-made to your hand? No worry or measuring and waiting for
the making and fitting ... Women will come to it, sooner or later.
There's no good reason why costumes and wrappers shouldn't be
ready-made and worn satisfactorily. Just a little looking in a light,
roomy department, exactly the thing you want chosen, and there's
the end. A perfect fit, and less to pay very likely, than if you'd
suffered the usual martyrdom.*[33]

Catering to all tastes, the store continued to operate a dressmaking and tailoring service on the premises. By 1900, 115 seamstresses
were employed in this workroom, and a dress or suit of individual
choice as to style, fabric, and size could be made in three to four
days. With silk priced at thirty-five to fifty cents a yard, a dress
requiring some fifteen yards of material, plus the necessary twelve
yards of lining, and all the boning, fastening, and trimmings cost
less than fifteen dollars, including the four- or five-dollar dressmaking charge.[34] With the difference in cost only marginally less for a
ready-made dress, many women preferred to maintain the fashionable edge by wearing custom-made garments. Perceptions of quality were also still a problem. The ready-made garments manufac-

tured earlier had been produced for a very limited market. Commonly referred to as 'slops,' they were worn primarily by the lower elements of society. Consumers therefore had to undergo a period of re-education where this merchandise was concerned.

By the end of the decade much of this doubt and hesitation had been overcome, and many manufacturers (John Northway and Son is one example) found it almost impossible to keep up with their orders. Such was the pace of expansion that some Toronto employers were compelled to seek out new pools of labour in smaller towns. Retailers came to perceive the many advantages to be gained by purchasing garments locally. Small initial orders could be placed and successful lines repeated and restocked in a matter of days.[35] No longer would orders have to be placed for the whole season at the risk of discovering that some lines were unsaleable. Company or even locally manufactured goods also helped to solve the problem, noted in the mid-1890s by the manager of the mail order department, that by the time the catalogue was issued some lines were already sold out.[36]

With the addition of further properties on Albert and James streets, Eaton's own manufacturing operations underwent considerable expansion. Women's coats, dresses, capes, skirts, and furs, and men's clothing were gradually added to the list of goods produced. Each line was introduced with the sure knowledge that it not only would sell quickly but would produce the necessary profit. Eaton's did not encounter the problem suffered by Macy's, which found that manufacturing small quantities of certain lines (bicycles and mattresses for example) was not the way to achieve optimum efficiency and adequate manufacturing profits.[37] By 1899 the Eaton factories employed more than seven hundred workers operating nearly five hundred sewing machines and producing 4,500 complete garments every day. Harnesses and saddlery, bamboo furniture, tents, flags, picture frames, and upholstered goods were also manufactured in company facilities.

In 1897 the Eaton company explored the possibility of further diversification, with regard first to the production of paint, and secondly to the possibility of establishing a packing house for the shipment of 'some of our dead meat across the water.' In the former case Timothy Eaton appears to have held the largest percentage of capital stock in a company styled the Paint Oil and Chemical Company, with the balance being held by E.Y. Eaton and other senior executives of the T. Eaton Company Limited. The packing house does not seem to have progressed beyond exploratory enquiries.[38]

The Eaton factories, like the store's departments, operated as separate entities and were obliged to show a profit. Although their total production was intended for sale either in the store or through the mail order catalogue, the procedure followed by both store and factory personnel was identical to that with external manufacturers. Orders were placed only after negotiations regarding prices, delivery dates, and discounts, thereby ensuring competitive rates.

The production, acquisition, and introduction of merchandise were, though important, only primary links in the chain of operations required to move merchandise from the store to the consumer. During this decade, one other activity gradually grew in importance – the promotion of the merchandise. Merle Curti suggests that most advertisements before 1910 appealed to the rational, logical, and sensible side of human nature.[39] Eaton's advertisements generally followed this pattern. There were occasions, however, when Timothy Eaton urged his advertising writer to 'Talk as big as you like – as wild as you like in keeping with the magnitude of the business.' The 'loyal political speeches,' no doubt referring to the democratic and informative tone of advertisements in the 1880s, were then set aside and replaced by insertions offering 'blood and thunder' sales. Special sales and bargain days were introduced to overcome both seasonal slackness and weekly inactivity. At first the store offered regular goods on these bargain days, but at very special prices. In 1894 the advertising manager urged the importation of special goods for the Friday bargain day. In his view, a bargain, if retailed properly, would not detract from the image of quality projected by a store whose reputation was now well established.[40]

The annual white sale, first introduced in January 1893, and the August and February furniture sales, introduced in 1895 and 1896 respectively, were initiated to overcome the sluggish trade customary at these times. As advertisements pointed out:

We can't afford not to improve with the years. We can't afford to rest content with laurels already won. The secret of our success is in reaching out to better things ... The idea is to make January the busiest of months by offering special inducements. The customary way is to expect dull conditions during January, and abide by them. Our way is to create business and induce active trade by reason of sheer gain. There's no longer any excuse for a dull day ... The old time merchant hibernated in August, but progressive stores today are more than ever alert.[41]

Advantage was taken on every possible occasion to keep the store's name before the attention of the public. Trade cards, akin to today's baseball and football cards, were much sought after by scrap-book collectors. These carried store advertising on one side and nursery and fairy-tale characters on the reverse. Fans, another give-away item in the heat of the summer, similarly blazoned the company name for all to see. After-hours musical programs, animated electrical exhibitions representing Peary's trek to the Antarctic, and a patriotic column commemorating those who had fallen in the Boer War were all means of attracting customers to the store.

It is not known how much was spent by the Eaton company on advertising, but by 1891 advertisements were inserted regularly in several Toronto and regional papers. While it seems unlikely that the advertising budget matched the $5,000 weekly expended by John Wanamaker, Timothy Eaton would have agreed with the statement made by his counterpart in Philadelphia that 'Advertising is the leverage with which this store has been raised up. I do not see how any large and successful business can do without liberal advertising.' On the other hand, Timothy Eaton regarded advertising as a staff, not a crutch. On occasion he ignored the requests of department managers for more coverage and insisted that the regular insertions be cut back. By doing this, he claimed he could then see just who or what was responsible for moving the merchandise –

the advertisements or his sales staff. When the advertising copy did not suit him, Timothy Eaton's favourite comment was, 'What reams of paper and barrels of ink are wasted by men who never think.'[42]

By the mid-1890s the Eaton store had become, in its own words, 'Canada's Greatest Store.' As later observers and historians have pointed out, most merchants endeavoured to develop and perfect a distinct image for both store and management. Like many of his fellow department store owners, Timothy Eaton and his advertising staff tried to ensure that this image responded to public trends and attitudes. The store in a sense developed a personality of its own, one that was fostered and maintained in all its appeals to the general public. The concept of a store committed to serving the consuming public was reiterated and expanded to include shoppers at all levels of society:

Your store ... we like the word 'your.' There's something personal in it. We might call this 'the people's store,' but 'your store' comes nearer home than that. It is comprehensive, all embracing, individual. It finds you out in the mansion, and in the cottage, on the east side or on the west, the oldest and the poorest, the richest and the youngest – your store ... Your store stands for something better than money making. It stands for diligent, watchful, faithful service for present and far absent customers.[43]

This concept of 'your store' assumed greater importance as the attacks on the store increased during the decade. Profitable survival depended to a large degree on maintaining the special relationship with the customer.

It is surely no coincidence that the 1890s saw the generation of some company-created myths regarding the early beginnings of the store. Foremost among these was the idea that Timothy Eaton was the first merchant to introduce the concepts of cash only and one fixed price – and that there had been resistance to his ideas. 'Nobody sold for cash in those days. We had to. We hadn't money or credit enough to do anything else ... Nobody marked the price on everything and stuck to it. The rule was to jockey, to haggle, to chaffer, to ask one price and take another. Nobody had the pluck to make a fair price to being with ... Wise heads wagged and gave us six months! Your sharpness saved us ...' This theme was constantly repeated in subsequent material, with the customer always accorded almost equal responsibility for the growth of the store. 'There's no difficulty in getting you to buy ... You are interested that the business always leads. You and we, working together, keep it growing ... '[44]

The presentation of these ideas occurred at about the same time that the store began to come under severe attack from many quarters because of its perceived encroachment on other commercial interests. As Michael Bliss observed in his wider study of the period, 'The creation of myths is bound to occur when actors are challenged to justify their roles either to the public or to themselves.'[45] The use of the slogan 'The Greatest Good to the Greatest Number' could also be seen as an appeal to counteract the many derogatory statements regarding department stores – and the Eaton store in particular – then appearing in the press. This controversy and Eaton's other reactions are discussed in greater detail in chapter 10. In the broadest sense, as the catalogue pointed out, Eaton's was no different from any of the other large stores in American and European cities. It was 'doing for Toronto' what Wanamaker, Macy, Marshall Field, Jordan Marsh, and the Bon Marché had done for Philadelphia, New York, Chicago, Boston, and Paris.

We won success because we deserved it ... we managed to do the right thing at the right time.[46]

9

A Department Store: The Human Element

> 'When the responsibility is loaded on your shoulders you
> will then begin to feel that you are a somebody ... the
> load ... helps you to grow stronger.'
> Timothy Eaton, February 1898

The changes in a store that had grown from a small retail outlet to
one covering almost ten acres of floor space were apparent not
only in the diversity of its merchandise but also in the number of
employees required to staff such an enterprise. The continuing
success of the store was now to a large degree dependent on the
skill, expertise, and attitudes of this vastly increased work-force.
The installation of pneumatic tubes to move cash between the
departments and the central cashier and of conveyor belts to move
goods between stock-room, store, and delivery departments
advanced productivity only if operated efficiently. Technology
could never wholly take the place of store employees.

In August 1889, before the real commencement of the manufacturing department, the number of employees at the Eaton store
totalled 350, up from the 36 noted in 1879. This total fluctuated
as workers were hired to cope with seasonal trade but, as Table 9
shows, the overall figure was constantly augmented as new merchandising areas were developed. By December 1899 the total work
force had risen to well over 2,500. This included all personnel
employed by the T. Eaton Company Limited – buyers, departmental managers, sales or mail order clerks, warehouse or delivery

men, factory workers, office employees, maintenance men, and so on. Such growth affected both the character and the nature of the work-place, and the situation was further complicated by personnel problems at all levels of activity. Stringent efforts had to be made to summon forth the desired attitudes of co-operation, loyalty, and enthusiasm. The old close relationship that had existed in the past between Timothy Eaton and his employees was of necessity replaced by one that was directed and governed by more formal procedures as he was compelled to delegate greater authority and responsibility to senior employees. Furthermore the chance of coming into any kind of contact with the 'Governor' was immeasurably reduced by a series of accidents that confined him to a wheelchair in the late 1890s.[1]

His reduced involvement in the daily routine of the store did not mean that Timothy Eaton had abdicated responsibility. He continued to be closely involved in all matters concerning store operations. One observer later remarked that those who considered 'themselves the power behind the throne' were 'there for no other purpose than to veil and cloak the hand that held the whip.'[2] On occasion his behaviour seemed unnecessarily petty. One employee who had risen rapidly to the rank of departmental manager was reprimanded for removing his jacket to assist his staff with the placement of merchandise. Timothy Eaton, witnessing this act, stated quite firmly that any department realizing a profit of $1,000 a week could afford a man to run it with his coat on.[3] The comment made by one employee that you could speak to Sir John without quaking in your boots suggests that this was not the case where Timothy Eaton was concerned. He was noted for his acts of individual kindness and generosity, however. Many employees whose health resulted in long absences from work received gifts of money and sufficient coal for the long Canadian winter. One junior clerk related how Timothy Eaton sprang to her defence when a display of gas globes fell in her department. Witnessing the accident as he progressed through the store in his wheelchair, he absolved her from blame.[4]

In one respect Timothy Eaton was more fortunate than many of his Toronto competitors, for the continuity of the business was assured by the active participation of several able family members. The Walker store was bought out by W.A. Murray and Company in 1897 when no family member could be found to carry on the business, and the Robert Simpson store passed into the hands of three Toronto financiers on the death of its founder in late 1897.[5] By the mid-1890s Timothy Eaton had two sons and several nephews actively involved in various managerial capacities.[6] The constant opening of new sections and departments also called for an increasing number of experienced employees. Managerial skills thus came to assume a much greater importance in the hierarchical structure as subordinate personnel moved to fill positions of responsibility. As Timothy Eaton pointed out to his son Edward, 'When you can use others to do the work, it is much better to let things go than attempt to do everything yourself.'[7]

Delegation of authority and its assumption by subordinate personnel was not accomplished without difficulty. At a time when professional managers were only just beginning to make an entrance into the retail field, many new managers had much to learn about the fine art of management. Many would discover that their new position required more than just the 'buying and bossing' that such a job had entailed in the past. Some managers were accused of throwing their weight around or playing favourites; others of attempting to run a department single-handed, or conversely of spending too much time talking to travellers and too little attending to what was going on in their departments. Several senior personnel argued for the appointment of assistant managers to mitigate these problems.[8]

In an effort to foster a continuing sense of co-operation and community among the staff, meetings were held in the store at which grievances and ideas were aired. Always willing to listen to proposals for innovations, Timothy Eaton asked that his staff provide him with detailed information on every matter under discussion. Then, as he observed, 'any suggestions that you have to offer, have them all laid out ready and I will give you my judgement on the matter.'[9] By training his staff to do their homework before approaching him with a problem or new idea, he could then deal quickly and effectively with all but the most complex matters. The advice given to John Craig Eaton on the occasion of his promotion to the position of vice-president reflects this background of expectation and perception. 'Can you say Yes or No? Can you decide which at the right time? That might be difficult. That's all you have to do.'[10]

Some problems facing management, however, would not yield to snap decisions, but required instead the active compliance of the whole work-force. One complaint raised by numerous managers in the store was that of lack of co-operation,[11] an indication that the constant induction of large numbers of new employees prevented the development of an overall awareness of the store's operations. Departmental specialization may have been a major factor contributing to this problem. The overriding desire for departmental profits in a sense placed each manager in competition with every other departmental manager. Susan Porter Benson has suggested that in some respects departmentalization undermined a store's overall efficiency, citing the complaint made by one American executive that departmental personnel became more department-minded than store-minded.[12]

It is also clear that many members of the staff considered their own jobs either more important or more onerous than those of the buyers, for instance, who were felt to occupy easier positions, while others strongly resented any suggestion of interference from the invoice or check offices. As the store increased in size, cost accounting and the subsequent detailed analysis of every item relating to departmental expenditure would become the tool by which the manager, and ultimately the owner, could determine the extent of past and present success and plan future strategy. The implementation of a uniform procedure for the collection of statistics was often greeted with exasperation rather than overwhelming enthusiasm. The paperwork generated by the accounting and controlling departments increased enormously and created additional burdens for managers who formerly had concerned themselves only with the purchase of merchandise and the general management of subordinate staff, tasks that had been accomplished largely intuitively and by rule of thumb.

Timothy Eaton urged his managerial staff to work together to further the store's success. Exhorting them to 'be up to the requirements of the times,' he made use of the familiar contemporary models, the industrious ant, the busy bee, and the well-disciplined soldier. In this respect he was very much a product of his times.

What would be thought of a soldier who would take out his watch when on duty to see when the parade would be over? He would expose himself to discipline. It should be so here ... To get the right idea of the value of time, and the results of combined effort and what diligence will accomplish, watch what is going on at an ant hill. Watch them in the early morning, watch them until your eyes will no longer help you and the sun has withdrawn its light, and you will see such devotion to work, such good order ...

Suggesting that managers should have perfect control over their staff and firmness enough to have all instructions faithfully carried out, he also urged them to be thoughtful and considerate to all in their charge: 'When you discover in a young person anything which he or she should be corrected for, speak to them alone and never before customers.' He also emphasized that 'none of us are too wise to learn, even from our juniors.'[13]

Although he expected his managers and buyers to abide by his strict sabbatarian principles when on company business, no such proscriptions were placed on their private lives. He earnestly believed that any person exposed to proper Christian behaviour could, from the example set by others, be persuaded to improve. The furor in Toronto over the issue of Sunday street cars was discussed at a meeting of Eaton buyers in April 1897. Timothy Eaton, as might be expected, delivered a strong statement opposing the introduction of such a service, and most of his executives present, at least in principle, supported his view. One manager had sufficient courage to express the opinion that such a service would benefit those who had no other form of transportation. His employer does not seem to have taken offence, and Lowry, the manager in question, continued to work for him for some considerable time. This, however, did not prevent Timothy Eaton from trying to convince Lowry that the running of Sunday street cars would result in a city no longer fit to be called Toronto the Good.[14]

Recognizing that human individuality and free will were natural, God-given endowments, Timothy Eaton held firmly to the view that faith, hope, and charity would triumph over the feeblest constitution. Employees dismissed for using bad language were reinstated after demonstrating a desire to improve. One such employee who had been twice so dismissed and twice reinstated also received his wages and a ton of coal when ill health caught him badly prepared for cold weather. In this respect Timothy Eaton manifested some of the typical attitudes of Victorian paternalism. A long letter of criticism and complaint to the relatively inexperienced young manager of the London office, for example, is a model of how to temper angry reprimands with solid practical advice. Urging the manager to send no more trash and to confine himself to the sending of samples and the filling of repeat orders, Timothy Eaton ended by praising him for the manner in which he had so rapidly organized the shipment of goods.[15]

Timothy Eaton expected his managers to tread a very fine line between demonstrating individual leadership and putting the good of the whole company before personal ambition, while also remembering that sales volume was the primary indicator of managerial ability. Sales and profits acquired ever greater importance as the number of employees who did not by their own actions generate income for the store increased. This branch of the work-force, classified as 'expense staff,' comprised all personnel from the mail order department, general and check offices, and various workrooms, as well as bundlers, engineers, cashiers, delivery men, and maintenance staff. By 1896 expense staff closely matched the number of employees on the sales force. During 1896 the number of employees in this expense category increased from 528 in April to 689 by the end of that year. The salaries paid to non-productive personnel became a matter of general concern for operators of all large stores, not just the Eaton store. One American department store owner, writing to find out about wage costs in Canada, complained to Timothy Eaton that the ten to fifteen dollars paid to floor walkers at his New York store ate into his profits.[16]

It is not known whether the increase in these expenses or the unsubstantiated reports in 1894 that the company was experiencing financial difficulties was responsible for the careful study of company expenses made by John James Eaton in 1895–6. Primarily concerned with discovering ways and means of reducing costs, this investigation also disclosed severe disparities in wages and salaries. No uniform rule existed regarding the rate at which staff members could expect to receive increases in salary or wages. The practice was that if an employee demonstrated an energetic and enthusiastic attitude then advancement was possible, or as one employee put it, 'You take an interest in your work and Eaton's will take an interest in you.'[17]

This appears to have been a very satisfactory method for departmental managers whose performance came under the direct scrutiny of the 'Governor.' In 1899 some executives had taxable incomes ranging from $1,200 to $2,600 a year. But until the late 1890s no formal mechanism existed to ensure that regular wage reviews were carried out at the lower levels of employment. Advancement was wholly dependent upon the whims of a departmental manager, whose own first concern was departmental profitability. Each departmental head operating independently could, if he chose to do so, achieve a greater rate of profit by maintaining low rates of pay. *Saturday Night* blamed such managers for the preponderance of low wages in the retail industry.[18]

The study by John James Eaton demonstrated that 497 of the 766 members of the sales staff (64 per cent) were receiving wages of $5.00 or less a week, and of this figure some 30 per cent were in receipt of $3.00 or less per week. The study also revealed the existence of 21 female sales clerks whose wages after service ranging from two to nearly six years amounted to only $3.00 or $3.50 per week, an amount comparable to that received by other employees with only one year's service. Although wages for male members of the staff were on the whole higher, it was further discovered that some 57 married employees in both sales and expense categories were receiving less than $8.00 a week, two in sales, for example, receiving only $5.00 a week, and a further 16 and 20, in the sales and expense categories respectively, only $6.00 weekly. John James

Eaton therefore recommended that the rate for married men in either sales or the office begin at $8.00 per week and for those in the shipping, express, or parcel departments at $7.00. No such general ruling was made with regard to female wages, although between 1 March and 1 October 1896 some 260 advances of salary were recommended and approved. The rationale that seems to have been adopted was that those who had been at the same rate for several years either be advanced or dismissed.[19]

These advances had very little impact on the standard rates. In December 1896, 233 sales clerks and 242 employees classified as expense staff were still receiving $3.00 or less per week. Most of these 475 employees were probably female. Starting rates for females continued to average around $1.50 to $2.00 a week for cash girls and bundlers, and $3.00 to $3.50 for junior sales clerks.[20] These continued to be widely accepted as the going rates throughout much of North America. The *Dry Goods Review*, in criticizing the abysmally low wages paid to salesgirls in the United States, incorrectly observed that 'it is not charged that this state of things exists in Canada.' For girls still living at home such wages were tolerable; but as Jean Thomson Scott demonstrated in her 1892 study of conditions of female labour in Ontario, if this small income contributed to the support of a widowed mother and dependents, the general health of the whole family suffered from the lack of an adequate diet. For those compelled by circumstance to live away from home, life was extremely difficult. Inexpensive room and board at the YWCA cost $2.50 a week, leaving little for such necessities as weekday lunches, shoes, repairs, and toiletries, to say nothing of clothes for employees who were at all times expected to present a neat and attractive appearance.[21] The high incidence of tuberculosis served to undermine even further the fragile health of those living in already tenuous circumstances.

In Jean Thomson Scott's opinion, the inability to attain any great expertise or advancement in the store was responsible for the general depression in wages. Large stores like that operated by Timothy Eaton employed more girls between the ages of fourteen and twenty than most factories and, despite the enormous expansion in business, such jobs offered the same level of remuneration as twenty years earlier. With most girls only too willing to work for whatever was offered, employers were able to maintain these low rates. With an increasing number of unskilled females entering the work-force, clerking of any description in a retail store attracted large numbers of women and girls. Many girls considered it superior in status to domestic service and, in some cases, to unskilled factory work. This attitude of superiority, characterized by one contemporary journalist as a 'particular form of mental measles,' was also held responsible for the lack of trade union organization amongst retail clerks. They certainly did not appear to fit the stereotype conjured up by the term 'shopgirl,' with its overtones of 'inferior class position, poor taste in speech and dress and possibly low moral state' suggested in a recent study by Susan Porter Benson. According to Benson the greatest problem facing store owners was the inherent class contradiction implicit in the employment of working-class saleswomen whose job required them to behave in a genteel fashion when dealing with members of socially different classes. By dealing thematically with material drawn from a wide variety of American sources and embracing a period of enormous change, 1890–1940, Benson over-emphasizes this aspect of class-consciousness, which, as far as can be judged from the limited sources available, certainly did not exist at the Eaton store. Far too often Benson has projected views, attitudes, and ideas present in mid-twentieth-century society onto an environment that in many cases was only just becoming aware of the social contradictions she enlarges upon so extensively.[22] The paternalistic world governed and directed by Timothy Eaton and, one suspects, most of his contemporaries was one that was accepted by the majority of unskilled female workers, who were only too happy to obtain paid employment in an environment that was both pleasant and superior in quality to that of either domestic or factory work.

Although Wayne Roberts states that by 1891 women had barely begun to penetrate the fields of cashiering, bookkeeping, clerking, copying, or sales, the few figures available suggest that the Eaton store was in the forefront of this trend. Like their counterparts on the sales counters, most clerical jobs called for relatively little skill beyond the ability to read and write. Of the eighteen clerks employed in the check office, fourteen were unmarried females engaged in verifying invoices. There were complaints that, by working for lower wages, women were moving into positions formerly held by men and were thus putting their male colleagues out of work. Richard Wilkins, employed by R. Walker and Sons, testified before the Royal Commission on the Relations of Capital and Labour in 1887 that two or three girls could be hired for the price of one man.[23]

In fact with the general expansion in the retail industry and the increased demand for managers, buyers, heads of departments, and floor walkers, as well as supervisors in the administrative offices, more opportunities for young men were being created. Largely because of the nature of the work in the maintenance and delivery departments of the Eaton store, for example, more men than women were employed in the expense categories. In December 1896 there were 443 men and 261 women employed in this category, and wage rates were on the whole similar to those for sales. The introduction of a wider range of heavy merchandise also offered opportunity. Departments such as furniture, hardware, and farm and sports equipment hired primarily male clerks. The number of males employed in all categories at the Eaton store therefore did not suffer a noticeable decline. In April 1896, with 250 females and 330 male employees on the sales staff, the proportion of men to women in this category was greater than that in some comparable American stores.[24]

Some eight months later, to cope with the usual seasonal rush, the number of female salesclerks rose to 463 while that of males dropped to 308 and reflected the company's desire to reduce selling costs. Average selling costs in 1891 had amounted to approximately 6.36 per cent, but by December 1896 these had been reduced to 4.86 per cent.[25] This saving was not accomplished without some loss in the area of service.

The number of unskilled young workers, both male and female, entering the retail industry – many of them, as Michael Bliss points out, undisciplined and exuberant teenagers – was probably partly responsible for the numerous complaints regarding carelessness, neglect, and inefficiency. Such difficulties were undoubtedly aggravated by the frequent addition of temporary workers during times of peak demand. This problem was a common one and was not confined solely to the Eaton store. One Eaton buyer reported that assistants at Chicago's Siegel Cooper store exhibited little interest in their jobs, at times ignoring the customers completely despite the large number of floor walkers constantly in evidence.[26]

Timothy Eaton urged his staff to remember that 'good service, faithfully rendered, should characterize every member of the staff from the cash boy to the leader.' By marrying the old custom of service to the newer concepts of one price, cash, and satisfaction guaranteed, Timothy Eaton had gained a multitude of new customers. He took pride in pointing out that the store was run as nearly as possible in the customers' interests. Indifference, rudeness, or carelessness that damaged this public image could ultimately result in lower sales and increased expense costs. Exchanges of merchandise generated by bad selling or delayed delivery of merchandise resulting from neglect in sending items down to the parcel department[27] created an impression of poor service and also increased unit costs.

Shop-lifting was also a growing problem. Several managers claimed that the loss of goods by theft was largely the result of indifferent or inattentive sales clerks, some of whom lounged behind the counters as though propping up a fixture. But it seems that the easy accessibility to merchandise by customers was a contributing factor, for all department stores were troubled by theft. Most, including Eaton's, overcame their initial reluctance to prosecute offenders. In cases where charges were laid penalties were frequently severe. In 1895 a Markham woman and her daughter were sent to prison for six to eighteen months in an attempt to put a stop to their activities. Another offender was sentenced to seven days in prison for the theft of a six-cent comb from the John Eaton Company.[28]

In 1897 the assistant superintendent of the Eaton store was sworn in as a special constable and given the power to arrest shop-lifters upon store premises. A few years later profound disagreement erupted over the question of whether floor walkers had the power to apprehend those believed to have been stealing merchandise. Because of the real difficulty it had in getting convictions, the store obtained written confessions from several shop-lifters along with promises to refrain from ever entering the store again. Where children were involved, they were taken home to their parents.[29]

Despite enormous changes in the industry, little thought had been given to the establishment of formal employee training programs. Several of the larger American stores had begun to take steps in this direction,[30] but the Eaton store continued to rely, as it had in the past, on the steady influx of experienced salesmen from Great Britain to fill the more responsible positions. These men were then responsible for providing on-the-job training for unskilled beginners. Many of the personnel problems stemmed from inexperience with company procedures and lack of awareness of managerial expectations. To fill this gap the store adopted a custom practised by merchants and retailers from time immemorial and instituted a lengthy list of rules. Reading books or papers, writing letters, sewing or making fancy work, cleaning fingernails, chewing gum or tobacco, and eating fruit or nuts while at work were all strictly prohibited. Loud noisy talk, quarrelling, loafing, assembling in groups of two or more for conversation, and striking a cash boy were all considered grounds for immediate dismissal. The workforce was governed by a series of bells indicating staggered lunch hours and departure times by departments at the end of the day. The store also urged customers to report employee incivility.[31]

The formal regulations implemented by most large employers and the constant spate of articles in trade magazines suggest that this problem was general in retailing. A visiting Englishman, observing the general air of equality and familiarity displayed by North American shopgirls, remarked that such free and easy ways 'would be met with rebuke in an English shop.'[32] In one sense such egalitarianism was probably bound to encounter difficulties when confronted with the almost religious zeal expected by many nineteenth-century employers. Store brochures proclaimed that: 'The Eaton spirit is the combined faith and enthusiastic loyalty we have for the store and for our fellow employees ... the spirit of the store too, demands the customer's satisfaction at any cost.'[33] Such statements carry overtones of a kind of secular creed, and Eaton's was not alone in attempting to cultivate and advance such attitudes amongst its employees. Those working at Wanamaker's had to hold to the company rule of four:

> *With all my strength,*
> *With all my mind,*
> *With all my heart,*
> *With all my will,*
> *I serve the public at the Wanamaker stores.*

Employees at Hudson's Detroit store were expected to subscribe to the company creed, which began 'I believe in Hudson's because into its makeup have gone the finest thoughts of those at its head.'[34]

This emphasis on dedication was tempered by the government's growing interest in the daily lives of the working public. The retail industry, unlike the manufacturing sector, had been confronted with little government interference in the operation of its business. Although legislation had been passed regarding hours and general working conditions, the erection of more modern buildings and the gradual shortening of the working day had eliminated the need for strong campaigns like those launched by Margaret Bondfield in England and the National Consumers League in the United States. However one issue did attract attention. The question of shop seats was first raised in the 1880s by the Toronto Humane Society, and by 1888 sufficient support had been generated to effect the passage of remedial legislation. The clause relating to this issue was contained in the Ontario Shops Regulation Act, which dealt primarily with the closing of shops and the hours of labour for children and young persons. Section 7 stated that: 'The occupier of any shop in which are employed females, shall at all times provide and keep therein a sufficient and suitable seat or chair for the use of every such female, and shall permit her to use such seat or chair when not necessarily engaged in the work or duty for which she is employed in such shop.'[35] Many saleswomen, compelled by the nature of their work to spend almost the whole working day on their feet, suffered a breakdown in health. As Margaret Carlyle, one of the factory inspectors, pointed out: 'In many respects the women employed in mercantile houses are under a more wearisome strain than those employed in factories and workshops. There is double exaction from employer and customer, more cramped and confined position, less freedom of movement.' Dr Oldwright, a former chairman of the Toronto Board of Health, also confirmed that the health of shopgirls compared unfavourably with that of other workers.[36]

Given the general attitude of employers and their desire that their clerks create an appearance of bustling activity, it is hardly surprising that this ruling was something of a dead letter. Girls found sitting at the Walker store, for instance, were told that they were wearing out their clothes. Jean Thomson Scott found in 1892 that many employers obstructed the law by giving employees work to do in order to keep them busy when they were not actually serving. By 1899 it was found that while establishments violating this section of the act always complied immediately with the regulations when notified of the lack of seats, 'whether employees are allowed to use them was another question.'[37] As a topic on which few could agree it attracted both attention and criticism. One writer in the *Dry Goods Review* stated that it ought not to be necessary to compel merchants to behave in a sympathetic manner towards their clerks. But another, while agreeing that employers should provide chairs for sales clerks to use when they were not busy, wanted it understood that this was not meant to encourage their latent laziness. One critic, however, sternly decried such laxity: 'Now sir, who ever heard of a dry goods clerk who has been trained to the business, that during his hours of labor needs ever be without something to do ... I am sure even you would consider a farmer insane who would provide chairs and umbrellas for his hands in the harvest field.'[38] And yet the question of long days spent entirely on one's feet surfaces in much of the literature of the period. The problem afflicted both sexes. The pain and fatigue experienced by sales clerks is perhaps best expressed by a researcher who worked as a clerk when undertaking a study of women in department stores in 1899 when she stated: 'It seemed to me that my thoughts were always centred on my feet.'[39]

Although the Eaton store offered pleasant surroundings for both customer and employees, the matter of shop seats proved a considerable bone of contention. Early in 1890 the Eaton store was subjected to a thorough inspection by government officials. Although no complaint appears to have been lodged against the company, Timothy Eaton strongly resented the fact that the inspection had been carried out without prior warning. In a letter to Staff Inspector Archabold, he drew attention to 'a few facts relative to the care and comfort of the female department in the store, which Mr. Vaughan may have overlooked, the place being very large, and unless your representative found a good guide to show him all around, he may have missed some important parts.' The business hours of the store were much shorter than those prescribed by legislation. 'Instead of 12 hours our people work only ten, with one hour off for dinner ... and during July and August from 8 a.m. to 2 p.m. on Saturdays.' The bulk of the letter was concerned with what Timothy Eaton referred to as the principle of 'the greatest amount of good to the greatest number of persons.' In this context it mentioned the Saturday half-holiday during the summer months. On the matter of shop seats Timothy Eaton abruptly informed Archabold that: 'We have at present 196 females at work. We are not aware of a dissatisfied person in the whole company. We have 580 stools and chairs. Females coming into the store may elect a sitting or standing position, as we have 75 places in the store for persons who are so situated that they have to sit all the time. We find young, active people prefer the active to the sitting departments.'[40] He was supported in this view by the company doctor, who at Timothy Eaton's urging stated that he felt the use of seats was not beneficial to employees.[41] Sales clerks were obviously not encouraged to sit down on the job. Since no reference was made in the letter to Staff Inspector Archabold as to the displacement of the 580 chairs and stools, it has to be assumed that this count included the many seats provided before each counter for customers, as well as more than one hundred chairs in the lunchroom, and the thirty in the general office.

The prevalence of tuberculosis accounted for many of the calls made by Dr Cotton in his capacity as Eaton company physician. Another Toronto doctor, who had been called in to attend to two female employees who had collapsed in the store, advised Edward Young Eaton that:

I believe that every employee who looks habitually sickly, pale and fagged out should be sent to the Company's physician for examination. For no matter what the cause of their ill health the public are almost invariably sure to blame the T. Eaton Company. And no matter how unjust such a statement undoubtedly is, still it is not a good policy, nor is it pleasant to allow a loophole by which your store can be blamed for any person's ill health or subsequent loss of life.[42]

As the operator of a store staffed by large numbers of highly visible employees, Timothy Eaton could not afford to project an image of exploitation. Some time in the late 1880s, the company encouraged the implementation of a primitive medical scheme organized and carried on by Eaton employees. Space was supplied in the store for the regular attendance of a practising physician, and a medical committee arranged for regular visits to sick employees. Those suffering prolonged ill health continued to receive their regular wages as well as gifts of coal.[43] Mrs S.G. Wood, speaking at the 1894 meeting of the National Council of Women, reported that:

Two years ago one of my own girls* was taken ill with typhoid fever. She was employed by Eaton & Co. She failed to appear at her work one morning, and at twelve o'clock the Matron was sent to see her. A doctor was sent for who declared the disease to be typhoid fever. She was sent to the General Hospital, and for five weeks Eaton & Co. paid all her expenses for the doctor and for the wine required for her. When convalescent she was sent to the Convalescent Home for three weeks, Eaton & Co., bearing the expense.[44]

As the crusade for smallpox vaccination took effect, the company offered a twice-daily dressing station in the drug department for

* Girls' Friendly Society

those suffering from sore arms and ultimately arranged for the company doctor to hold regular vaccination clinics. Because of the unstable nature of much of the early vaccine, some employees experienced considerable pain and scarring but received compensation for the time lost following vaccination. In more than one case, this amounted to several weeks.

The reduction of store hours continued throughout the decade. Beginning in 1890, six o'clock closing was extended to Saturdays with the exception of a few days before Christmas. By 1892 early closing movements in many Ontario towns led not only to the introduction of a shorter working day, but also to wider acceptance of a half-holiday during July and August. In 1895 hours at the Eaton store were further reduced during the heat of summer to five o'clock daily and one o'clock on Saturdays. Although several stores followed Timothy Eaton's lead, many of Toronto's dry goods stores continued to remain open late both on weekday and Saturday evenings.[45]

As long as sales volume continued to increase at a healthy rate, a shortened work week was one way of remunerating one's employees and cutting overhead costs while also enhancing the company's reputation. Generating little effect on the debit side of the company's ledger, it probably resulted in a considerable saving of overhead expenses, since, as the *Dry Goods Review* observed, longer hours helped to swell the profits of the gas and electric companies.[46]

The attention paid by both trade unions and provincial legislators to working conditions encouraged several of Eaton's female employees early in 1897 to approach a member of the provincial legislature about the problem of lunchtime accommodation. Apparently customers had objected to the use of the store lunchroom by employees, and this had resulted in their exclusion from this facility. The salesgirls insisted that they were compelled to leave the store to obtain their midday meal, since they were not allowed access to lunchroom facilities provided for women working in the Eaton factory. In response to Timothy Eaton's objections to statements made on the subject, J.W. Dryden, the Ontario minister of agriculture, acknowledged that the whole matter may have been a question of misunderstanding on the part of the clerks.[47] Since a lunchroom was provided in the store for Eaton employees, it has to be assumed that this facility was suffering from the strain imposed by continued growth. It is not known what subsequent action was taken in this matter.

Many Victorian employers felt that in offering reasonable working conditions and a fair day's wage in return for a fair day's work they had more than fulfilled their side of the bargain. The contemporary adage 'keep no drones about you, none who are not true to the interests of the company' was constantly cited and widely practised. Timothy Eaton, like many other nineteenth-century businessmen, strongly resented anything that restricted his freedom of activity. This unquestionably accounted for his refusal to deal with labour organizations. Any employee demonstrating anything like an interest in the foundation of a trade union was treading on very thin ice. By the 1890s, trade unions had achieved sufficient strength to stage annual Labour Day parades in several large urban centres. Several company upholsterers who participated in one parade were promptly dismissed. Letters addressed to Timothy Eaton by union officials regarding this matter received only perfunctory replies.[48]

Timothy Eaton would no more have thought of interfering in the business ethics or behaviour of one of his suppliers than he would have expected an outsider to demand changes in his. This attitude in large part has been responsible for his inclusion by labour historians among the ranks of sweat-shop employers. The 1896 *Report on the Sweating System in Canada*, for example, noted that there was 'no evidence that the manufacturers ... keep themselves informed as to the rate of wages paid' or 'as to the conditions of the shops or houses in which the goods were made.'[49] During the 1890s Timothy Eaton was only one of the many Toronto manufacturers producing clothing for men and women, but the high visibility accorded the Eaton store into the twentieth century has provided detractors with a whipping boy known to all.

As the demand for ready-made clothes escalated, many individuals with little experience rushed to enter what was thought to be an extremely lucrative business. By 1901 some 18,000 garment workers were employed in 189 establishments. Many large tailoring establishments, however, had the bulk of their work completed by outside workers on a sub-contract basis, and it was this practice that led to the greatest abuse. With small family-oriented operations ignored by provincial legislation, some small contractors grossly exploited their workers, like the one on Elizabeth Street, mentioned in evidence given before the 1896 commission, who kept his family of five stitching from five in the morning until eleven or twelve o'clock at night.

In 1894 the *Toronto Daily Star* discovered that, in their desire to obtain work, many contractors frequently miscalculated costs and lost everything. One wholesale clothing manufacturer, a Mr Love, had originally run a grocery store. As something of an amateur expert on the question of contracting work out, he admitted that the growing competition had led to a decline in wages. Indeed Love questioned whether anyone would be foolish enough 'to keep a girl working for six dollars when he could get a better one for four.' Louis Gurofsky, a union organizer, went further and declared that he considered three dollars a fair wage for a female factory worker.[50]

Because the manufacture of ready-made clothing had grown to enormous proportions in a very short space of time, it allowed for intense exploitation during a period of depression and unemployment. Exploitation was aggravated by the influx of highly skilled artisans in the needle trades from eastern and western Europe. It is difficult, given the attitudes of the day, to know what Timothy Eaton could have done to ameliorate the situation, other than increase his own payments, a step he was understandably reluctant to take in view of the competition. One only bucked the tide if it did nothing to jeopardize the business. With pants being made in Toronto for ten cents a pair, and people 'breaking their necks' to get this work[51] on the one hand, and merchants offering suits and dresses for sale at prices even the poorest could afford, all concerned were caught in a vicious self-perpetuating cycle.

During this decade the Eaton factory system underwent constant expansion; by 1900 it employed more than 700 workers, with a further 115 in the dressmaking department. Protected by provincial legislation, their working conditions were uniformly good. Contemporary photographs show large well-lighted rooms with sewing machines ranged in rows and operated by both men and women.[52] As legislation regarding hours of work and general working conditions tightened, wages became the only item in a manufacturer's costs that allowed a measure of flexibility. The wages paid by the Eaton company caused some girls who had grown tired of sales work to become work-room operators, for the simple reason that blue-collar jobs paid better wages.[53]

Labour relations were not entirely problem-free, however. A strike of Eaton cloak-workers in the summer of 1899, about which little information exists, was presumably due to disagreement over the hand stitching of linings for garments. The company was reported to have brought in strike-breakers from New York and was denounced by the Toronto Trades and Labour Council as unworthy of the patronage of organized labour. The tyranny cited in the union circular perhaps had something to do with the way in which the workers were paid. By far the largest percentage of workers in the Eaton factories – nearly 80 per cent in 1897 – were paid on a piece-work basis. Louis Gurofsky, a union organizer for the garment workers, claimed that in most factories where the piece-work system prevailed the power was never turned off, with the result that 'the employees eat their dinner in five minutes, [and] put the rest of the meal hour in at work.'[54] The daily hours of work at the Eaton factories were from 8:00 a.m. until 5:00 p.m. with one hour allowed for dinner, well within the limits of ten hours a day prescribed by the Factory Act. The company was thus breaking no laws if workers chose to cut short their own midday break.

Lack of archival material prevents a full, systematic, and comparative analysis of issues relating to Eaton employees in the store and factory. Despite the growth of the labour movement, as in the past, union activity continued to be largely confined to skilled artisans and tradesmen. Most young female sales clerks regarded their occupation as a temporary way station on the road to the more permanent goal of marriage and demonstrated little interest in the possibility of being unionized. Those garment workers, on the other hand, who did join unions could do so only half-heartedly, for any active involvement would bring, as it had with the upholsterers, instant dismissal.

It seems likely that the percentage of factory expenses in the form of rent, light, heat, etc., along with the large item of raw material was considerably higher than that in the store and necessitated stringent attention to detail to enhance profitability. Wages, for example, for a six-month period in 1897 amounted to more than 28 per cent of output, compared to an average of just under 5 per cent for the store.[55]

The factory departments, like those in the store, were run independently by individual managers. Workers were thus exposed to abuse by managers whose first concern was profit. Timothy Eaton and his senior managers were well aware that this possibility existed and were also aware that such objectionable behaviour could damage the store's reputation. When Eaton learned on one of his visits to the factory that some girls were being charged for the thread they used, a common practice in many workshops at that time, he ordered the immediate cessation of this practice.[56]

The overwhelming desire for departmental profitability compelled managers in both store and factory to be constantly on their guard against extravagance and waste. Cost was the primary factor in most decisions and has been responsible for the lean reputation given to the Eaton company by later observers. In the 1930s when the store was once again under attack, R.Y. Eaton declared that department stores had taken the lead in establishing minimum wages for both men and women, and that this had occurred well before 1900. He also stated that Timothy Eaton was a pioneer in this field.[57] This was not the case. Wages for the large percentage of the Eaton work-force, whether in the store, office, work-room, or factory, continued at the same low levels of some twenty years earlier. This was especially true where entry-level jobs were concerned. While it could be argued that employees had benefited from the introduction of shorter hours, this had effected no great loss for the company. Sales continued to increase at an annual rate of about 25 per cent and, despite the steady growth in the number of employees, the company managed gradually to reduce its selling costs and, one assumes, its production costs. Some of this saving was achieved by maintaining low wages.

10
Hostility and Reaction

'Remember this, that the greatest number of sticks and
stones are found under the good apple trees.'
Timothy Eaton

Toronto in the late nineteenth century manifested many of the
characteristics found in other western cities that were undergoing
rapid industrialization and urbanization. Dynamic and industrious,
in its hasty advance to the twentieth century it gave little thought
to those who were either displaced or overwhelmed by this process.
The rapid growth of population and the widespread increase in
living standards were contributing factors in the growth and expansion of many of Toronto's larger retail outlets. Many young men
who lacked both experience and capital felt encouraged or tempted
to venture into what appeared to be a profitable endeavour, that
of meeting the demand for cheap goods. Despite the constant
establishment of numerous small stores, the actual number of dry
goods stores within Toronto gradually declined from 135 in 1889
to about 109 in 1893. Although this sector of the industry had
always suffered a high rate of transiency, financial breakdown
seems to have occurred with greater frequency during the late 1880s
and early 1890s. The financial pages of contemporary journals
regularly carried the lists of those forced into assignment. As in the
past, many failures were attributed to the lack of sufficient capital.
The comprehensive study undertaken by Bradstreets in 1891 of the
bankruptcies that had occurred over the past several years revealed

that out of more than 1,084,000 traders, fully 85 per cent had capital of less than $5,000.[1] This problem had an adverse indirect impact on the whole industry, for as one old retailer remarked: 'I can say that more injury has been done to my trade through the bankrupt stocks of men who commenced with little or no capital being thrown upon the market than from anything else.' In the words of one observer, 'In this hustling age, capital is what is wanted.' And yet optimistic aspirants, noting the success of a Timothy Eaton or a Robert Simpson, continued to enter the business relying solely on easy credit from suppliers.[2]

While the community in typical Victorian fashion simply castigated the economically unfortunate for lack of moral fibre and financial capability, there may have been some truth in the observation that Toronto had developed too rapidly. The overzealous development of commercial property had provided Toronto with more store frontage than any other comparable city. In May 1893 it was estimated that there were nearly 140 vacant stores along Yonge Street and a further 212 on Queen.[3] Many people believed that the larger stores, and more specifically what were coming to be known as departmental stores, had vastly intensified competition and were responsible for much of the problem. This belief often produced expressions of great hostility against the big stores.

In Toronto the Eaton store was probably the exemplar in this move towards departmental store status, although several other enterprising merchants had also increased their stock and enlarged their physical space. By 1895 Robert Simpson was operating from a large newly erected five-storey building on the southwest corner of Yonge and Queen streets. Like Timothy Eaton, Robert Simpson had gradually added a wide variety of merchandise to his stock-in-trade and had vigorously promoted the operation of a mail order department. W.A. Murray, first established in 1854 at 21 King Street East, expanded in the mid-1880s into several adjacent stores. By that time his annual sales amounted to $500,000 and the store had begun to manufacture certain lines of clothing. The Murray store, conducted on the departmental system, employed some three hundred clerks and operated a thriving mail order department. Murray's was officially incorporated in January 1897 with a capital of $600,000. R. Walker and Sons, located at 33–43 King Street East (also known as the Golden Lion) and acknowledged by its contemporaries to be one of the oldest business houses in the city, underwent considerable expansion both in physical size and variety of stock.[4]

Departmental stores on both sides of the Atlantic drew the scorn and wrath of those who could not compete with this new manner of doing business. As one Englishman observed in 1893, 'It is an age of big combinations, and those who cannot or will not fall in with the new order of things are frequently left behind or crushed.' Few traditional merchants were prepared to recognize the basic changes that had occurred in the industry. By and large they simply refused, through lack of either capital or foresight, to adjust to the more progressive methods of retailing. As one local commentator observed in 1896, some of the stores on King Street were 'too slow for anything' and lagged twenty years behind the bigger stores. Objections to these bigger stores had been slow to develop in Canada. Similar concern had been expressed in New York in the 1870s and even earlier in Great Britain.[5]

Departmental stores were regarded by many as 'the modern curse' to both capital and labour. Numerous pamphlets and articles drew attention to their methods of retailing. The tone was often emotional and occasionally vicious. Departmental stores were accused of forcing merchants out of business, increasing the number of vacant stores in the city, exploiting young women and children, and effecting a decline in the provincial birth rate. They were also held responsible for working conditions in the garment trade, unemployment rates, and the depreciation of city property. Rural merchants denounced mail order departments for effecting the destruction of small country stores from Halifax to British Columbia. (The fact that Eaton's ran a parcel delivery express through the Annapolis Valley, overloading already heavily burdened post office cars with merchandise, only added to the injury inflicted by rural residents who went past their local stores to obtain money orders for catalogue goods.)[6]

These latter complaints were aggravated by the endeavours of the Patrons of Industry, who had themselves entered the wholesale market. To enable them to supply farmers with cheaper goods through large co-operative purchases, the Patrons had received the active assistance of wholesalers. Retailing goods at an advance of 12 to 15 per cent on wholesale prices, both they and the wholesalers were attacked for contributing to the ruin of legitimate merchants in small towns and villages. One Patrons' supply house in Toronto, operated by Joseph Dilworth of 51 Colborne Street, offered everything from 'a needle to an anchor' at cut prices.[7] Animosity was directed at any store that appeared to achieve its success by resorting to untraditional methods. Guinane Brothers at 214 Yonge Street, which was reported to be the largest shoe store in Canada, was blamed for creating more havoc in the shoe trade in Toronto than the departmental stores. Paranoia regarding any type of competition was such that in 1891 Toronto City Council banned peddlers from working the city's main streets. The ban apparently had little effect, for in 1895 Timothy Eaton complained about the obstruction caused by banana peddlers congregating around the store's main doorways.[8]

Despite the overwrought tone of much of the Canadian writing, many of the charges contained an element of truth. Some ordinary stores in other areas of the city were reported to be prospering, but the presence of the two large Yonge Street stores, where you could 'purchase anything from a bicycle to a toothbrush,' was having an adverse effect on the merchants of Yonge and Queen streets. Few merchants were willing to accept the view expressed by one writer 'that the day of the small dealer was passing into darkness.' Yet in the space of just four years at least four dry goods stores located just north and south of the Eaton store were forced into assignment.[9]

Because of the diversity of the merchandise carried by departmental stores, criticisms and complaints were not confined to the dry goods trade. As one observer in the *Monetary Times* noted:

The existence and increase of enormous concerns such as Eaton's, Simpson's, Walker's, which are no longer dry goods shops alone, but bazaars which trench upon the business of druggists, booksellers, crockery men, picture dealers, are a growing menace to the small retailer. The system is eating up the smaller men, many of whom can no longer pay their former rent, if indeed they can continue in business at all.[10]

Much of the problem derived from the lingering belief that every merchant, whether capable or incompetent, had a right to expect a profitable return for his efforts. Defending the premise put forward by one observer that 'there is no use being in business if you cannot make a decent profit,' many merchants chose to ignore the five pointed suggestions necessary for business success quoted by the *Monetary Times* – 'Buy Cheaply, Pay Smartly, Cry Loudly, Sell Quickly, Cash Only.' Complaints were made that the cash system drove those of moderate means out of business and that lack of proper credit prevented someone with character from attaining success, thereby severely curtailing opportunities for young men.[11] Although the gospel of success, as Michael Bliss points out, places the responsibility for a businessman's fate squarely into his own hands,[12] there were few merchants who were willing to take this concept one step further and endorse the idea of wholly unregulated competition. Few could respond as Timothy Eaton had done when he expressed the belief that competition encouraged those with ability.

It has never been possible, it never will be possible to confine business within certain bounds or to portion it off between stores on an equality basis. One has ability: another has not. One is enterprising to reach out for the best of everything you happen to need; another satisfies itself with the commonplace, and charges more in proportion. No two stores are alike. Shoppers look around, and compare and decide for themselves which is most deserving of their patronage.[13]

Some of the most acrimonious criticisms aimed at departmental stores were to be found in the pages of the *Canadian Pharmaceutical Journal*. Because the Eaton store was retailing drugs and patent medicines at 'dry goods prices,' it became a prime target of the pharmacists. The intensity of the outcry undoubtedly proceeded from the realization that such competition would severely damage long-established profit margins ranging from 100 to 200 per cent.[14] The Eaton store was not the only offender or innovator. Drugs and patent medicines were carried by several of the other large stores in Toronto. The time-honoured custom of stocking patent medicines followed by many rural and small-town general stores had been carried over into numerous stores, both large and small, in urban locations.

The progress of Eaton's drug department was hampered by problems with both the supply of goods and the question of legality. The Ontario Society of Retail Druggists and that of the Toronto Retail Druggists tried repeatedly to persuade wholesalers and manufacturers not to supply Eaton's with patent medicines and drug preparations. These efforts met with little success, for Timothy Eaton was always able to find other suppliers, many of them in Great Britain. As one company pointed out, 'Messrs. Pears do not care to whom they sell their soap so long as it is sold.' These efforts were further weakened as many retail druggists, despite assertions to the contrary, personally reduced prices convinced that the 'only logical way to retain business' was to remove the advantage gained by department stores by fighting 'the evil with its own weapons.'[15]

To draw attention to the fact that many stores were breaking the law by retailing drugs and patent medicines, the *Canadian Pharmaceutical Journal* regularly listed suicides said to result from the public's ready access to poisonous substances and compounds. Both the Eaton and the Simpson stores were taken to court by the Ontario College of Pharmacy for allowing an unlicensed person to retail such merchandise. The costs entailed in prosecuting offenders subjected the college to considerable financial strain and frequently resulted in only token fines for those prosecuted. On one occasion, the Eaton company was fined for an act, which, as the *Canadian Pharmaceutical Journal* was forced to admit, was committed by every drugstore in Toronto. Legal recourse was further limited by the fact that few patent medicines listed the make-up of their contents on labels. It was not until 1908 that the Ontario College of Pharmacy succeeded in obtaining the required amendments to the Pharmacy Act regarding the registration and proper labelling of patent medicines.[16]

The aggressive character of many retail merchants during this decade provided visible evidence of the changes that had occurred within the industry. Practices initially introduced by Timothy Eaton, Robert Simpson, and other like-minded merchants had been called into being by the opportunities presented in the increased demand for goods. Increased competition demanded greater effort. It is surely no coincidence, for example, that Eaton's advertisements grew from a small insertion to a full page by 1900.

The behaviour of Timothy Eaton's nephew John Weldon Eaton shows the lengths to which some merchants were prepared to go. John Weldon Eaton, the eldest son of Timothy's brother James, had begun his business career at his father's store in London and had subsequently managed James Eaton's store at 84–90 Yonge Street. The failure of this store in August 1894, with liabilities of $132,348 (vastly in excess of its assets), created an opportunity for an older Toronto company, Thomas Thompson and Son, to take advantage both of the Eaton name[17] and of a prime location on Yonge Street.

Some time in the spring of 1895 the John Eaton Company was incorporated with an authorized capital of $2,000. This was increased a few months later to $100,000. As the credit rating makes clear, John Weldon Eaton held only a nominal financial interest; by far the largest proportion of the stock was held by members of the Thompson company. The original intention to locate the John Eaton store in James Eaton's old quarters at 84–90 Yonge Street was foiled by the fire that destroyed the Simpson store in March 1895. Instead the new store was located at the corner of Yonge and Temperance streets in a large four-storey building. The John Eaton store commenced business on a very large scale. Not for John Weldon Eaton or his Thompson backers the opening of a small store followed by gradual expansion; the store opened as a full-blown department store retailing everything that could be purchased at any of the larger stores. Trading both on the connection with his Uncle Timothy and on that with the store previously owned by his father, James Eaton, John made constant reference in advertisements to the 'little Eaton.'[18] 'When will all the people learn that the little Eaton is in town doing business – the little Eaton, that keeps open on Saturday nights – the little Eaton that will be open on Thursday night for the benefit of the thousands who want to shop – the little Eaton who sells cheaper than any house and yet can pay bigger wages.' And in a dig at Timothy Eaton's new slogan, the new Eaton store urged Torontonians to be sure to patronize 'Canada's Greatest Coming Store.'[19]

Timothy Eaton's public response to such advertisements was merely to talk about general business tactics. It was plain whom he had in mind. One advertisement that appeared shortly after the opening of the rival store declared: 'Evolution: Those people who're always beginning at the top are sure to reach the bottom sooner or later. For 25 years we've been learning your wants better and turning each day's experience into a betterment. That's natural law in the business world – the gradual development of very big results from very small beginnings.'[20] By October 1895 the advertisements for the John Eaton store, always large, aggressive, and bombastic in tone, were announcing not only that it was the most popular, progressive store in Toronto, but also that 'we've built this great business up in about four months.'[21]

The fact that much of the early stock was acquired from merchants forced into receivership allowed for the sale of goods and merchandise at rock-bottom prices. Men's flannelette shirts were offered at fifteen cents each, men's suits at only $4.97, and women's mantles at the ridiculously low price of forty-five cents each.[22] This prompted Timothy Eaton to observe that new goods from England were always the focus of attention at his store.[23]

Despite statements by several later writers, there is no firm evidence that Timothy Eaton took legal action against his nephew. But he certainly had cause to be severely provoked by his nephew's aggressive sales techniques. The advertisement placed in the 1896 City Directory, for instance, was an exact replica in both type and layout of that placed by the T. Eaton Company in the 1895 directory. The only visible difference was in the name, John Eaton instead of T. Eaton. Advertisements declaring that 'the giant store on Yonge Street never pushed harder for business than it's doing now. It realizes that the younger and growing and popular "Eaton" store is steadily pulling the trade from its doors'[24] were undoubtedly a thorn in the side for both Timothy Eaton and his management. In a letter to his son Edward, Timothy declared that:

One would think to look at the adds Mr. Rose was writing for Tomsons as well as ours ... What is Bilger doing he can't see this. Their aim is to make believe it is all the same ... from what I gather they think The name Eaton will sell in Toronto – no doubt it has a wonderful power & people are so stupid they will not notice the difference. See you keep the prices low is the only leaven you have to counteract their game. Thus far you have no reason to complain judging from the increase of the sales each week.[25]

In March 1896 the capitalization of the John Eaton Company was increased to $500,000. In the following month plans were announced for the construction of a huge extension at the back of the property. By the early summer Torontonians were offered the services of a hair-dressing salon, a dental department, maid service to care for customers' children, a mail order catalogue, and the largest restaurant in the city.[26]

The September 1895 credit rating, which had declared that all the directors of the John Eaton Company bore respectable characters and were giving close attention to the business, was ultimately open to question. A fire in May 1897 completely destroyed both building and stock and brought to light a slightly different picture. It was discovered that the Bank of Toronto had taken charge of all insurance policies to secure loans of $207,000, leaving a further $136,178 unsecured. The *Dry Goods Review* questioned the ease with which the company had been able to acquire goods and credit. The subsequent lengthy court inquiry revealed that heavy use had been made of duplicate invoices, which had grossly inflated the value of stock on hand.[27]

The failure in December 1897 of the Army and Navy Clothing Company store (also operated by members of the Thompson family) revealed similar irregularities. As a minor shareholder in the John Eaton Company, John Weldon Eaton escaped much of the blame connected with the case. He moved almost immediately to New York where he was employed briefly as an advertising manager for Bloomingdale's. This apparently did not offer the fullest scope for his 'ambition, energy and hope,' and on 19 July 1897, just some eight weeks after the fire in Toronto, he established his own advertising agency in New York. The success of this venture, if there was success, was short-lived, for John Weldon Eaton died in Toronto in 1900 at the age of thirty-two.[28]

Attacks on the department stores came from other directions. By the beginning of 1895, the growing hostility had generated considerable public and political sympathy for the sufferings of the small merchant. The matter was brought before Toronto City Council by Alderman Davis. A special committee was appointed to consider the advisability of levying a graded business tax or licence to protect retail merchants, druggists, and others against the 'ruinous practices of monopolists in the centre of the city.' A public meeting called by the mayor on 1 March 1895 in support of this measure was attended by some four hundred shopkeepers and several representatives of the mechanical trades.[29]

So intense was the hostility that the fire that completely destroyed Robert Simpson's new store on the night of 3 March was considered by some to be a direct outcome of the agitation against departmental stores. Damage of more than $750,000 was inflicted on properties on both sides of Queen and Yonge streets. The Eaton store, where automatic sprinklers and an independent system of fire protection had been installed whenever expansion or renovations had been made, suffered only minimal damage. On the issue of fire protection Timothy Eaton was greatly ahead of his time. The Simpson store apparently had no such protection. Indeed on the night of the fire the huge Simpson store was manned by only one night-watchman as opposed to the six on duty at the Eaton store.[30]

The scale of the damage and the fact that a man had lost his life in the fire seemed to drain some of the emotional venom from the newspaper columns, although the more objective focus on taxation was perhaps a contributing factor. In the past the Toronto *World* had published highly emotional letters conjuring up visions of tombstones 'To the memory of dear little Jane,' whose death was attributed to the fact that 'departmental stores would not supply needful medicine at night time,' and had called upon the clergy to urge business to follow the teachings of Jesus so that the majority would not suffer from 'the hoggishness of a few' who wanted all the trade to themselves. In contrast, the *World*'s lead article on 6 March 1895 suggested that the small stores must find a way to compete and that an elimination of the credit system might prove most effective. 'If it is a fact that the departmental stores have come to stay, the best thing for those whose interests are adversely affected by them will be to recognize the fact as soon as possible and cut their cloth according to the new ideas. They may as well understand at the beginning that they will be powerless to close up these large establishments.'[31] As the *Monetary Times* confessed, it was not very clear just what the municipal council could do to discourage such establishments, but it pointed out that 'these stores represent a transition in the mode of doing business ... Whether we like it or not, the tendency is this way at present. The trouble is that only a few of those now in trade can take advantage of the new method; one great departmental store causes hundreds of small stores to disappear.' Although similar themes were pursued in the pages of trade journals, some suggested that, instead of weeping and reviling, small stores should 'adopt the newest methods' and 'keep a-hustling.' As one realist remarked, large departmental stores were efficiently and economically run and you could not find fault with that.[32]

Given the intensity and extent of the bitterness within the commercial community, the Eaton company could not wholly ignore public opinion. Efforts were made through the medium of the regular daily advertisements to present the other side of the question. Asserting as it had done so often in the past that 'the question of *value* had everything to do with trade' and that since 'People want to *save* money ... they come or send to where money can be saved,' one advertisement declared: 'No man, no set of men can interfere with the law of *progress* ... Instead of trying to stop the sun, suppose our enthusiastic friends get together and *investigate*? It'd be a heap sight more interesting than chasing after shadows and meddling with honest people's business.' One long statement, sarcastically entitled 'A New Comedy,' drew attention to the many reasons for the store's success – larger store, improved facilities, better service, foreign buying service, cash discounts in buying and selling strictly for cash, enormous variety of stocks – and suggested that unlike the sleepy, less successful merchants whose only concern was for their profits, the Eaton store had been of direct benefit to thousands of families throughout Canada.

All this is talk you say. Perhaps so! But so long as foolish sentimentalists disregard the law of progress, we shall 'let slip the dogs of war,' and give them something to think about ... What use in the world are such men as Edison and Watts with their new fangled notions about electricity and steam upsetting business at every turn, and changing the complexion of trade life? And what a pity Toronto isn't the little village it used to be, and all its merchants as careless and indifferent as they once were? ... This is emphatically an age of PROGRESS. *The golden age is before us, not behind, and those who're unwilling to keep up with the procession will have the decency to* STAND ASIDE.

Whatever the intent of such comments, the tone and content of several of these statements can have served only to exacerbate tensions. One typical advertisement declared that: 'This store has been blessed with more *free advertising* than other houses pay for in *years*. No end of complaints are lodged against the business, but it keeps right on growing, serenely unconscious of foolish criticism. The more people talk the better we are satisfied. *Keep it up gentlemen*.'[33] Such claims seemed to more than justify the comment made by the *Canadian Pharmaceutical Journal* that 'the Eaton Company loses no opportunity to make capital out of passing events.'[34]

Advertisements openly deriding the efforts of wholesalers and commercial associations demonstrated the contempt Timothy Eaton felt for those members of the retail industry:

The Retail Druggists Association is the authority that prices are to go up and a combination of manufacturers is the lever to be used in upsetting this business. We're ready gentlemen! We accept the change! Drugs and patent medicines will continue to sell here at dry goods profits and the results of higher prices elsewhere will be vastly larger sales here. We've no objections. At no time have we had any trouble in getting all the goods we want, and the men who can stop us now are rarer than white crows.[35]

Timothy Eaton was little affected by the criticisms. When asked by Joseph Atkinson what he intended to do about the charges, he remarked that 'he would just continue to keep store.'[36]

Furthermore, Eaton paid little attention to the complaints of wholesalers who had served him well in the past. The companies of both John Macdonald and H.S. Howland and Sons, in an attempt to arrest the decline of the Toronto wholesale industry, questioned Timothy Eaton's decision regarding the supply of merchandise from local wholesalers. Macdonald drew attention to favours extended to Eaton's by his father in the 1880s and questioned the fairness of instructions stipulating that Eaton buyers should 'buy nothing from John Macdonald & Co.'[37] Howland's representative went farther and offered to meet competitive prices, urging that local wealth be kept in the city.

We have heard for some time past that it is the policy of the departmental stores in Toronto, and of your good store in particular, not to patronize the wholesale merchants and manufacturers of the city of Toronto, except where absolutely necessary, that is, when you run short of goods and cannot wait to bring them from a distance: your policy being to buy outside of Toronto wholesale merchants or manufacturers at even prices or in some cases, preferring to pay a little more rather than patronize local concerns. It is hard for us to believe that you are assuming this position, although from the amount of business which we are doing with you, it looks as though your buyers are under some such instructions.[38]

An investigation by a local newspaper appeared to confirm this suspicion and cited an instance where Timothy Eaton had countermanded the order placed by one of his buyers from a local supplier. One wholesale merchant interviewed by the *Daily News* considered it a very serious matter that a local store purchased the bulk of its goods abroad. As he pointed out:

The wholesale men of Toronto pay large taxes into the city coffers. Their employees are paid fair salaries, an ordinary clerk receiving from ten to fifteen dollars a week. Our business is not carried on by a staff of shop girls at two dollars a week. Still we must suffer from the competition of such stores as T. Eaton & Company. This house had not even the good grace to purchase goods in the city where they make their money. T. Eaton & Company has gradually been estranging itself from the Toronto wholesale houses until now almost all their purchases are direct importations from abroad. Where T. Eaton & Company formerly had the largest account with us, their purchases now average no more than $100 a month.[39]

These complaints reflected the changes in the retail and wholesale industry in general and also at the level of earlier close relationship. Little would be gained by direct appeal. Indeed Howland's representative's reference to the 'policy of the departmental stores of Toronto, and of your good store in particular' was ill advised. Timothy Eaton used the reference to a 'departmental store' to sidestep the real question and to fudge the whole issue of merchandise supply:

Your private note of yesterday to hand, which is rather amusing to read, and is very difficult to understand. I really think you must be joking. Kindly accept our thanks for the very elaborate information you have given us, and as you say you don't believe it, helps to make it more amusing. As you request an early reply, beg to say and wish it distinctly understood, that we do not understand the Policy of the Departmental Store in Toronto, and wish it distinctly understood that this is not a Departmental Store, any more than yours is, or any other place of business. You must have been reading 'Saturday Night,' or consulting with 'North' and 'West' 'Enders'; they talk about Departmental Stores in profusion. I do not think it is the business of any respectable house to listen to the twaddle of the street, or what street gossip you may hear. We know nothing of Departmental Stores or their Policies; we are simply here doing business at 190 Yonge Street, and would recommend you to investigate a little closer what you seem to have heard, and when you have done this, believe all you see.[40]

As his advertisements suggest, Timothy Eaton was guided by the actions of the general public: 'The great public is fully competent to decide what it wants without any help from the disgruntled politicians or unsuccessful merchants. This store is big and powerful, because it considers the interests of customers on a par with its own. There's no patent about it. Anybody can do the same if they work hard enough and wait long enough.'[41]

And yet it seems likely that there were occasions when there was more than just cause for complaint. Some managers, with or without Timothy Eaton's knowledge, appear to have overstepped the general bounds of commercial ethics, but perhaps these came under the heading of 'considering one's interests.' Complaints were received from several suppliers regarding the unsanctioned use of brand names on company-manufactured textile and medical preparations. Furthermore in 1898 the company was convicted of applying false trade descriptions to goods.[42] In replying to one complaint Timothy Eaton again fudged the issue and did not fully address the real problem. Pointing out that the action taken by his company had not affected the sales of merchandise supplied by the British company, he declared that: 'We would not take it on ourselves to advise you in any way to curtail your business on account of our action in the matter. We have invariably done fairly well with any lines we got from you and will probably be in a position to say the same in the future, as we ask no more than to be on an equal footing with our competitors and we will look after the rest.'[43] The tone of this letter, while polite, is similar to several others suggesting quite firmly that the Eaton store was a private business and could be run as the owner dictated; outside interference was neither appreciated nor tolerated.

The crusade against departmental stores continued. By 1896 the retailers of Toronto had gained the support not only of a considerable number of aldermen but also of Mayor Fleming, who declared that he would do what he could to increase the assessment rate on departmental stores.[44] The issue of municipal taxation had long been a source of considerable ill-feeling in Toronto. The businessmen of the city at both the retail and the wholesale level particularly resented the tax on property, known as the personalty tax, which was levied annually on a merchant's stock-in-trade. This was in addition to the normal tax assessed on land and buildings. In times of economic depression the personalty tax created serious financial difficulties for merchants with large inventories. Many felt especially resentful because they also carried a heavy taxation burden imposed by customs duties. Letters and articles continually denounced the inherent injustice of taxing the invested capital of enterprising merchants, while ignoring funds invested in savings banks, stocks, mortgages, fine furniture, and paintings. As several reports argued, the tax was directed at 'the bone and sinew' of those who were most active in building up the community and whom it was in 'the city's interest to favour.'[45] One proposal, for a business tax to replace the personalty tax, received strong support during the early 1890s.[46]

Over the years numerous unsuccessful resolutions and petitions requesting a change in this law had been placed before the Ontario Legislature and the Toronto City Council. The recommendations of various commissions appointed throughout the previous two decades had resulted in a number of amending acts but had done nothing to remove the merchants' essential grievance. The 1893 *Report of the Commission on Municipal Taxation*, for example, affirmed continued belief in the taxation of personal property, since it ensured that speculators could not evade their responsibilities and were brought within the cognizance of the assessor.[47] In the meantime many merchants either vastly minimized the amount of their taxable inventories or claimed inflated debt exemptions as a means of avoiding taxes.[48] The comments made by Board of Trade executives, who argued that the assessment act bred corruption, perjury, and disrespect for the law and placed those who would not lie at a disadvantage, would seem to confirm this. The value of Timothy Eaton's assessed personal property, for example, rose from a low of $2,000 in 1871 to $20,000 in 1890; these figures certainly did not represent an accurate valuation of stock on hand (see Table 7). Since the taxable value on land and buildings rose from just under $7,000 in 1869 to more than $57,000 in 1890, perhaps he felt that he was contributing his fair share of taxes to the community chest. From 1890 to 1895, the considerable increase in store size raised the annual taxable value of personal property or stock from $20,000 to $50,000.[49]

The formation of the Association of Retail Merchants in April 1897 consolidated support for the implementation of a special tax on departmental stores, a recommendation that had been advanced early in the previous year. This Toronto association, headed by E.M. Trowern, one of the leading retail jewellers in the city, followed the example set by similar American organizations and lobbied for provincial legislation.[50] Bills proposing the implementation of special taxes on departmental stores were brought before the Ontario Legislature in 1897 and 1899, but in each case lack of precision in the wording of the proposed legislation rendered them unacceptable to a wide majority of commercial interests. The 1897 bill, if passed, would have severely penalized rural general stores, and since nothing in that of 1899 defined a retailer, the proposed legislation would have presented a threat to the livelihoods of both wholesalers and manufacturers. Edward Gurney, in a speech to the Toronto Board of Trade, asserted that taxation should not be aimed at certain classes with the intention of driving them out of business. In his view, this would drive business away from a developing city, since it could be claimed with some justification that Toronto taxed capital and enterprise.[51]

Actions undertaken by other taxpayers were more successful. The complaint lodged in 1895 before the Court of Revision by Isaac B. Johnston, a boot and shoe merchant on Queen Street East, resulted in an increase of Eaton's assessment on personal property for 1896 to $100,000.00. Not satisfied with this result, Isaac Johnston lodged another complaint before the Court of Revision regarding Eaton's assessment in 1897. Johnston drew attention to the enormous depreciation in assessments that had occurred in the last eight years and stated that the departmental stores were largely responsible for this decline. To reinforce his argument he asserted that the Eaton store had paid taxes on only $80,000.00 out of a total stock of $609,666.00. Citing a municipal tax payment by the Eaton company of only $1,172.00, Johnston declared that it barely covered the cost of police protection for the block bounded by the store. He therefore proposed the implementation of a progressive tax on turnover. The Eaton company took exception to this accusation of wilful dishonesty and announced in one of its advertisements that all the figures cited by Johnston were grossly inaccurate. The estimated value of stock assessed had amounted to $426,766.00 and the company held receipted tax statements to this effect amounting to $7,930.52. But as the Eaton advertisement pointed out, 'Evidently elections are coming and aldermen and would-be aldermen must talk – they want votes.'[52]

Timothy Eaton's public statements regarding his practice of paying cash for all merchandise ultimately worked to his own disadvantage. One could hardly make such statements and then expect to claim tax exemptions for debts outstanding on stock. The appeal by the company before the Court of Revision in 1898 was dismissed when the company failed to furnish sufficient information to show reason why judgment should be withdrawn. Assessment on personal property for the years 1898 to 1900 inclusive was increased to $200,000 annually.[53]

By 1900 agitation and unrest were sufficiently widespread to bring about the appointment of a special commission to investigate fully the question of municipal assessment laws. As it had in the past, the personalty tax would come in for a great deal of criticism. One widely circulated view was that, since most legislative bodies were controlled by lawyers and professional politicians, ignorance had allowed the passage of measures that were bad for business.[54]

Since little possibility existed for immediate legislative action, the Association of Retail Merchants continued the attack made earlier by Johnston and other taxpayers against the Eaton store. Their 1900 case before the Court of Revision resulted in a further increase in the Eaton store's taxation rate. On this occasion, the Eaton company made a determined attempt to reverse the decision and provided extensive information regarding land, buildings, plant, stock, and outstanding debts. In addition, the municipal assessment department conducted a thorough examination of the whole Eaton operation, going so far as to inspect shelving and count the number of arc lamps in the store. Claiming outstanding debts amounting to nearly $630,000, the company argued that these should be deducted from the assessed value of personal property, as the current by-law directed. Stock at this time was valued at $855,847. These exemptions were allowed on personal property and thus reduced the assessed value to $203,944. The Appeal Board, headed by Judge McDougall, refused to accept the company's depreciated values on plant and fixtures, however, and increased this assessment to $467,209 from the previously assessed rate of $426,027. The result of the appeal by the company nevertheless reduced the overall assessed value by $301,728. The Association of Retail Merchants was incensed that Judge McDougall had upheld the company's practice of charging money on loan from the bank as a debt against stock in order to claim it as an exemption. As Trowern testified before the Ontario Assessment Commission in 1900: 'while they will come out and tell you that it has a good moral effect on the country to be able to say, "We buy for cash"; when you bring them before the Court of Revision they say "We owe for everything." '[55]

The findings of the OAC ultimately resulted in the passage of remedial legislation. The bill passed by the Ontario Legislature in 1904 not only abolished the personalty tax and replaced it with a new business tax, but, to the great satisfaction of the Association of Retail Merchants, the act contained a special tax, similar to that implemented in Prussia, for department stores.

Every person carrying on the business of what is known as a departmental store or of a retail merchant dealing in more than five branches of retail trade or business in the same premises or in separate departments of premises under one roof, or in connected premises where the assessed value of the premises exceeds $20,000, for a sum equal to 50% of the assessed value of the said land and premises in addition to the full assessment of said land and premises.[56]

Whether this would act as a deterrent for other enterprising Toronto merchants would remain to be seen, but at least it gave the appearance of some kind of support for the smaller merchant.

Competition was a constant given for any merchant carrying on a business in nineteenth-century Toronto, and accompanying this was the ever-present fear of failure and bankruptcy. Whether the rate of failure for small merchants increased as the century drew to a close is not clear; what is apparent is the extent to which small businessmen began to lay the blame on visible external forces rather than merely accepting failure, as they had in the past, as a more or less natural consequence of normal pressures in the market-place. In addition, the adoption by both retailers and wholesalers of cash or shorter credit terms effected changes in the industry that were increasingly felt by those with limited resources. Those who had failed could no longer entertain the thought of settling their affairs and immediately re-establishing themselves in business as they would have in the past. Economic circumstances now militated against this possibility.

The competition offered by such stores as Eaton's, Simpson's, or even Jamieson's and the Guinane shoe store seemed to leave little room for those willing to serve a limited market. By the 1890s many of the sectors projected an image wholly aggressive in outlook that was in striking contrast to the earlier more dignified behaviour of the older merchants. The general acceptance of cash terms and fixed prices had encouraged bigger businesses gradually to introduce other innovations that few small merchants could match. Shorter hours, Saturday half-holidays, city-wide deliveries, waiting-rooms, parcel checks, restaurants, and the huge variety of merchandise were all made possible by volume trade.

In this respect it could perhaps be argued that the Eaton store and others like it had effected a general improvement in the industry. As far as the ordinary consumer was concerned, the increasing volume of sales achieved by the Eaton store demonstrated quite clearly that the average Torontonian had no complaint to direct at a store that gave both service and value.

11

Timothy Eaton: The Final Years

'Mr. Eaton is entitled to a foremost place among the
leaders of the modern commercial revolution which has
given the retail trade a new and higher standing
in the commercial world.'
Globe editorial, January 1907

Toronto at the turn of the century was witness to a vastly different
retail industry from that which had been in evidence when Timothy
Eaton first opened his store at 178 Yonge Street in the winter of
1869. King Street was no longer regarded as the prime location for
retail stores; Yonge Street as far north as Bloor Street drew shoppers
from all over the city. By 1907 the number of dry goods stores in
the vastly enlarged city had fallen to ninety-one. Of this number
only one was to be found on Yonge Street, and there were none at
all in the immediate vicinity of the Yonge-Queen intersection, an
indication of the impact the department stores had had on this
sector of the retail trade. The true magnitude of that impact is more
evident when one considers that Toronto's population rose from
208,140 in 1901 to more than 380,000 by 1911. The city then
stretched from Jane Street in the west to Victoria Park in the east,
and well beyond St Clair Avenue in the north. To accommodate
this spreading urbanization, the Eaton store by 1903 instituted
regular deliveries to Mimico, Victoria Park, Lambton Mills, Rich-
mond Hill, and Cooksville.

The company continued to expand its physical space for store, mail order, and factory facilities. Property was acquired on Louisa and James streets in 1899, on Yonge Street in 1900, on Albert Street in 1901, and on Louisa Street and Trinity Square in 1903. Further acquisitions were made on Yonge and Queen streets in 1904 and 1909. By 1908 Eaton property covered some twenty-two acres of prime downtown land.[1]

In 1904 Timothy Eaton reached the traditionally allotted span of three score years and ten, by which time he had been in business as apprentice, clerk, and merchant for fifty-seven years. Although the accidents he had suffered had restricted his physical mobility, they had little effect on his ability to promote and oversee further growth. Neither he nor his store demonstrated any signs of slowing down or falling behind. The continued increase in store space allowed for further expansion of departments and merchandise. Shot-guns, revolvers, rifles, cartridges, and accessories were added to the sporting goods department in 1900. In response to numerous inquiries, buggies, cutters, and sleighs, priced from $35.00 to $78.75, were offered in the Fall-Winter catalogue of 1902–3.[2] The variety of merchandise expanded further and ranged from graphophones for office dictation to parquet wood tiles for home installation: 'Any good carpenter can do the job.' In 1905 the curtain and carpet departments more than doubled in size. In the following year a selection of bathroom equipment made its appearance in the hardware department. Two years later the toy department achieved independent status from sporting goods. The first portable electric vacuum cleaner was added to merchandise in 1909.[3]

New services were also added. In 1901 the restaurant opened on the third floor upgraded a facility formerly located in the basement. By the spring of 1902 the catalogue carried a notation stating: 'A nos Clients Français: Nous préférons que vous vous écriviez en Anglais, mais si vous ne pouvez pas, alors veuillez écrire distinctment en Français. En envoyant vos ordres mentionnez toujours la page du Catalogue et le numero de l'article.'[4]

One new service, the deposit account, instituted in 1904, grew out of the apparent success of the employee savings account. Nevertheless, before it was formally implemented the whole matter was carefully investigated. A visit was made to the Macy store in New York to study the workings of the deposit account system that had been in operation there for nearly two years. Originally established to overcome the objections of customers who did not like carrying cash, Macy's operated the service as a selling expense at a cost to the company of approximately $1,000 a month. Interest of 4 per cent was paid by the Macy store on average deposits, and an annual Christmas bonus of 2 per cent was made on net purchases for the year.[5]

Although the Eaton store had no intention of discontinuing its cash-only system, the deposit account allowed a customer to offset purchases against a prior credit balance paid into the account. Interest at the rate of 5 per cent was paid by Eaton's on outstanding balances. This rate was sufficiently attractive that many customers used their accounts as subsidiary savings accounts. The main thrust of this service, aside from the convenience it offered for impulse purchases, was directed at Toronto's more well-to-do citizens, many of whom were still accustomed to buying on credit. As an attempt to expand this market the service had some success, for, some two years after the introduction of deposit accounts, the store had more than seven hundred active accounts, and by 1914 this number had risen to 4,500. Funds deposited with the Eaton company were secured by holdings of government securities equal in value to the total amounts on deposit.[6]

The personnel responsible for the promotion of store and merchandise continued to seek new ways of drawing people to the store. The display windows fronting on Yonge and Queen streets frequently contained items usually reserved by more conservative stores for interior display. An enormous Easter egg displayed in the store in 1906 housed an eight-piece orchestra complete with piano. The annual Santa Claus parade, a promotional device that would ultimately become a Toronto tradition, first came into being in 1905. For several days before the great day, Eaton's advertisements carried messages purporting to be from Santa Claus and detailing the progress of his journey from the 'far north,' in this case Winnipeg. Santa Claus arrived by train at Union Station and travelled from there to the store seated on a huge packing case atop a horse-drawn wagon. A fashion show held in the store in August 1908 not only created something of a precedent but generated considerable comment. On this occasion, Eaton's was the first Canadian store to use living models (brought in from New York) in the presentation of imported French directoire gowns. The *Dry Goods Review* devoted three pages to the event.[7]

The store continued to advertise heavily in many of the Toronto papers. The *Toronto Daily Star*, for example, now carried a full-page advertisement in each daily issue. For those shoppers who did not read the *Star*, these advertisements were widely displayed throughout the store in specially made frames.[8] In an attempt to reach a wider audience, the McKim advertising agency in Montreal was hired to place weekly full-page advertisements in papers throughout Ontario and eastern Canada. But hostility towards department stores still prevailed in many rural centres, and few local publishers could be persuaded to sign contracts with a retailer operating in direct competition with local merchants.[9]

The catalogue, therefore, continued to be the most effective promotional publication. By 1904 the company was printing 1.3 million catalogues annually. The *Dry Goods Review*, commenting on the influence wielded by this publication, stated that 90 per cent of the students at a year-end examination at one Gananoque school provided precise details about the Eaton store and its merchandise when asked to write an order for goods as though it were the genuine article. As the *Dry Goods Review* observed, the young people of Canada were 'getting a correspondence school education with Eaton's Catalogue as the text book.'[10] By 1907 the influence of the catalogue had spread beyond the shores of Canada. Postcards requesting copies were received from expatriate Canadians living in several European countries, as well as China, Jamaica, India, and Mexico. The Reverend William Elliott in Hiroshima, Japan, wrote that hundreds of dollars were sent annually from Japan to Montgomery Ward and that some of this might quite easily be diverted to Canada if Eaton catalogues were made available.[11]

Despite this apparent success, there appears to have been continuing uneasiness regarding the growth of mail order sales. Consideration was given to the possibility of issuing quarterly or even bi-monthly editions of the catalogue in addition to the regular twice-yearly publications, with the intention of increasing the business and bringing the company name more frequently to the attention of the public. In order to improve service, the mail order department moved into its own building at 14 Albert Street in 1903. In 1909 it took over two more buildings on Louisa Street, and at this time mail order stock was totally segregated from that carried in the store.

Sales volume, whether generated by city shoppers or mail order customers, became a matter of overwhelming importance. The constant physical expansion of store space and the consequent increase in overall expenses demanded that the volume of sales escalate proportionately. According to Ralph Hower, the Macy department store by the turn of the century had almost exhausted the possibilities of diversification. Efforts then had to be made to increase the number of shoppers, and to persuade them to make larger purchases.[12] The constant stream of directions and instructions to department managers suggest that this was also the case at Eaton's. Each item of merchandise intended for inclusion in the Eaton catalogue was to be subjected to extremely careful attention, bearing in mind that 'it should be made to speak out in the matter of *style* and *price* in such a way as to *convince* the readers.' The motto should be '*every item a seller.*' Those customers receiving the catalogue who purchased only certain lines 'must be *forced* into buying by the values offered on other items.' As one such notice urged, 'every department [must] sell to *every* Eaton customer not to only between 5% to 25% of available mail order customers as at present.' Mail order customers who never bought anything from the catalogue were regarded as 'deadheads' and removed from the mailing list.[13]

In an attempt to increase mail order sales several new inducements were added to the store's services. In 1905, as a means of reducing customer freight charges, the company advanced the idea of 'club orders.' Neighbours were urged to order goods 'at one time and in one letter.' By having merchandise so requested mailed in one parcel customers could save up to 75 per cent on freight rates. To further increase the volume of mail order trade the company assumed all freight and express charges on orders of twenty-five dollars or more. In 1907 merchandise could be exchanged at no cost, as the company assumed all postal charges. One senior executive kept a close watch on the sales of farm products for each province to show that the opportunity existed for a greater volume of sales if the mail order department went after them.[14]

With city customers, the stress was placed on increasing the traffic during slow periods by advertising special sales. To give departments more leeway in this effort, the normally required gross gain was considerably reduced to allow goods to be marked and sold even closer to established company margins than usual. Attention was drawn in 1907 to the 15 per cent increase in public spending calculated from the receipts of the Toronto Street Railway and customs duties. From this calculation it was estimated that 'any business or part of a business increasing less than 15% is losing ground and the competitor gaining.' Each department manager was therefore urged to 'aim at a big increase and not rest content with less than 25% increase. That will lower the expense per cent enough to show sufficient profit.'[15]

The search for sales was undoubtedly responsible for the physical expansion of the store outside Toronto. To this end John Craig Eaton actively promoted the idea of an Eaton store in Winnipeg, convinced that if they did not do so some other large retail company might, thereby severely reducing their western market.[16] By the 1890s the enormous growth within the city of Winnipeg had reduced the dependence of retailers there on eastern suppliers and wholesalers. Western shoppers' demands were now being met by local suppliers, and these customers were no longer so willing to rely on mail order services in the east, no matter how prompt.

Despite some misgivings regarding the problem of managing a store so far from Toronto, Timothy Eaton agreed in principle with his son and the usual investigations were made. As a first step, arrangements were made for the company to present a display of store merchandise at the 1899 Western Industrial Fair in Winnipeg. By early 1904 the Eaton company was in possession of a large number of properties assembled privately on a block of land with a frontage of 266 feet on Portage between Donald and Hargrave streets.[17] Some risk was incurred by locating away from the centre of retail activity at Portage and Main streets, but it had not been possible to secure sufficient property in the central area. Timothy Eaton thus would repeat an experience similar to that of 1869 when he located on Yonge Street, well away from the fashionable shopping district on King Street.

The first sod was turned on the site on 27 July 1904, and the store opened for visitors at 2:30 p.m. on Saturday 15 July 1905 and for business the following Monday. Its opening was timed to coincide with the influx of visitors attending that year's Western Industrial Fair.[18] More than 250 experienced employees were invited to move to Winnipeg to manage the operations of the new store; they were given the option to return to their old jobs in Toronto after a year if they decided they did not like the western city, but less than 20 took advantage of this offer.

During the course of construction Timothy Eaton received a number of discouraging reports as to the size of the store and its almost certain failure. The financier E.R. Wood, who visited the site when construction had just begun, informed Timothy Eaton that the hole in the ground was so big that it would never be needed during his lifetime. One manager, with a notable lack of foresight, declared that not only was the Winnipeg store in the wrong location, but that the western city was not big enough to support such a store. As a result the projected six-storey building was reduced to five storeys and then had to undergo constant expansion to cope with the flow of business. Such results utterly confounded those who had also predicted that the west was not ready to discard the credit system of doing business. By 1910 an eighth storey was added and the building extended farther south on Donald Street.[19]

With the opening of the Winnipeg store separate catalogues were published, and those produced in Winnipeg contained some merchandise more suitable for the western market. Some losses were initially experienced in the shoe department and in some of the clothing lines, since those first stocked were not of a sufficiently heavy quality. Sheepskin coats and jackets were added. Greater stress was placed on durability and value. Fur jackets, priced to sell at $150.00, were included in the stock of merchandise along with heavy tweed suits at $4.50.[20] Much of the merchandise was similar to that in the Toronto catalogue, and in most cases the prices were identical.

The increase in population in most large western cities during the next ten years was simply enormous. Winnipeg's population rose from 90,153 in 1906 to 163,000 some ten years later, and similar growth was demonstrated throughout the west. The few existing figures for the Winnipeg store indicate that sales volume there increased from $2,686,320 in 1905 to $14,407,166 in 1915.[21]

No complete figures are available regarding the sales figures at the company's Toronto store. Assuming that sales volume at the Eaton store in Toronto doubled every five years – a somewhat conservative estimate – then sales at the main store rose from $6,732,000 in 1901 to $26,928,000 in 1911. The company's gross sales for all outlets rose from $22,488,000 in 1907, to $53,367,000 in 1914, and $141,320,000 in 1920, indicating that the volume of sales doubled every five years in the last decade of the nineteenth century and continued to increase but at a faster rate in the first two decades of the twentieth. By comparison, sales of the Simpson company, despite its entrance into the Montreal market with the purchase of the John Murphy stores, rose from only $1,250,000 in 1898 to $14,081,451 in 1914, barely a quarter of Eaton's volume.[22]

This growth was matched by continuing concern with cost and further attempts at self-sufficiency. In the late 1890s efforts had been made to free the company from the payment of heavy insurance premiums. An insurance fund was established and regular amounts set aside 'equal to the amount which would otherwise be paid for premium in effecting insurance on [company] buildings and fixtures.'[23] By underwriting some of the cost of the safety of its own buildings, plant, and merchandise, the company was able to make use of funds that would otherwise have been permanently lost to it.

In 1901 the Eaton company established its own typographical plant and printing department. Despite statements to the Toronto Typographical Union that 'they had no desire to do "aught that would conflict with the Union's rule and that they would conduct a union office," ' it soon became clear that the company did not intend to run its printing department under union rules. The resulting strike on 16 May 1902 brought work on the catalogue to a standstill. Timothy Eaton therefore recruited a manager from gentlemen's furnishings, J.S. Lowry, and gave him authority to hire typesetters to replace those out on strike. By supplementing non-union men with salesmen drawn from his own department, Lowry got the catalogue out on time. The boycott of the Eaton store organized by the Toronto typographers, received the active support of the printing community and was said to have inflicted some damage on Eaton's sales. Largely because of disagreements between the Toronto local and its American headquarters, which refused either to consent or give support to a widening of the strike to all newspaper offices, the strikers failed to achieve their objective of a union shop.[24]

In 1909 the Eaton company expanded the activities of its print room to include the production of school-books. The huge contract awarded to the company for half a million school readers and textbooks was an attempt by the Ontario government to break what the papers referred to as the 'School book ring.' The tender submitted by Eaton's amounted to just over thirty-nine cents for a set of five books and effected enormous savings to Ontario taxpayers. The retail price of forty-nine cents for the set, down from the dollar and fifteen cents charged previously, generated further savings for Ontario parents. Since the Eaton name appeared in each book, the Booksellers' Association censured this widespread promotion of a private business. In its opinion the Eaton company already received sufficient assistance from the Post Office in the promotion of its business through the unreasonable dumping of mail order literature. (The envelopes containing the catalogues routinely carried a notice addressed to the local postmaster requesting him kindly to give the enclosed catalogue to someone who would appreciate it, if it had not been called for in two weeks.)[25]

The establishment of the printing department was just one aspect of the company's continuing expansion into manufacturing and production. The introduction of Eaton brand names – Acme in 1905 and Teco in 1907 – were further measures designed to gain greater control and perhaps to increase demands for company manufactured goods. As the concept of trademarks gained greater credibility, the store could avoid those brands subject to a specific resale price by producing its own lines. In the 1890s the Eaton company had wielded sufficient power to have its name stamped on a number of items, such as silverware and cutlery. Sales volumes now allowed for the production of entire lines manufactured to company specifications.

By January 1905 the Eaton company had seventeen different manufacturing departments producing goods ranging from an enormous variety of ready-to-wear clothes to harnesses, upholstered goods, check books, (the sales books used by the cash sales clerk), and ice cream. These were in addition to the company established for the production of drugs. Because of the speed with which the ready-to-wear industry had grown, Toronto manufacturers had been faced with a shortage of female labour. To overcome this difficulty the company opened a whitewear factory in Oshawa in 1903 and a ready-to-wear factory in Montreal in 1909.[26]

In 1901, as a result of rumours that Eaton's would open a factory in Hamilton, the company had been approached by civic personnel from Hamilton, Brampton, Oshawa, and Peterborough, all anxious to obtain this source of employment. Each municipality listed its advantages and offered additional benefits ranging from cheap power to tax exemptions.[27] Since Oshawa already housed several large manufacturing plants employing some 2,400 workers, it was assumed that, if suitable employment were provided, little difficulty would be experienced in securing a large female work-force. By October 1909, nearly 150 workers were employed by Eaton's at this plant.

As in the past, the growth of the company was paralleled by similar increases in the number of workers employed in all sectors of the organization. With the opening of the plants in Oshawa and Montreal, the number of workers directly employed in Eaton factories and work-rooms in 1909 rose to more than 4,500 from 400 in 1899. If one includes all workers in the factories and the store, employees rose from 2,475 in 1898 to 4,900 in 1903 and nearly 8,800 in October 1909. By 1910 Eaton's employed 11,700 workers in its stores, factories, and mail order and buying offices.[28]

By 1906 and possibly earlier, the classification of personnel underwent some change and was broken down into eleven or twelve categories. Those working in the store were divided into four categories – sales, mechanics, mail order, and expense – instead of the earlier two – sales and expense. A caretaking department, classified under the heading of maintenance, was established to look after general cleaning and minor repairs throughout the store. Supplies used in the course of these duties were charged to the retail department concerned, instead of to general expense. This was no doubt intended to discourage waste in matters of departmental housekeeping.

By 1909 the sales staff at the Toronto store had risen to 2,156 but represented only one-quarter of the total payroll. Manufacturing in one form or another now accounted for well over half the total number of employees in Toronto, while expense and mail order employed 1,260 and 449 respectively. Since only totals for each category are given, it is impossible to know just what these numbers represent in terms of executive, management, clerical, or unskilled help, or to arrive at a ratio of male to female employees. In 1906 the city's assessment rolls listed the names of 514 male and 170 female employees at the Eaton store. Since those listed represent only a fraction of the total staff employed at that time (3,080), it seems likely that these were managerial personnel in receipt of wages and salaries above a certain level. As might be expected, men at this level vastly outnumbered their female counterparts.

To raise the sales staff's level of competence, attempts were made to attract a better type of saleswoman. A minimum wage of six dollars a week was established for a first-class saleswoman at the age of eighteen, and steps were taken to increase this to seven dollars. A formal dress code was introduced in 1909, dictating that clothing during working hours was to consist of a black dress or a black skirt and a white shirtwaist.[29]

Hours of work for all company employees, whether in the store, a factory, or the mail order department, were further reduced in

January 1904. The store then closed each day at 5:00 p.m. Hours were again reduced in 1913 when the doors opened at 8.30 a.m. instead of 8:00 a.m. The Saturday half-holiday during the summer months of July and August was extended to June in 1907 and May in 1910.[30]

The material relating to the actual executive management of this enormous operation during the first decade of the twentieth century is extremely limited, but what there is points to the possibility of some stress and internal upset. This was brought about by a number of factors, not least of which was the considerable delegation of authority necessitated by the personal adversities that afflicted Timothy Eaton around the turn of the century. The early death of Edward Young Eaton in October 1900 at the age of thirty-seven from Bright's disease, coming so soon after Timothy Eaton's own accidents, which had confined him to a wheelchair, was a severe blow to his constitution and prevented him from attending the regular meetings for shareholders from 1900 to 1902.[31] Matters that Timothy Eaton had normally handled himself were thus placed in the hands of other senior personnel, for John Craig Eaton, at the age of twenty-four, was not yet ready to step into his brother's shoes.

Although Timothy Eaton was willing in the interest of business expansion to allow his senior staff a fairly large measure of initiative and independence, it appears that some executives arrogated more responsibility to themselves than was intended. Several reports hint at a power struggle by three or four senior executives to oust a number of their colleagues. For the period in question, 1899 to 1902, they seem to have achieved a fair measure of success. During this period the number of shares taken up increased from 2,700 to 4,950, and several members of the staff were unhappy with the way this was managed. Although the Eaton family at all times held more than 80 per cent of distributed shares, the holdings of several senior non-family members underwent some expansion. The investigation of store operations undertaken during the mid-1890s had concentrated wholly on wages and day-to-day expenses and had directed little attention to activities of senior personnel. Procedures such as those involving the distribution of shares or payment of bonuses had been ignored. Possibly the fact that the company secretary changed four times between 1891 and 1895 had prevented the development and implementation of proper formal procedures where these matters were concerned. As early as 1896 Timothy Eaton had complained to Edward that some members of the London office had not received their July bonuses and that they did not know whether or not they held company shares.[32]

Matters came to a head in the late summer of 1903 with the sudden dismissal of four senior executives. The comments made by one employee in the *Dry Goods Review* cast some light on the problem:

One after another have been given the reins of management only to find themselves eventually dropped ... The persistent growth of the business carries some of them to heights they never dreamed of, and it isn't to be wondered at that heads got turned and egotism became rampant, with comparatively little to fall back upon when the end came ... one only has to study the developments of the last year or two to see how easily and quickly the best of them are 'thrown.'[33]

Because of the speculative nature of much of the material, it is only possible to arrive at a very limited conclusion. Perhaps some senior non-family personnel felt that John Craig Eaton's comparative youthfulness created an opportunity for them gradually to assume a greater measure of control.

The steps taken to remedy the situation included the promotion of several family members. Robert Young Eaton was appointed to the position of secretary-treasurer and Robert Wellington Eaton of store superintendent. Timothy Eaton remained as president, with John Craig Eaton as vice-president. By 1907 management of company operations had once more returned to an even keel. Responsibility for certain aspects of store operations was divided amongst senior executives. John Craig Eaton assumed responsibility for everything connected with mail order sales; Robert Young Eaton, all other sales; Robert Wellington Eaton, store operations and services; J.J. Vaughan, general office and accounting; Harry

McGee, building construction and renovations; and W.G. Deans, everything connected with factory production.

The sudden death of Timothy Eaton from pneumonia at 10:20 a.m. on Thursday, 31 January 1907, stunned the commercial community. As one employee put it, 'This was one crisis the Governor couldn't beat.'[34] He had, however, created an organization that could withstand this loss. It seems likely that had it not been for the early death of Edward Young Eaton, Timothy Eaton would have surrendered control around the turn of the century, for in 1898 he had talked of wanting to step down.[35] For a man whose mental powers remained undiminished, the strain imposed by his physical limitations must have been especially discouraging.

All Eaton stores and factories were immediately closed, as were the offices in London and Paris, and they remained so until the following Monday. Timothy Eaton's death and his funeral on Saturday, 2 February, received wide coverage in newspapers across Canada. In each case the editors wrote glowing tributes lauding his moral influence in the commercial revolution and his keen discernment of the public's needs. More than 230 carriages followed by several thousands of mourners on foot accompanied the stern Irish merchant to his final resting placing in Mount Pleasant Cemetery.[36]

Timothy Eaton left an estate of $5,250,000, all, as the *Dry Goods Review* pointed out, 'the result of operations in the Toronto retail trade.' In the opinion of its editor, Timothy Eaton's success demonstrated the soundness of the cash-only principle.[37]

When John Craig Eaton assumed the reins of power, one of his first actions was to regain complete control of all company shares. Those held by employees were replaced by company bonds of equal value but carried no voting rights. In future all financial decisions would reside in the hands of the president.[38] Members of the staff could thus benefit from the growth of the company, but no information regarding profits or other financial arrangements would be revealed. Just as Timothy Eaton had gradually removed all possibilities for external interference or obstruction in the day-to-day operations of the Eaton store, so by this action John Craig Eaton removed the final possibility for intervention by internal agents in company operations and activities.

Conclusion

'Nature abhors a vacuum and this is why we fill it up.'
Eaton advertisement,
Daily News, 4 August 1886

In 1852 Timothy Eaton left the store at Portglenone with little more than a thorough grounding in the day-to-day operations of a large general store. At the time of his death some fifty-five years later, he left not only two thriving department stores and numerous manufacturing establishments, but also the solid foundations on which the enormous Canada-wide chain would be erected.

Like many successful men of business his ascent to the top had not been achieved without some setbacks, and at no time during his early years could his later success have been regarded as a foregone conclusion. Indeed there were several occasions – the openings of the bakery in St Marys in 1860, the first Toronto store in 1868, the one at 178 Yonge Street a year later, the wholesale enterprise on Scott Street in 1881, and the new store at 190 Yonge Street in 1883 – when he might have joined the ranks of those he despised, for on each occasion the external economic circumstances offered an environment hostile to business success. But he did not fail, and on each occasion he managed to rise above his own difficulties and those imposed from outside.

These handicaps were offset by several factors that favoured his eventual success. The enormous growth of industrialization and the consequent increase in the number of those earning regular wages are the first that spring to mind. In addition, the constant increase in population growth and the steady rise in the standard of living provided an ever-expanding market for the goods and novelties being produced in great volumes. Competition for business was fierce, however, and the number of failures remained at a high level, despite the increase in both demand and supply. Timothy Eaton's store at 178 Yonge Street in 1869 was just one of many small dry goods stores in Toronto. Indeed when compared to those operated by some of his larger competitors, it was easily overlooked. What then were the factors that were responsible for the store's great success?

The character of the man himself has much to do with this, for Timothy Eaton possessed an iron-willed determination. He sincerely believed that hard work and right Christian living would be rewarded with success. In this respect he was probably no different from thousands of other Victorians who had absorbed the optimistic attitudes expressed in the practical maxims of the day regarding hard work, thrift, punctuality, and a proper observance of the sabbath. Although his own observations would constantly remind him that the optimistic hopes so expressed did not always accord with reality, his positive attitude was buttressed by a personality of great independence. The comment found in his notebook, 'If almost Starved depend upon yourself and not upon others,' brings this home with great force.

Several reports suggest that, despite his Scottish ancestry, he occasionally demonstrated traits more in keeping with an Irish temperament. Indeed one contemporary felt that Timothy Eaton's motto should be that of the Donnybrook Fair – 'Whenever you see a head, hit it.'[1] This was a man who would brook no opposition nor allow himself to be swayed by external forces. From the evidence contained in his own letters, he was a man of few words, abrupt, plainspoken, and direct. An Italian proverb written in his notebook, 'Beware of men who praise you to your face. They are ever to be suspected,'[2] suggests that he had little use for those who would flatter and fawn. Impervious to most attacks of criticism, he had little sympathy for those who refused to demonstrate similar forcefulness and tenacity in their business relations. One contemporary who had been close to him for several years later remarked that he was completely lacking in sentiment. So far as it is known, he did not pray, as John Macdonald had prayed, to be delivered from inordinate attention to worldly objects.[3] The Eaton store, the central focus of his life, would provide him, the ninth child of a small Ulster farmer, with the means to become a 'somebody.'

Determination and strength of character did not by themselves automatically result in commercial success. Throughout this period many men imbued with the same determination entered the ranks of small businessmen only to suffer great personal and financial loss. But in Timothy Eaton's case this determination was reinforced by a further characteristic that contributed in large measure to his success. His adherence, whether conscious or instinctive, to the admonitions in the biblical parable of the five talents ensured that he made the fullest possible use of every opportunity.

It could also be argued that not only was Timothy Eaton in the right place at the right time – for location was clearly of vital importance to commercial success – but that circumstances directed his attention to the right business. Were it not for the difficult matter of 'licquors,' Timothy might have gone on to establish himself as just another merchant in the Toronto grocery trade. Instead, his purchase of the business formerly owned by Jennings and Brandon was something of a stroke of luck. Although situated in the unfashionable environs of Yonge and Queen streets, it offered several distinct advantages – a low rental, a well-frequented intersection, and a business with some reputation. But what was ultimately more important, he entered the trade now acknowledged as the advance guard for all the changes that were occurring in the retail industry – dry goods and drapery. Of all the department stores in existence today, only one – Harrods – began as a grocery store rather than a dry goods store. As David Alexander points out, the dry goods trade 'was the first trade to manifest [the] unmistakable characteristics of modern retailing,' for it was the one trade in which 'the retailer had few processing functions.'[4]

With the bulk of his capital invested in the stock so desired by the new working class, Timothy Eaton could focus his attention exclusively upon improving sales techniques and increasing volumes. Moreover a new store with all the features of a cheapjack store (the word 'cheap' appeared endlessly in his early advertisements) attracted workers whose financial credibility and social status perhaps made their custom unwelcome at the older traditional stores. The fashionable character of King Street may have made many wage-earning workers feel ill at ease. The fact that all Timothy Eaton's early flyers were distributed to this new sector of the population demonstrates that he was fully aware of the opportunities offered to the merchant who was prepared to cater to their needs. Clothing his ideas in 'the currency of honest merchandise and square dealing,' he was, as another employee put it, 'remarkably successful in giving the people what they wanted and in the way they wanted it.'[5]

In many respects he was still a country man at heart, and this was reflected in occasional turns of phrase. When writing to James about problems at the St Marys store in 1873, he advised, 'let both grow together until harvest – Then have a good Thumping Auction Sale.' On another occasion in the depth of winter, he wrote to a new supplier that 'It is an awkward time of the year to be sowing seed, but we may have a harvest before August.'[6] He obviously regarded his endeavours in shopkeeping as closely akin to farming; both could reap only the harvest of what had been sown.

The preparation that went into every new undertaking left little possibility for failure. Nothing was left to chance, from the introduction of a new line of merchandise to the opening of a new department or a large physical expansion. It was surely no accident that each large physical expansion, whether in Toronto or Winnipeg, was scheduled to coincide with the opening of an annual industrial exhibition.

Timothy Eaton's own early experiences had also compelled him to recognize that times were changing and that the merchant who wished to survive had to change with the times. The introduction of cash terms and one fixed price were the first concrete indications of many such changes in the retail industry. By the 1850s and early 1860s such concepts were being practised by many of the larger stores not only in Toronto but in some of the province's smaller rural centres. Many local stores, however, of necessity continued to hold on to older ways for fear of losing existing patrons.

Timothy Eaton, on the other hand, as a new merchant, could freely introduce any concept he chose, since he did not have to wean a following of older customers away from the more traditional methods of shopkeeping. Nevertheless it must be admitted that the state of his own finances and his complete lack of familiarity with customers drawn from a large population of social strangers urgently dictated the wisdom of cash sales. In a society where increasing numbers of workers were drawing a regular weekly wage, such a concept made excellent sense. By selling for cash Timothy Eaton was able to undercut merchants who were still dependent on credit. With no outstanding customer accounts, nearly every cent taken in across the counter could be ploughed back into the business. This income was used initially to reduce a heavy debt load, but as time went on it was also put to energetic use for the expansion of both store and merchandise. Perhaps in stepping out of character and adopting practices utilized by only the bigger stores in Toronto, Eaton provoked the ridicule G.G. Nasmith speaks of in the early years. But in an aggressive environment each merchant was compelled by necessity to find ways of capturing as big a share of the market as possible. Unfettered by the chains of tradition, Eaton could approach each new idea, project, or obstacle with an open mind.

In an attempt to overcome his constant difficulties he was always on the look-out for good ideas, for, as he himself would have been the first to admit, he was in business to make money. The conclusions he drew from his keen observations on the commercial scene, whether in Toronto or elsewhere, were matched by his willingness to introduce and adopt innovative concepts, merchandise, services, and procedures. Ideas introduced into other stores in both the United States and Europe were swiftly adopted by the Eaton store. Indeed the number of occasions when innovations introduced by John Wanamaker rapidly made their appearance at the Eaton store suggests that this was more than a coincidence. But as Timothy Eaton himself acknowledged, 'Whilst I am not the originator of the system, which is the work of many brains, I know the working of every cog and when anything goes wrong I can put my finger on the spot and say, there lies the trouble.'[7]

Whether he was selling three pairs of stockings for sixty cents, two hats for the price of one, and drugs at dry goods prices, closing early on Saturday afternoons, or introducing bus services from train or boat stations, waiting-rooms for his customers, and electric illuminations throughout the store, his prime objective was to draw customers to his store. It seems likely that this search for sales and the resultant profit margin was occasionally used to justify means not wholly in accord with the constant assertions regarding honesty. Perhaps Timothy Eaton regarded such actions under the heading of 'humbug.'

The gradual introduction of a wider range of merchandise led to the greater separation of stock. The early implementation of an efficient transfer system within the store not only increased the number of sales each employee could make, but also allowed for the establishment of really effective departmentalization of goods. Just as some wholesalers had benefited from the departmentalization of their merchandise, so too did Timothy Eaton. Specialization by departments allowed for the expansion of variety and choice that comes with merchandise breakdown, while the store gained the profits that resulted from the overall aggregation of stocks. With each department controlled by a senior member of the staff, profitability was no longer left to chance.

The growth of the Eaton store from dry goods outlet to department store demonstrated the extent to which Timothy Eaton and his staff had progressed in the art of business administration. Managing the small store at 178 Yonge Street was a wholly different proposition from running the company covering several city blocks in 1907. Despite some setbacks, this was accomplished with relative ease, largely due to the fact that, once problems were recognized, immediate steps were taken to resolve them. The studies undertaken by John James Eaton in the 1880s and 1890s, the streamlining of the delivery system by Edward Young Eaton, and the constant care given to stock control, costing expenditure and selling costs, discounts, interest payments, and margins helped the company guard against waste and avoid conservative complacency.

Concern with expenditure was carried to surprising lengths. In a recent article relating to the introduction of new business methods at the Hudson's Bay Company, David Monod discusses the emergence in the 1920s of the theory of 'turnover' as the most important of retail objectives, with the volume of customers demanding more consideration than that of profit.[8] Even a cursory glance at material relating to the Eaton store, and indeed at even earlier sources relating to British commerce in the 1840s, indicates that this 'new' theory was widely understood and recognized prior to 1900. Certainly Timothy Eaton and his managers gave every evidence of using turnover to great advantage well before the turn of the century. Indeed, as early as the 1870s Timothy Eaton was regularly counting the number of customers patronizing the store on a daily basis, and his early letters demonstrate his concern with turning over stocks rapidly.

At a time when a merchant could be accused of culpable carelessness for financial negligence and when the accounting and bookkeeping side of any business was still very primitive, the Eaton store was something of an anomaly. The greatest possible care was taken to ensure that every cent counted and was made to do twice and sometimes three times the work it had in the past.

The early introduction of sophisticated methods of accounting with regard to cost and price analysis also ensured adequate profit margins while allowing bargain prices for customers to be maintained. Merchandise was priced to allow for profitable margins, not only on initial sales, but also on possible stock clearances. As might be expected, profit margins on slow-moving merchandise, such as furniture and pictures, were higher than on fast-moving goods such as Misses suits, which had a turnover rating of ten times a year. The close checks kept on every item of merchandise allowed for increasingly rapid turnovers, especially in those departments that retailed goods in high demand. Profit margins were then adjusted accordingly.

That such accounting methods were not in wide use is evident from comments made by contemporary observers. The spectacular failure of the wholesale house of Samson, Kennedy and Gemmel showed the effects of reckless and ultimately destructive negligence where pricing and cost analysis were concerned. It seems highly likely that the John Eaton store that burst upon the retail field in 1895 would ultimately have experienced a correspondingly spectacular collapse. The fire of 1897 that revealed the store's rash operational methods merely hastened the fatal day. In both cases goods were placed on the market at prices too low even to cover expenses.

Gene Allen's observations regarding the difficulties facing new wholesale houses in the 1870s could quite easily have been applied to both the wholesale and the retail trade in the 1880s and 1890s, for any merchant entering the dry goods trade after 1880 'faced stiff competition from two directions' – from older dealers 'who had had time to establish good connections' with suppliers and from newer firms that specialized in a narrow line of goods. 'Success,' as Gene Allen pointed out, 'went not to all those who adopted changes in business organization, but principally to all those who made them first.'9 The great five-cent store opened by Frank Woolworth in Utica in 1879 is the classic example of a first in the marketplace. By establishing an even cheaper line of merchandise than his competitors, Woolworth overcame commercial barriers and successfully established himself in an increasingly difficult market.

In this respect Timothy Eaton represents another classic example, especially when a comparison is made between his business and that of his closest competitor, Robert Simpson. When Simpson first opened his store in 1872 at 184 Yonge Street, it was almost identical in size and layout to Timothy Eaton's, and his pace of expansion seemed to match that of his Irish rival. The subsequent disparity in sales figures is of such magnitude that it cannot be attributed solely to Simpson's apparent reluctance to draw attention to his store at 184 Yonge. Instead it would seem to indicate the existence of significant fundamental differences in approach and management between the two companies.

Although material relating to Robert Simpson's early years in Toronto is almost non-existent, it is commonly believed that he directed his appeal to the traditional middle-class housewife. This would go some way to explain why his sales figures lagged so dramatically behind Timothy Eaton's, since he had entered a highly competitive market that was served by a large number of active and well-established merchants. Timothy Eaton, on the other hand, by addressing his appeal to the newly solvent wage earner, tapped a market that was just beginning to grow and that could then form a broad base of support as the tone and style of that market improved. But given the growing demand for dry goods and the fact that both Simpson businesses were sufficiently successful to make expansion necessary, it seems likely that this was not the only factor involved.

Lack of sources prevent even the simplest discussion of the way in which Robert Simpson managed or operated his department store, so that any conclusions regarding this aspect of his career have to be drawn from the limited material relating to the years he spent in Newmarket. Although Robert Simpson demonstrated many of the attributes of an entrepreneur, it seems likely that he lacked the superior management skills demonstrated by Timothy Eaton and continued to run his large organization in a highly personal and intuitive manner, perhaps ignoring many of the administrative and accounting aspects that would prove so important as the store grew in size. In this respect it has to be assumed that only minimal attention was paid to the all-important issues of volume, turnover, costing, and profit margins. Moreover, his ability to delegate real authority and to introduce frequent business innovations may have been hampered by a lack of assistance from close relatives and a failure to encourage initiative in subordinates.

This certainly was not the case at the Eaton store, where delegation of authority was a constant given. Indeed, contributions by family and staff were largely responsible for much of the change demonstrated in the store, especially in the area of administration. The interest and initiative continually demonstrated by many individual employees was not only welcomed but taken for granted by Timothy Eaton. In this respect Eaton was extremely fortunate, for he had the active help and co-operation of a constant stream of talented assistants who filled the positions of the first professional managers in the Eaton store. From Hugh Robb, who provided the necessary fancy goods expertise in the early 1870s, to John James Eaton, who tightened expense costs, and Harry McGee, who was given total responsibility for the construction of the Winnipeg store, employees provided help that proved to be invaluable.

As the store increased in size, more authority was delegated, and the chains of command became more complicated. But Timothy Eaton's capacity to accept and utilize the expertise and organizational abilities of others allowed him to profit, in more ways than one, from the fullest possible use of all available resources. Although he remained the pre-eminent figure, directing operations until the end of his life, his staff were obviously a constant source of strength. As one economist has observed, 'the ability to hold together an able staff, to delegate authority, to inspire loyalty' – all managerial functions – play just as important a role in the achievement of entrepreneurial success as the propensity to be 'bold, rugged and ruthless.'[10] Despite reports that point to a personality that was both abrupt and outspoken, Timothy Eaton was indeed able to inspire feelings of great loyalty in many of his employees.

The dedication demonstrated by his departmental managers and buyers was often similar to that of any successful independent merchant. Each department manager was responsible not only for the purchase and the sale of the merchandise carried in his department, but also for a full share of all administration and selling costs. Most of these managers, like Timothy Eaton, had begun at the bottom and had learnt their trade and their new managerial skills on the job. The changes experienced over the course of their business lives had confronted them with both obstacles and opportunities. For many of these men management, administration, and training of large numbers of employees was a wholly new experience. This was complicated to a degree by the entrance of women into the retail work force.

While the working lives of nineteenth-century saleswomen, and for that matter salesmen, have not been entirely ignored, they have not received as much attention as other occupations. This is curious when one considers the enormous increase in their numbers and the conditions under which many early sales clerks worked. When

Timothy Eaton first opened his store in 1869, he had the assistance of four people, only one of whom was female. By 1910, well over five thousand women were employed by the company in a wide variety of capacities: as saleswomen, managers, and buyers; as factory operatives and forewomen; and as clerical personnel in the accounting, general, cash, and mail order offices. Many of these positions had either not existed in the past or else had been filled by men.

With the expansion of the store the opportunity for the large majority of this work-force to acquire any great level of skill was considerably reduced. The wages paid by Timothy Eaton to his sales clerks in the 1870s, for example, suggests that these employees had some degree of skill. The three female clerks received wages ranging from four to six dollars and the males from nine to ten dollars, rates higher than average in the later decades of the century. Increased regimentation, division of labour, and job specialization greatly reduced the need for a highly skilled work-force. Transactions, whether in the office or in the store, could now be handled by a staff of largely inexperienced workers under the supervision of a skilled manager. The wages paid to many female workers, therefore, remained low throughout this entire period.

The Eaton store did offer one benefit not often found in other Toronto stores. Beginning in the 1870s Timothy Eaton set in motion the reduction of hours of work for his employees, a reduction that continued throughout his career. By 1910 Eaton employees across Canada worked an average of forty-three to forty-eight hours a week, a great change from the more than seventy demanded in 1869.

The reduction in store hours made possible by a careful study of sales statistics that clearly demonstrated that sales volume would thereby suffer no appreciable decline is but one consequence of the company's increased efficiency in accounting. This constant attention to detail gradually allowed for an increasing measure of further independence.

Timothy Eaton's early efforts to reduce interest payments to suppliers offering long credit terms led to a gradual transformation in his methods of supply. In his desire to obtain better prices and terms, he bypassed the traditional lines of supply through local wholesalers and gradually established contacts with suppliers and manufacturers in Great Britain, Europe, and the United States. With a greater supply of capital at his command, he then concentrated on the issue of discounts and, by persuading suppliers to grant more favourable terms, sixty days at $2^{1}/_{2}$ per cent rather than ten days at the same rate, secured even greater savings.

To ensure greater efficiency, separate buying organizations were established in various foreign centres. By 1913 the Eaton company had offices in London, Manchester, Leicester, Belfast, New York, Paris, Berlin, and Zurich. This move and the company's expansion into the actual production of goods and merchandise, especially after the 1890s, brought about a steady drop in prices. The savings achieved by importing unfinished goods and manufacturing a wide range of ready-to-wear clothing effected economies that in turn could be passed on to a growing army of satisfied customers. The Eaton company entered this market at a time when few reputable brand names for ready-to-wear clothes existed. With the demand for this merchandise still on the increase, a merchant with a recognized reputation thus occupied a position of some significance in the market-place.

There were of course limits to the possibilities of such vertical integration and, in line with past practices, the company manufactured only those items that demonstrated fast rates of turnover and highly acceptable profit margins. From the few figures available it can be seen that the manufacture of men's suits, ties, shirts, and underwear, boys' clothing, and the whole range of women's clothing from underwear and shirtwaists to suits and furs more than met these requirements, with turnover rates of five to ten times a year and net profit margins ranging from 5 to 11 per cent.[11] By manufacturing those goods that experienced the greatest demand, the company could also respond quickly and immediately to the customer's needs. The manufacturing operations would increase in importance as the volume of mail orders grew. Delays in filling orders could create huge backlogs of paperwork and mar the company's stated guarantee of prompt service and immediate satisfaction.

The mail order service, introduced in 1884, not only strengthened the public perception that the company would not rest in its desire to serve the customer, but was responsible for creating solid markets for each future branch store. The success of the Winnipeg store amply bears this out. The care taken to ensure that sales volume continued to increase was the paramount concern of all senior executives. Thus sales could not be jeopardized or threatened by the bestowal of approval or encouragement to special interest groups. By 1900 departmental managers were directed to 'Discountenance the 17th March and 12th July colours and ribbons' being worn by employees. This is a very real indication of the change that had occurred, for in the early years Timothy Eaton himself had sported a sprig of shamrock in his buttonhole on St Patrick's Day. By the turn of the century every effort was directed at maintaining sales volume at a very high level. Timothy Eaton at all times kept his finger on this important aspect of his business, and even when vacationing in Muskoka insisted on receiving daily reports regarding store sales.[12]

The democratization of luxury, a term used by contemporary observers and later historians, suggests not only the increased acquisitiveness of the whole population but also the extent to which the variety of merchandise had expanded to include articles formerly out of the reach of all but the wealthy. The introduction of paper patterns that could be successfully utilized by the home sewer along with the production of less expensive fabrics allowed even the lowest-paid clerk to outfit herself in a copy of the latest fashionable ensemble from Paris. And this is but one example. Timothy Eaton, and other enterprising merchants throughout the western world, responded to the growth in demand and supply by acknowledging no limits to their stock-in-trade.

The most important factor responsible for the increased demand for goods was the steady rise in the number of industrial and white-collar employees – including an increasing number of women and young girls in receipt of a weekly wage. As Neil McKendrick points out, 'it was the[ir] increased propensity to consume and increased ability to do so ... which largely decided whether [a merchant's] efforts would succeed.'[13] By appealing initially to this wage-earning sector of the population Timothy Eaton successfully brought count-less numbers into contact with consumer society.

In this respect he was probably unique, for many of his contem-poraries – Lyman Bloomingdale, Marshall Field, William Whiteley, Rowland Macy, and the Straus brothers – like Robert Simpson, catered predominantly to the middle class and the emerging white-collar workers. Indeed, the Macy store, at the urging of Jesse and Percy Straus, moved to a new location closer to Broadway when it was perceived that the district around the original store was attract-ing more people from the lower classes. Timothy Eaton recognized, as possibly few other merchants at the time did, that the industrial working class, like their rural counterparts, looked for quality when buying goods. The term 'cheap' was acceptable when it referred to cost but not when it referred to the nature or character of the article. The fact that many shoppers operated on a limited income did not mean they they wished to be fobbed off with poor-quality merchandise. 'Nice goods' continued to exert their appeal.

By recognizing and responding to a demand that was not only not being met but may have been largely ignored, Timothy Eaton at the very outset of his Toronto career created a secure niche for himself and one that would form a solid base for future expansion. Ultimately he attempted to appeal to all sectors of the population, thus ensuring that the Eaton store would continue to maintain its leading edge in the retail field. By 1896 one advertisement could freely state: 'This store is becoming more and more a shopping-place with fashionable ladies. That means we're selling more rich and exclusive things, and more of the novelties that are limited to one or two of a kind. Aristocratic styles come with the growth of the trade.'[14] As the older stores such as Walker's and Murray's declined and passed from view, the Eaton store, the pre-eminent department store in the province, and the Robert Simpson store, by taking up much of the slack, were able to augment and expand their own share of the market.

But there was yet one further element that was vital to the success of this Irish merchant, and one moreover that was regarded by most of his peers as fatal to the possibility of success – namely, competition. Throughout Eaton's entire career, competition was the one factor that remained constant and that could never be ignored. Timothy Eaton regarded competition as a given and something to be used. His strong sense of independence never allowed him to appeal from weakness for a fairer deal as many of his contemporaries did in the 1890s. Competition for Timothy Eaton represented a prime ingredient in the life of his trade. Each service introduced, each new item of merchandise added to stock, each expansion of store space was set in motion with the prime objective of overcoming competition and increasing volume and sales. His ability to draw constant attention to the store may have disgusted his competitors, but he could never be accused of hiding his light under a bushel. The onset of each new difficulty merely gave further evidence of his willingness to experiment and to branch out in different directions in order to ensure the survival of the store. In this respect the consuming public was co-opted as an active partner in the establishment of a sound financial enterprise.

Timothy Eaton's career and the rise of his department store cover a period of well over fifty years. A study of such scope provides not only an insight into the growth of the department store, but also an in-depth look at an industry in the process of change. The last three decades of the nineteenth century had seen a transformation of both the retail industry and the market-place to which it catered. The most noticeable change in Toronto was the movement of retail stores from King Street to Yonge Street. Although Timothy Eaton and Robert Simpson have been credited with the responsibility for effecting this change, it seems likely that such a move was already underway when Timothy Eaton first opened his store at the corner of Queen and Yonge streets. The actual growth of population severely limited the extension of old and new outlets on King Street, and the introduction of the streetcar service in 1861 opened the way for considerable growth further north on Yonge Street.

Evolution in the less tangible realm of attitudes and behaviour was probably responsible for the greatest changes. Despite the introduction of many 'personal' services, the market-place was now governed by an air of detachment in an environment of highly impersonal competitive trading that was in striking contrast to the earlier close traditional personal relationship that had existed between merchant and customer. The aggressive tactics adopted by many of the larger stores and the fierce competition that resulted led to the elimination of many small retailers who were either unable or unwilling to change.

The subsequent animosity directed at departmental stores in particular resulted in a campaign first to amend the municipal assessment laws and ultimately for special legislation directed at curbing or restraining the activities of department stores. H.H. Fudger's comment before the Ontario Assessment Commission in 1900 that there was 'nothing in the volume of our business or in the nature or conduct of it that should subject it to any additional or special taxation' was the expressed view of someone who had profited from the changes introduced by Robert Simpson. Fudger could hardly be blamed for adopting this view, for, as he pointed out, special taxation would discriminate against something that the public itself had encouraged.[15]

The vehemence of the attacks brought the whole issue of retailing methods out into the open. Although it is doubtful that many small retailers either in Toronto or elsewhere in Canada would have agreed with the tributes praising Timothy Eaton's moral influence on the commercial revolution, most shoppers would have agreed that he and others like him had effected great improvements to the retail trade, not just in Toronto, but throughout Canada. As one contemporary observer stated: 'The advent of Eaton's great store in Winnipeg brought about not only a revolution in the prices of the vendor, but in the ideas of the buyer; and two and a half years after my first visit to the city I found a marked improvement in the value for money displayed in shop-windows.'[16]

By 1900 and in some cases even earlier, many merchants began to adopt the practices of the larger stores. What could not be accomplished by the Eaton stores in Winnipeg and Toronto yielded eventually to the pressures and popularity of the mail order system. The gradual change to a cash system of doing business attracted adherents in centres all across Canada. The complaint put forward by rural merchants that such a system was not possible where customers were mostly agricultural labourers and farmers was repudiated by the manager of a large Toronto store who declared that 50 per cent of his department's annual cash sales were to rural customers. Many rural stores found that their customers preferred the reduction in prices that resulted from a change to the cash system.[17] This change was not welcomed by all merchants, but eventually most realized that to persist with the old methods would ultimately result in failure. As one Nova Scotia resident declared:

Up until the early 1900s the local merchants had the field all to themselves and with no outside competition charged the natives all the traffic would bear. Then, along came Eaton's catalogue with its alluring bargains, bargains that is, compared to what the local people were forking over for the same grade merchandise. Naturally a howl arose from the outraged merchants [who] resented the invasion of outside competition and the threat to their overcharging.[18]

From the late 1890s the *Dry Goods Review* urged its readers to adopt new methods and meet the competition offered by department stores. At the turn of the century it sponsored a series of articles written by local merchants entitled 'How I Planned My Campaign to Meet Mail Order Competition.' To combat the influence of the mail order service many stores not only offered to meet Eaton's prices but kept a current Eaton catalogue on hand so that customers could compare local prices against those in the catalogue. One long article in the *Canadian Journal of Fabrics* suggested that smaller stores should make themselves more popular by allowing shoppers to view the goods without being pressured to purchase. In the writer's opinion, this had more to do with the success of the department store than any other characteristic. As he pointed out, whether the item purchased cost five cents or a fortune, each customer was 'treated with the same amiable indifference.'[19] His remarks provide an apt commentary on the changes that had occurred within the retail market-place.

Timothy Eaton, the entrepreneur who transformed his small dry goods store into a mammoth concern containing nearly a hundred departments, was responsible for much of this change. By his decisions and his actions, he set in motion a chain of events that actively combined with and took advantage of other forces emerging in the market-place. The sheer weight of manufacturing output, pressure of population growth, and consequent demand created needs that could not be met by small shopkeepers operating with older and more traditional methods. The mass production of goods, as Michael Miller points out, required 'a retail system far more efficient and far more expansive than anything small shopkeepers' were able to offer.[20] From the point of view of sales volume alone a large department store provided a market-place geared to a constant high rate of turnover along with the opportunity for wide exposure both in the store itself and through the medium of a large advertising budget. Stores offering these features not only acquired a competitive edge over smaller more conservative merchants but possessed the power to demand lower rates from suppliers, thereby increasing their competitive edge.

Timothy Eaton, as just one player in such a market, served as a vital link between the producing and consuming ends of the economy. By responding in an active manner to recognized demands he ensured both his own success and the success of his store.

Appendix: Tables

TABLE 1
Timothy Eaton, Kirkton store
Stock, book account, and liabilities at year end, 1857–60 inclusive
(in dollars)

Year	Stock	Book account	Liabilities
1857	1,177	N/A	N/A
1858	N/A	N/A	N/A
1859	999	723.50	1,588.50
1860	663	N/A	N/A

SOURCE: Eaton Archives, Timothy Eaton, *Memorandum 1857–1866*

TABLE 2
Timothy Eaton, Kirkton store
Amount of stock purchased from Adam Hope, June 1859–Nov. 1860
(in dollars)

Date	Dry goods	Groceries	Hardware	Cash remitted
June 1859	—	139.47	—	25.40
Sept. 1859	214.43	43.65	—	60.00
Nov. 1859	111.66	113.92	—	200.00
Dec. 1859	213.95	265.13	—	301.08
Jan. 1860	—	10.60	—	—
Sept. 1860	1,031.61	375.40	15.06	403.22
Oct. 1860	115.90	8.04	83.70	1,103.62
Nov. 1860	—	—	47.75	165.00

SOURCE: Buchanan Papers, 32/026910, 026912; 86/060724–26, 060794,
060690–92; 32/026042–44, 026954; 86/060830, 060824, 060878

TABLE 3
Timothy Eaton, St Marys store
Stock, book accounts, and liabilities at year end,* 1861–8 inclusive
(in dollars)

Year	Stock	Book account	Liabilities
1861	N/A	N/A	N/A
1862	N/A	N/A	N/A
1863	3,915.82	N/A	N/A
1864	5,121.00	4,104.00	6,620.00
1865	5,074.00	4,224.00	N/A
1866	6,285.00	7,866.00	9,388.00
1867	N/A	N/A	N/A
1868	11,000.00	5,000.00	13,500.00

* Year end seems usually to have been the end of January.
SOURCES: Eaton Archives, Timothy Eaton, *Memorandum 1857–1866*;
Buchanan Papers, 25/21372-73

TABLE 4
Timothy Eaton, St Marys store
Amount of stock purchased from Adam Hope, Jan. 1861–Oct. 1863
(in dollars)

Date	Dry goods	Groceries	Hardware	Cash remitted
Jan. 1861	19.62	61.81	3.80	550.00
Apr. 1861	1,737.78	268.87	162.48	1,206.60
June 1861	388.54	37.72	539.78	549.00
Aug. 1861	105.15	—	84.00	50.00
Sept. 1861	2,820.92	155.02	73.83	—
Aug. 1862	131.10	—	11.50	—
Sept. 1862	74.59	65.00	9.09	300.00
Oct. 1862	1,199.29	—	24.92	399.50
Oct. 1863	434.74	6.57	—	317.11

SOURCE: Buchanan Papers, 86/060938, 060944, 060785, 060958, 060964, 061023, 061008, 061047, 061085

TABLE 5
T. and J. Eaton Account, Bank of Montreal ledgers
Annual totals of payments, deposits, and discounts,
17 Oct. 1862 to 31 Dec. 1867
(in dollars)

Year	Payments	Deposits	Discounts
1862*	6,323.04	5,087.36	1,860.21
1863	22,803.51	14,156.13	8,564.16
1864	27,119.82	12,700.48	12,688.10
1865	43,410.84	22,387.75	20,750.59
1866	38,324.79	23,263.47	14,914.36
1867	35,561.44	25,148.66	10,744.42

* Three months only
SOURCE: Bank of Montreal ledgers

TABLE 6
T. and J. Eaton Account, Bank of Montreal ledgers
Monthly totals of payments, deposits, and discounts,
17 Oct. 1862 to 31 Dec. 1867 (in dollars)

Year	Month	Payments	Deposits	Discounts	
1862	Oct.	1,661.76	2,226.00	—	
	Nov.	3,521.07	2,090.36	1,296.95	(5)*
	Dec.	1,140.21	771.00	563.26	(1)
Total		6,323.04	5,087.36	1,860.21	
1863	Jan.	2,157.43	1,712.00	200.00	(1)
	Feb.	1,039.30	913.00	214.85	(1)
	Mar.	1,791.71	894.71	543.92	(1)
	Apr.	1,459.00	689.41	781.58	(1)
	May	626.10	628.53	168.82	(1)
	June	1,630.63	729.00	729.57	(4)
	July	1,413.62	1,138.60	298.60	(1)
	Aug.	783.26	854.98	98.80	(1)
	Sept.	2,823.58	1,462.00	1,171.99	(4)
	Oct.	2,647.58	1,960.00	791.31	(4)
	Nov.	2,759.63	1,715.40	978.09	(3)
	Dec.	3,671.67	1,458.50	2,586.63	(4)
Total		22,803.51	14,156.13	8,564.16	
1864	Jan.	2,093.73	838.00	—	
	Feb.	1,676.92	986.67	642.16	(1)
	Mar.	1,475.48	601.83	697.99	(2)
	Apr.	986.25	291.00	815.99	(2)
	May	1,722.31	815.00	908.54	(2)
	June	2,089.15	1,145.00	941.16	(5)
	July	726.59	577.00	—	
	Aug.	1,765.28	992.82	787.58	(3)
	Sept.	2,040.28	1,014.00	1,173.55	(3)
	Oct.	4,091.52	1,554.00	2,397.22	(7)
	Nov.	3,617.46	1,344.16	1,710.31	(5)
	Dec.	4,834.85	2,541.00	2,613.70	( )
Total		27,119.82	12,700.48	12,688.10	

TABLE 6 (*continued*)

Year	Month	Payments	Deposits	Discounts
1865	Jan.	3,770.39	2,031.00	1,476.14 (3)
	Feb.	2,829.43	924.00	1,894.48 (5)
	Mar.	3,979.01	600.00	4,204.12 (6)
	Apr.	4,621.39	1,316.87	2,321.69 (4)
	May	7,280.20	1,800.67	5,458.89 (8)
	June	3,046.43	1,921.25	1,465.37 (4)
	July	1,744.65	744.50	695.34 (3)
	Aug.	1,600.73	972.50	870.44 (3)
	Sept.	3,846.58	3,441.79	996.55 (1)
	Oct.	6,468.56	4,873.85	856.04 (2)
	Nov.	2,587.35	2,521.82	318.38 (2)
	Dec.	1,636.12	1,239.50	193.15 (1)
Total		43,410.84	22,387.75	20,750.59
1866	Jan.	2,246.54	1,610.50	590.49 (2)
	Feb.	2,075.69	2,223.53	—
	Mar.	3,900.34	2,670.22	1,070.89 (4)
	Apr.	2,983.22	1,716.64	1,118.85 (2)
	May	4,058.34	1,899.70	2,178.54 (6)
	June	2,496.13	2,312.00	397.47 (1)
	July	1,239.07	948.00	—
	Aug.	1,571.41	177.00	1,475.94 (2)
	Sept.	896.33	1,097.00	—
	Oct.	7,003.04	3,877.38	2,977.34 (3)
	Nov.	6,335.87	2,685.00	3,634.75 (4)
	Dec.	3,518.81	2,046.50	1,400.09 (3)
Total		38,324.79	23,263.47	14,914.36

(*continued*)

TABLE 6 (concluded)

Year	Month	Payments	Deposits	Discounts	
1867	Jan.	2,491.73	2,336.36	241.57	(1)
	Feb.	2,453.18	1,679.10	772.40	(2)
	Mar.	2,339.00	970.00	1,242.20	(4)
	Apr.	1,959.08	1,140.00	1,065.90	(4)
	May	2,135.47	1,442.50	485.23	(2)
	June	2,933.36	1,555.00	1,315.97	(3)
	July	1,516.03	923.12	716.63	(2)
	Aug.	3,860.86	1,406.00	2,439.27	(6)
	Sept.	3,051.95	3,087.50	—	
	Oct.	7,262.80	5,336.08	2,465.25	(3)
	Nov.	3,159.23	2,555.00	—	
	Dec.	2,398.75	2,718.00	—	
Total		35,561.44	25,148.66	10,744.42	

* The numbers in brackets refer to the number of discounts received each month.
SOURCE: Bank of Montreal ledgers

TABLE 7
Timothy Eaton, Toronto store
Annual totals: sales, stock, personal property assessment, and
approximate liabilities, 1869–96 (in dollars)

Year	Annual sales	Stock	Assessed personal property	Approximate liabilities
1869	2,248[a]		5,000	
1870	25,417		4,000	69,780
1871	44,136		2,000	31,093
1872	56,547		2,000	42,946
1873	53,449	40,966	2,000	38,142
1874	67,985	39,636	3,000	34,743
1875	64,204	28,290	3,000	27,331
1876	78,104	32,236	3,000	26,136
1877	112,657	33,756	3,000	21,678
1878	114,187	49,472	3,000	65,556
1879	134,083	49,909	3,000	29,459
1880	154,979	53,789	4,000	30,768
1881	16,149[b]	54,720	4,000	16,604
1882	137,801[c]	57,428[d]	4,000	52,513
1883	237,769	62,219[d]	3,000	80,445
1884	248,229	113,906	*	89,030
1885	334,166	85,747	6,000	58,402
1886		115,206	10,000	
1887		79,353	10,000	
1888			20,000	
1889			20,000	
1890	653,796[e]	367,594[e]	20,000	
1891	714,490[e]	445,304[e]	25,000	229,914
1892				
1893			33,000	
1894			30,000	
1895	2,921,470[f]		50,000	
1896	3,715,989		100,000	

* Unfinished building.
a Dec. only
b First two months only
c Last eight months only
d Yonge Street store only, Scott Street $38,383 and $41,145, respectively
e 1 Jan. to 8 July only
f Last six months an estimated 18 per cent more
SOURCES: Eaton Archives, Timothy Eaton, *Notebook*; John James Eaton, *Notebook*; Stock report, 8 July 1891

TABLE 8

Timothy Eaton, Toronto store

Sales: monthly totals (amounts have been rounded to the nearest dollar)

Month	1869	1870	1871	1872	1873	1874	1875	1876	1877
Jan.		1,802	3,910	4,196	3,489	3,876	4,765	4,099	8,050
Feb.		1,474	2,723	3,681	3,296	4,452	4,780	4,083	7,712
Mar.		1,205	2,376	3,083	2,747	4,166	4,900	3,198	6,988
Apr.		1,139	2,817	4,237	3,976	5,000	4,786	5,335	9,469
May.		1,992	3,771	4,726	5,899	6,070	5,446	8,118	11,510
June		2,130	3,439	4,505	4,915	6,484	6,424	8,706	11,156
July		1,112	3,295	3,935	4,755	6,168	4,924	5,635	8,350
Aug.		1,112	3,063	3,792	3,786	5,181	4,219	5,050	7,076
Sept.		2,094	3,523	4,435	4,154	5,871	4,905	6,346	7,665
Oct.		3,539	4,851	9,129	5,688	7,031	6,146	8,252	11,715
Nov.		3,862	5,154	5,272	6,197	6,582	6,328	9,649	10,935
Dec.	2,248	3,956	5,214	5,556	4,547	7,104	6,581	9,633	12,032
Total	2,248	25,417	44,136	56,547	53,449	67,985	64,204	78,104	112,658

Month	1878	1879	1880	1881	1882	1883	1884	1885
Jan.	7,337	7,182	8,403	8,344		15,450	13,285	16,541
Feb.	6,928	6,914	6,987	7,805		11,594	11,599	15,225
Mar.	7,165	9,475	9,584			14,436	15,660	18,533
Apr.	9,629	9,849	13,070		19,081	18,208	20,497	25,844
May.	12,118	14,276	18,395		19,870	20,731	25,604	30,395
June	11,617	14,033	16,484		13,701	21,081	25,950	34,597
July	8,591	11,173	12,588		11,975	17,056	18,629	26,138
Aug.	7,762	9,550	10,806		18,111	14,170	14,372	21,328
Sept.	9,662	12,795	14,187		17,781	26,165	21,881	30,220
Oct.	11,395	11,931	14,701		18,643	29,211	25,060	36,792
Nov.	10,626	13,096	14,195		18,639	23,798	25,975	35,577
Dec.	11,357	13,809	15,579			25,869	29,717	42,976
Total	114,187	134,083	154,979	16,149	137,801	237,769	248,229	334,166

SOURCE: Eaton Archives, Timothy Eaton, *Notebook*

TABLE 9
Timothy Eaton
Number of employees, 1869–1909

Year	Employees
1869	4
1871	5
1874	14
1876	25
1881	48
1883	175
1887	250–300
1889	350–600
1891	750–1,000
1893	1,250
1895	1,800
1897	1,600–1,900
1898	2,475
1902	3,700–4,500
1905	5,500
1907	6,190–6,925
1909	7,219–8,775

SOURCES: Compiled from various
sources, both printed and unpublished,
at the Eaton Archives

TABLE 10
Timothy Eaton, Toronto store
Number of employees, 15 Apr. to 15 Dec. 1896

Date 1896	Sales M	F	Total	Expense M	F	Total	Factory total	Overall total
Apr. 15			561			622	333	1,516
Apr. 21	330	250	580	278	250	528	342	1,450
Oct. 21			655			630	350	1,635
Dec. 3			697			670	403	1,770
Dec. 15	308	463	771	443	261	704	400	1,875

SOURCE: John James Eaton, *Notebook*

TABLE 11
T. Eaton Company Limited
Employee statistics, 1906–9*

Classification	1906		1907		1908		1909	
	July	Dec.	July	Dec.	July	Dec.	July	Dec.
Sales	1,396	2,155	1,635	1,811	1,629	2,163	1,848	2,156
Mechanics	63	100	71	202	60	61	161	196
Expense	934	1,371	1,058	1,324	991	1,481	1,088	1,260
Mail order	329	387	306	255	254	352	352	449
Work-rooms	358	363	403	357	423	385	431	560
Factory	1,995	2,262	2,660	2,922	2,736	3,016	3,281	3,651
Oshawa factory	111	111	118	113	131	120	136	145
Paris office	7	6	9	7	7	7	8	7
London office	12	16	19	21	23	20	24	23
Drug company	46	60	57	54	53	65	58	65
Farms	11	12	11	9	10	9	11	10

* This table does not include employees at either the Montreal factory or the Winnipeg store.
SOURCE: Statistics compiled 1973 by the Eaton Archives from early ledgers

TABLE 12

Comparative sales figures for selected years (in dollars)

Year	Eaton's	Simpson's	Hudson's Bay	Macy's	Harrods	Bloomingdale's	Sears	Woolworth's
1850					5,000			
1859				90,000				
1868					246,000			
1870	25,417			1,024,621				
1877	112,658			1,873,205		184,184		
1879	134,083			2,924,132				12,024
1883	237,769			4,831,158		851,156		
1889				5,469,078	2,410,000			246,782
1895	2,921,470			6,907,144			750,000	
1896	3,715,989			7,095,729				
1898		1,250,000		7,058,955				
1899				7,825,141				4,415,110
1900				8,148,254			10,000,000	
1901	6,732,000			8,812,171				
1902				10,765,066	5,000,000			
1904				13,135,446				10,210,000
1907	22,488,000			16,779,425			50,000,000	
1911	45,613,000		4,592,000	16,575,590				
1914	53,367,000	14,081,451	8,000,000	17,289,057				
1918				25,827,948				107,000,000
1919	123,590,000	33,444,765	14,865,000	35,802,818				

SOURCES: Figures compiled from Maxine Brady, *Bloomingdale's*; Tim Dale, *Harrods*; Ralph M. Hower, *A History of Macy's*; John P. Nichols, *Skyline Queen and the Merchant Prince*; James C. Worthy, *Shaping an American Institution*; Canada, *Royal Commission on Price Spreads*, 1934; and material in Eaton Archives

Notes

EA   Eaton Archives
BP   Buchanan Papers
OA   Ontario Archives
CJF   *Canadian Journal of Fabrics*
CPJ   *Canadian Pharmaceutical Journal*
DGR   *Dry Goods Review*
RMJ   *Retail Merchants Journal*
MT   *Monetary Times.*

PREFACE

1 Michael Bliss, *A Canadian Millionaire: The Life and Business Times of Sir Joseph Flavelle, Bart. 1858–1939* (Toronto: Macmillan of Canada 1978): C.L. Burton, *A Sense of Urgency: Memoirs of a Canadian Merchant* (Toronto: Clarke, Irwin 1952); G. Allan Burton, *A Store of Memories* (Toronto: McClelland and Stewart 1986); Merrill Dennison, *This Is Simpson's* (Toronto: 1947); John W. Ferry, *A History of the Department Store* (New York: Macmillan 1960); Douglas E. Harker, *The Woodwards: The Story of a Distinguished British Columbia Family, 1870–1975* (Toronto: Mitchell Press 1976); Douglas McCalla, *The Upper Canada Trade, 1834–1972: A Study of the Buchanans' Business* (Toronto: University of Toronto Press 1979); Allan Wilson, *John Northway: A Blue Serge Canadian* (Toronto: Burns and MacEachern 1965)
2 Asa Briggs, *Friends of the People: The Centenary History of Lewis's* (London: B.T. Batsford 1956)
3 *Golden Jubilee, 1869–1919* (Toronto: T. Eaton Co. Ltd. 1919); Mary

Etta Macpherson, *Shopkeepers to a Nation: The Eatons* (Toronto: McClelland and Stewart 1963); G.G. Nasmith, *Timothy Eaton* (Toronto: McClelland and Stewart 1923); William Stephenson, *The Store that Timothy Built 1869–1919* (Toronto: McClelland and Stewart 1969)

4 When compared to similar studies elsewhere, this neglect is even more surprising. See for example: Hrant Pasdermadjian, *The Department Store: Its Origins, Evolution and Economics* (London: Newman Books 1954); Alison Adburgham, *Shops and Shopping, 1800–1914: Where and in What Manner the Well-Dressed Englishwoman Bought Her Clothes* (London: Allen and Unwin 1967); David Alexander, *Retailing in England during the Industrial Revolution* (London: Athlone Press 1970); Dorothy Davis, *A History of Shopping* (London: Routledge and Kegan Paul 1966); W. Hamish Fraser, *The Coming of the Mass Market, 1850–1914* (London: Macmillan 1981); Ralph M. Hower, *A History of Macy's of New York, 1858–1919: Chapters in the Evolution of a Department Store* (Cambridge: Harvard University Press 1943); Richard S. Lambert, *The Universal Provider: A Study of William Whiteley and the Rise of the London Department Store* (London: Harrap 1938); Michael B. Miller, *The Bon Marché: Bourgeois Culture and the Department Store, 1869–1920* (Princeton: Princeton University Press 1981).

INTRODUCTION

1 Ralph M. Hower, *A History of Macy's of New York 1858–1919: Chapters in the Evolution of a Department Store* (Cambridge: Harvard University Press 1943) 142, and 'The Effect of Managerial Policy upon the Structure of American Business,' *Business History Review* 16 (1942) 49; Dorothy Davis, *A History of Shopping* (London: Routledge and Kegan Paul 1966) 289–90; Michael B. Miller, *The Bon Marché: Bourgeois Culture and The Department Store, 1869–1920* (Princeton: Princeton University Press 1981)

2 Peter Samson, 'The Department Store, Its Past and Its Future: A Review Article,' *Business History Review* 55 (Spring 1981) 31

3 Douglas McCalla, 'The Decline of Hamilton as a Wholesale Centre,' *Ontario History* 65 (1973) 251

4 John H. Dales, 'Approaches to Entrepreneurial History,' *Explorations in Entrepreneurial History* 1: 1 (1963) 10

1 APPRENTICE MERCHANT

1 EA, Timothy Eaton to James Eaton, 28 April 1870

2 EA, John Eaton died 30 Jan. 1834, aged fifty years. There was some evidence of cholera in Ireland in 1834, and John Eaton was said to have died from exposure after caring for a sick neighbour.

3 Timothy was a Craig family name. Timothy Eaton was not named, as G.G. Nasmith relates, after one of his father's favourite books in the New Testament.

4 EA, Sir John Heaton-Armstrong, College of Arms, London, England, to Lady Eaton, 2 Sept. 1964

5 Ibid., see also M. Perceval-Maxwell, *The Scottish Migration to Ulster in the Reign of James I* (London: Routledge and Kegan Paul 1973) 230

6 T.W. Freeman, *Pre-Famine Ireland: A Study in Historical Geography* (Manchester: Manchester University Press 1957) 54, 59, 71–2, 289; William Fowkes Adams, *Ireland and Irish Emigration to the New World from 1815 to the Famine* (New Haven: Yale University Press 1932)' 3, 39–40

7 *The Parliamentary Gazetteer of Ireland, Adapted to the New Poor Law, Franchise, Municipal and Ecclesiastical Arrangements and Compiled with Special Reference to the Lines of Railroad and Canal Communication as Existing in 1847 and 1848* (Dublin: A. Fullarton 1850) vol. 1, 184; Samuel Lewis, *A Topographical Dictionary of Ireland* (London: S. Lewis 1849) vol.1, 141–2

8 W.H. Crawford, 'The Evolution of Ulster Towns, 1750–1850,' in Peter Roebuck, ed., *Plantation to Partition: Essays in Ulster History in Honour of J.L. McCracken* (Belfast: Blackstaff Press 1981) 151, 154; J.C. Conroy, *A History of Railways in Ireland* (London: Longmans, Green 1928) 21

9 Freeman, *Pre-Famine Ireland* 289; *Parliamentary Gazetteer of Ireland* vol.1, 184

10 EA, Family Research, Robert Clark, Ballymena, Oct. 1961; Timothy Eaton to James Eaton, 9 Oct. 1870

11 G.G. Nasmith, *Timothy Eaton* (Toronto: McClelland and Stewart 1923) 37

12 Freeman, *Pre-Famine Ireland* 309; Adams, *Ireland and Irish Emigration* 183, 217; H.J. Johnston, 'Immigration to the Five Eastern Townships of the Huron Tract,' *Ontario History* 54 (1962) 217

13 Nasmith, *Timothy Eaton* 39–41

14 EA, Harry McGee, *Notebook*, unpaginated. McGee was hired by Timothy

Eaton in August 1883 and was appointed a director of the T. Eaton Company Limited in Feb. 1893.

15 Nasmith, *Timothy Eaton* 43–4

16 EA, Professor N.C. Mitchel, Department of Geography, Queen's University, Belfast, 31 Dec. 1963

17 Quoted in Adams, *Ireland and Irish Emigration* 218–20; see also 18–19, 34, 49–51, 116, 174.

18 Ibid., 100–1, 123, 153–5; Helen I. Cowan, *British Emigration to British North America: The First Hundred Years* (Toronto: University of Toronto Press 1961) 290, 301

19 EA, Family Reminiscences, Mabel Reid Kerr, 11 Sept. 1961. William Reid, accompanied by his eldest son, came to Canada in 1832; the son subsequently died of typhoid fever before his mother arrived a year later.

20 Nasmith, *Timothy Eaton* 36–7; EA, ibid., Otto Eaton, July 1961. Robert was thought to have travelled first to Ottawa, where he was employed briefly as a woodsman. Here he met and married, about 1842, Margaret Young, the Canadian-born daughter of an Irish immigrant, George Young, then farming in the North Gower area.

21 St Marys *Argus* 22 Nov. 1934, 7; Donal Begley, 'The Journal of an Irish Emigrant to Canada,' *The Irish Ancestor* 6 (1974) 43–7

22 EA, Family Reminiscences, George Fraser Reid, 21 Aug. 1961

23 Elsie McLeod Murray, 'An Upper Canada "Bush Business" in the Fifties,' *Ontario History*, 36 (1944) 41

24 OA, MU 2110, Misc. Coll. 6, *Canada Company Circular* 1 Aug. 1849 and 1852

25 OA, GS 3345, *Georgetown Deeds* instrument 261C, 19 Dec. 1855; GS 535, *St Marys Deeds* vol. B, instrument 900, 17 Oct. 1856, instrument 1132, 20 Dec. 1856; St Marys *Argus* 1 Jan. and 7 May 1857

26 William Johnston, *The Pioneers of Blanshard with an Historical Sketch of the Township* (Toronto: William Briggs 1899) 24–5, 54

27 See, for example, St Marys *Argus* Feb. – May 1858.

28 Post Office Record Card for Kirkton Post Office, photo copy supplied by Canada Post, Western Division, Ontario, Aug. 1983

29 OA, GS, 1753–5, *Usborne Deeds* vol. 1, instrument 446, 28 Aug. 1858. When this property was sold in 1866 James Eaton received only $250 for it, suffering a loss of $125. *Usborne Deeds* vol. 3, instrument 485, 10 Jan. 1866, vol. 2, instrument 260, 15 Jan. 1859, instrument 42, 25 Feb. 1859

30 Johnston, 'Immigration to the Five Eastern Townships of the Huron Tract,' 213, 221–3; William Johnston, *History of the County of Perth*

from 1825 to 1902 (Stratford: W.M. O'Beirne 1903) 179, 220. Blanshard Township was largely settled by Ulster Irish.

31 Johnston, *History of the County of Perth* 542–3: in 1844, Milner Harrison, an English immigrant, arrived in St Marys, opened a general store, and by the 1850s was recognized as a businessman of some repute. W. Stafford Johnston and Hugh J.M. Johnston, *History of Perth County to 1967* (Stratford: 1967) 41: in 1832 John Cory Wilson Daly, an Ulsterman, arrived in Stratford where he had a store and post office, achieved some success, and later became a major landowner. Douglas McCalla, 'Adam Hope,' *Dictionary of Canadian Biography* vol. 11, 422–4: Adam Hope, a Scottish immigrant who came to Canada in 1834, by 1840 had established himself in business in St Thomas and by 1856 was recognized as a leading businessman in the London area. Frederick H. Armstrong, 'George Jervis Goodhue: Pioneer Merchant of London, Upper Canada,' *Ontario History* 63 (1971) 217–32: Goodhue, an American, moved to the London area in 1820, opened a small store, and by the 1850s had achieved recognition as a major landowner and moneylender.

32 Mary Quayle Innis, *An Economic History of Canada* (Toronto: Ryerson Press 1934), 99

33 EA, Timothy Eaton, *Memorandum 1857–1866*

34 EA, Reminiscences, Samuel Shier, 6 Oct. 1958; St Marys *Argus* 9 Sept. 1858; OA, *Township of Usborne Assessment Rolls 1857–1860*

35 See Eaton Advertisement, St Marys *Argus* 10 May 1861; *Canada Directory* 1851, 500–1.

36 BP, 32/026910, 026912, 026942–4; 86/060690, 060724, 060794, 060824, 060830; William Johnston, *Pioneers of Blanshard* 54

37 EA, Timothy Eaton, *Memorandum 1857–1866*

38 Douglas McCalla, *The Upper Canada Trade, 1834–1872: A Study of the Buchanans' Business* (Toronto: University of Toronto Press 1979) 78–9

39 EA, Timothy Eaton, *Memorandum 1857–1866*

40 BP, 86/060825

41 Henry Scadding and John C. Dent, *Toronto: Past and Present* (Toronto: Hunter Rose 1884) 212; Elsie McLeod Murray, 'An Upper Canada "Bush Business," ' 46

42 William Johnston, *History of the County of Perth*, 154–5; Adam Shortt, 'The History of Canadian Currency, Banking and Exchange,' *Journal of the Canadian Bankers' Association* 11:3 (April 1903) 206–10; McCalla, *Upper Canada Trade* 177–8

43 St Marys *Argus* 9 Sept. 1858

44 *R.G. Dun and Co. Collection* (Baker Library, Harvard University Graduate School of Business Administration), Perth County, Canada West, vol. 24 (12 Oct., 27 Nov. 1857, 7 May 1858) 28

45 OA, *Usborne Deeds* vol. 1, instrument 477, 1 Oct. 1858; *R.G. Dun and Co. Collection* Perth County, Canada West, vol. 24 (1 Dec. 1858, 7 Jan. 1859, 2 May 1860) 28; St Marys *Argus* 17 Mar. 1859

46 EA, Timothy Eaton, *Memorandum 1857–1866*

47 BP, 32/026788

48 McCalla, *Upper Canada Trade* 100; OA, GS 540, *Blanshard Deeds* vol. C, instrument 1553, 12 Jan. 1860, instrument 1586, 4 Apr. 1860; GS 537, *Blanshard Assessment Rolls* 1860

49 EA, Timothy Eaton to James H. Reid, Georgetown, 16 Nov. 1892

50 OA, GS 540, *Blanshard Deeds* vol. C, instruments 2070, 2071, 1725, 8, 9, and 30 Oct. 1860; see also BP, 32/027057-8, 027062.

51 OA, GS 537, *Blanshard Assessment Rolls* 1858–60

52 EA, Timothy Eaton, *Memorandum 1857–1866*, BP 86/060724-6, 060794, 060824-5, 060830-1, 060938

53 EA. All information relating to the Union Sabbath School had been taken from *Book of Minutes of Union Sabbath School Blanshard and Usborne, 1856–1865* unpaginated.

54 EA, pamphlet, Golden Jubilee Celebration, Kirkton Methodist Circuit, *The Story of the Years* 4–5; see also OA, Pamphlet, 1908, no. 94, Jubilee Souvenir of Methodist Church of St Marys, Ontario, 1908, 7. John Eaton, Timothy's father, had been an elder of the Seceder Presbyterian Church at Kirkinriola in Ulster.

2 THE EATON STORE IN ST MARYS

1 *Illustrated Historical Atlas of the County of Perth* Facsimile (Toronto: H. Belden 1897) x; William Johnston, *History of the County of Perth from 1825–1902* (Stratford: W.M. O'Beirne 1903) 408–28. While some contemporary sources, such as the *Historical Atlas*, add the apostrophe in St Marys, twentieth-century practice seems to follow that used by William Johnston and drops it.

2 St Marys *Argus* 1 Jan., 12 Mar., 30 Apr. 1857, 31 Jan. 1861

3 William S. Fox, ed, *Letters of William Davies, Toronto, 1854–1861* (Toronto: University of Toronto Press 1945) Preface by H.A. Innis, vi

4 St Marys *Argus* 13 May 1857

5 Ibid., 1 Jan., 7 Dec. 1857, 13 May 1858, 23 May 1861

6 Douglas McCalla, *The Upper Canada Trade 1834–1872: A Study of the*

Buchanans' Business (Toronto: University of Toronto Press 1979)
122; Elsie McLeod Murray, 'An Upper Canada "Bush Business," in the
Fifties,' *Ontario History* 36 (1944) 46

7 *R.G. Dun and Co. Collection* (Baker Library, Harvard University Graduate School of Business Administration) Perth County, Canada West,
vol. 24, 28; see, for example, Alex Emerson and Co., St. Marys, 28 Apr.
1859.

8 Adam Shortt, 'The History of Canadian Currency, Banking and
Exchange,' *Journal of the Canadian Bankers' Association* 11:3 (Apr.
1903) 207

9 Ibid., 11:1 (Oct. 1902) 26. Since there were no twenty-five-cent pieces,
English shillings remained in use to cover this deficiency.

10 Victor Ross, *A History of the Canadian Bank of Commerce* (Toronto:
Oxford University Press 1920) vol. 2, 420; A.B. Jamieson, *Chartered
Banking in Canada* (Toronto: Ryerson Press 1959) 11

11 Fox, *The Letters of William Davies* 102

12 William Johnston, *History of the County of Perth* 413

13 St Marys *Argus* 10 Jan. 1861; Canada, *Census* 1861, St Marys Personal
Folio 26, and Esquesing Township, Personal

14 BP, 86/060893; OA, *Blanshard Deeds* vol. C, instruments 1810 and 2083

15 St Marys *Argus* 1856–60

16 No evidence exists relating to the number of employees working for
Timothy Eaton, and the lack of assessment rolls for St Marys makes
it impossible to discover this. Given the size of the business he could not
have run it single-handed and presumably had young male assistants.

17 St Marys *Argus* 7 May 1857, 2 Dec. 1858, 10 Jan. 1861; EA, Information
from Miss Nettie Fairbairn, Oct. 1958

18 EA, R.Y. Eaton to J.G. McKee, 25 Mar. 1936

19 St Marys *Argus* 1 May, 24 Oct. 1861

20 BP, see, for example, 87/061425 and 25/21372-3; *Bank of Montreal
Deposit Ledgers* 17 Oct. 1862 to 31 Dec. 1867

21 *R.G. Dun and Co. Collection* Perth County, Canada West, vol. 24
(1 May 1863) 241

22 BP, 86/060887-8, 060893

23 *R.G. Dun and Co. Collection* Perth County, Canada West, vol. 24
(12 March 1863) 28; EA, Bank reference from the Commercial Bank
of Canada, 1864–7

24 EA, Timothy Eaton, *Memorandum 1857–1866*; BP, 25/21372-3

25 St Marys *Argus* 16 Oct. 1862; *Bank of Montreal Deposit Ledgers*

26 EA, Timothy Eaton, *Memorandum 1857–1866*; BP, 25/21372-3

27 BP, see, for example, 86/060892, 061092. See also G.G. Nasmith, *Timothy Eaton* (Toronto: McClelland and Stewart 1923) 57–8.

28 EA, Printed circular letter, J. and T. Eaton, 14 Dec, 1866; Eaton invoice, Oct. 1862

29 EA, Memorandum in Timothy Eaton's handwriting, about 1880s

30 OA, *St Marys Deeds* vol. D, instruments 2811 and 2812, 27 and 30 Apr. 1864

31 William Johnston, *History of the County of Perth* 431; *County of Perth Gazetteer and General Business Directory, 1863–1864* 137; St Marys *Argus* 16 Jan. 1862

32 EA, Rev. Dr Andrew B. Baird, 'Memories of St. Marys,' St Marys *Argus* 22 Nov. 1934

33 Ibid.

34 EA, Notes of a meeting on 'Sunday Street Cars' held at T. Eaton Co. Ltd offices, 22 Apr. 1897; Timothy Eaton, *Notebook*, 331

35 EA, Montreal *Daily Herald* 1 Feb. 1907

36 St Marys *Argus* 30 May 1861. Although copies of the *Argus* between 22 Dec. 1864 and 7 Jan. 1869 are no longer extant, I do not feel that I have overstated this argument, since Timothy Eaton did not resort to this medium at all from May 1862 to December 1864.

37 EA, Timothy Eaton, *Notebook* 331

38 BP, 87/061425

39 Ibid. See, for example, 86/060892, 061003, 061008, 061047, 061092, 061134. No further statement appears in the Buchanan Papers after Feb. 1864.

40 EA, Timothy Eaton, *Memorandum 1857–1866*; BP, 25/21372-3, 86/061092, 061134, 061047; *Bank of Montreal Deposit Ledgers* Oct. 1862 to Dec. 1867. In two separate three-month periods, one from Mar. to May 1863, and the other from Dec. 1863 to Feb. 1864, cheques were drawn on the Bank of Montreal account amounting to $3,876.81 and $7,139.92 respectively, while only $421.99 and $1,201.20 were forwarded to Buchanan and Hope, and this at a time when both quarters showed large overdue payments. Of course it is possible that these expenditures might also represent items other than payments for stock, such as rental or mortgage instalments, but it would appear that once the brothers had gained the confidence of their first supplier, a deliberate choice was made to hold the Buchanan account to terms and to channel available funds in a specific other direction. Even for part of the month of Oct. 1862, when $1,661.76 was paid out, only $399.50 of this was forwarded to the Buchanans.

41 R.G. *Dun and Co. Collection* Perth County, Canada West, vol. 24,

(18 Aug. 1872) 28; *County of Perth Gazetteer and General Business Directory, 1863–1864* 141

42 EA, Bank reference from the Commercial Bank of Canada, 1864–7

43 OA, *St Marys Deeds* vol. D, instruments 2632 and 2639, 27 Mar., 4 Apr. 1863, vol. E, instruments 3683 and 3855; see also *Blanshard Deeds* vol. D, instrument 2462 and 2463, 30 Jan. 1864. Some property was occasionally bought at public auctions or sheriff's sales at knockdown prices to enable the county to recover unpaid taxes, see *St Marys Deeds* vol. C, instruments 2575 and 2576.

44 OA, *Blanshard Deeds*, vol. D, instruments 2630 and 2736, 10 Jan. and 25 Sept. 1865

45 EA. Timothy Eaton's nephew later stated that, when the business relationship between Timothy and James was dissolved, it was understood that one brother would take half the net value and start up elsewhere. James decided at that time to stay on, so Timothy left and set up in Toronto. R.Y. Eaton to G.G. Nasmith, 1923

46 McCalla, *Upper Canada Trade* 110–12

47 EA, Marriage certificate, 28 May 1862, St Marys. James Eaton remained a bachelor until 4 July 1865, when he married Rachel Freeman of Georgetown.

48 EA, Timothy Eaton, *Notebook* 331

3 SHOPS AND SHOPPING

1 David Alexander, *Retailing in England during the Industrial Revolution* (London: Athlone Press 1970); W. Hamish Fraser, *The Coming of the Mass Market 1850–1914* (London: Macmillan 1981); James B. Jeffreys, *Retail Trading in Britain, 1850–1950* (Cambridge: Cambridge University Press 1954); Peter Mathias, *Retailing Revolution: A History of Multiple Retailing in the Food Trades* (London: Longmans, Green 1967)

2 Rosalind Williams, *Dream Worlds: Mass Consumption in Late Nineteenth-Century France* (Berkeley: University of California Press 1982) 2–7

3 Neil McKendrick, 'Home Demand of Economic Growth: A New View of the Role of Women and Children in the Industrial Revolution,' in Neil McKendrick, ed., *Historical Perspectives: Studies in English Thought and Society* (London: Europa Publications 1974) 208–10

4 Alison Adburgham, *Shops and Shopping 1800–1914: Where and in What Manner the Well-Dressed Englishwomen Bought Her Clothes* (London: Allen and Unwin 1967) 32, 173–4; W. Hamish Fraser, *Coming*

of the Mass Market 98, 118, 180–4; Daniel Boorstin, *The Americans: The Democratic Experience* (New York: Random House 1973) 99–100; Whitney Walton, 'To Triumph before Feminine Taste: Bourgeois Women's Consumption and Hand Methods of Production in Mid-Nineteenth Century Paris,' *Business History Review* 60 (Winter 1986) 541

5 Ralph M. Hower, *A History of Macy's of New York, 1858–1919: Chapters in the Evolution of a Department Store* (Cambridge: Harvard University Press 1943) 76

6 W.N. Hancock, *Is the Competition between Large and Small Shops Injurious to the Community?* (Dublin: Hodges and Smith 1851) 20; Alexander, *Retailing in England* 134–5; Harry E. Resseguie, 'Alexander Turney Stewart and the Development of the Department Store, 1823–1876,' *Business History Review* 39 (Autumn 1964) 315–20

7 William S. Fox, ed, *Letters of William Davies, Toronto, 1854–1861* (Toronto: University of Toronto Press 1945) 54, 60; Alexander, *Retailing in England* 82, 231–8

8 Hancock, *Competition between Large and Small Shops* 23

9 W.H. Ablett, ed., *Reminiscences of an Old Draper* (London: Sampson, Low 1876) 103; Fox, *Letters of William Davies* 43

10 Dorothy Davis, *A History of Shopping* (London: Routledge and Kegan Paul 1966) 290

11 Genevieve Leslie, 'Domestic Service in Canada, 1880–1920,' in Janice Acton et al, *Women at Work in Ontario, 1850–1930* (Toronto: Canadian Women's Educational Press 1974) 71

12 Alexander, *Retailing in England* 23

13 Ibid., 107, quoting from Anon., *Book of English Trades and Library of the Useful Arts* (1821); Adburgham, *Shops and Shopping*, 139–40

14 Charles Dickens, *Sketches by Boz* (London: Ward, Lock and Bodwen 1850) 124

15 Charles Knight, ed., *London* vol. 5 (1851), quoted by Adburgham, *Shops and Shopping* 97; Ablett, *Reminiscences of an Old Draper* 155

16 N. Coghill, *The Vision of Piers Plowman* quoted by Davis, *History of Shopping* 32, see also 188; M. Beer, ed., *The Life of Robert Owen by Himself* (London: G. Bell and Sons 1920) 28–9

17 Isabel Grubb, *Quakerism and Industry before 1800* (London: Williams and Norgate 1930) 19–23; Davis, *History of Shopping* 152, 183; Wayland A. Tonning, 'The Beginnings of the Money-Back Guarantee and the One-Price Policy in Champaign-Urbana, Illinois, 1833–1880,' *Business History Review* 30 (Summer 1956) 196

18 Beer, *Life of Robert Owen* 25–7

19 Hancock, *Competition between Large and Small Shops* 9; Davis, *History of Shopping* 187–9; Beer, *Life of Robert Owen* 17–19, 25–7

20 Hancock, *Competition between Large and Small Shops* 6, 15–16; Alexander, *Retailing in England* 107–9

21 *Report of the Select Committee on Manufactures and Trade 1833* Q 1425, quoted by Davis, *History of Shopping* 258

22 Dickens, *Sketches by Boz* 41–2; Arnold Bennett, *The Old Wives' Tale* (1911) 88–92; Williams, *Dream Worlds* 59; Hancock, *Competition between Large and Small Shops* 12–13, 24

23 A Draper's Assistant, 'Groans from behind the Counter,' *Chamber's Edinburgh Journal* 14 Mar. 1846, 173–5

24 Francis Wey, *A Frenchman among the Victorians* (New Haven: Yale University Press 1936) 145–6

25 Lee Holcombe, *Victorian Ladies at Work: Middle Class Working Women in England and Wales 1850–1914* (Newton Abbot: David and Charles 1973) 114–15; C.C. Taylor, *Toronto 'Called Back' from 1886 to 1850* (Toronto: William Briggs 1886) 17–18; Draper's Assistant, 'Groans from behind the Counter,' 174; Agnes Amy Bulley and Margaret Whitley, *Women's Work* (London: Methuen 1894) 51–2

26 Taylor, *Toronto 'Called Back' from 1886 to 1850* 18

27 M. Jeune, 'The Ethics of Shopping,' *Fortnightly Review* NS 57 (1 Jan. 1895) 124

28 Adburgham, *Shops and Shopping* 281–2, vii

29 Ablett, *Reminiscences of an Old Draper* 160–1; Alexander, *Retailing in England* 130; Jeune, 'Ethics of Shopping,' 124

30 Resseguie, 'Alexander Turney Stewart,' 311

31 Robert W. Twyman, 'Potter Palmer: Merchandising Innovator of the West,' *Explorations in Entrepreneurial History* 4:2 (1966) 62

32 Lloyd Wendt and Herman Kogan, *Give the Lady What She Wants: The Story of Marshall Field and Company* (Chicago: Rand McNally 1952) 34; Ralph M. Hower, 'Urban Retailing 100 Years Ago,' *Bulletin of the Business Historical Society* (Dec. 1938) 94–5

33 Herbert A. Gibbons, *John Wanamaker* (New York: Kenibat Press 1971) vol. 1, 84–5, 93; Resseguie, 'Alexander Turney Stewart,' 306, 319–20; Hower, *History of Macy's* 17 and chapter 3

34 John W. Ferry, *A History of the Department Store* (New York: Macmillan 1960); *R.G. Dun and Co. Collection* (Baker Library, Harvard University Graduate School of Business Administration) Toronto, County of York, vol. 2 (25 Nov. 1858, 18 Apr. 1859)

35 Charles Dickens, *American Notes for General Circulation and Pictures from Italy* (London: Chapman and Hall 1910) 244

36 *City of Toronto Directory* 1847–94; MT, see, for example, 29 Apr. 1869, 589, 23 Sept. 1870, 105, 19 May 1871, 787.

37 Gene Allen, 'Competition and Consolidation in the Toronto Wholesale Trade, 1860–1880,' unpublished paper, May 1982, 26; see also Douglas McCalla, 'The Toronto Wholesale Trade in the 1850s: A Study in Commercial Attitudes,' unpublished paper, 1965, 27–8.

38 Hower, *History of Macy's* 82–7

39 Taylor, *Toronto 'Called Back' from 1886 to 1850* 236; MT 29 Apr. 1869, 588

40 C.C. Taylor, *Toronto 'Called Back' from 1894 to 1847* (Toronto: William Briggs 1894) 44; J.E. Middleton, *The Municipality of Toronto* (Toronto: Dominion Publishing1923) vol. 1, 507

41 Henry Scadding and John C. Dent, *Toronto: Past and Present* (Toronto: Hunter, Rose 1884) 255, quoting from *Canadian Illustrated News* 3 Sept. 1870

42 *City of Toronto Directory* 1856 and 1869

43 Taylor, *Toronto 'Called Back' from 1894 to 1847* 27

44 Ibid., 27–8

45 T.W. Acheson, 'The Nature and Structure of York Commerce in the 1820s,' *Canadian Historical Review* 50 (1969) 411; *City of Toronto Directory* 1847–8; see also Toronto *Globe* 17 Jan. 1860; Perth *Courier* 6 Jan., 22 Apr. 1865.

46 Toronto *Globe* 17 Apr. 1860; *R.G. Dun and Co. Collection* York County, Canada West, vol. 2, (28 July 1858) 41

47 *MT*, 25 June 1869, 714

4 A NEW BEGINNING: TORONTO

1 *Globe*, 22 Oct. 1866; Canada, *Census* 1871

2 G.G. Nasmith, *Timothy Eaton* (Toronto: McClelland and Stewart 1923) 67; EA, Letter from F.W. Murdy, 10 Dec. 1930

3 *City of Toronto Assessment Rolls* 1869

4 Gene Allen, 'Competition and Consolidation in the Toronto Wholesale Trade, 1860–1880,' unpublished paper, May 1982, 39

5 See, for example, MT 25 Feb. 1869, 444, 29 Apr. 1869, 589, 20 May 1869, 637, 17 June 1869, 700

6 Newmarket *New Era* 30 Dec. 1870; MT 9 Dec. 1870, 327–8

7 *MT* 17 June 1869, 700, 8 Dec. 1871, 444

8 EA, Letter from Mrs Stuart Shier, 3 Dec. 1958; Timothy Eaton to James Eaton, 19 Feb. 1870

9 *City of Toronto Assessment Rolls* 1869; assessment taken 17 Apr. 1869. Timothy Eaton lived at 12 Gloucester Street from 1869 to 1876, except for part of 1870 when, for some reason, the family moved briefly to 75 Grosvenor Street. EA, Timothy Eaton to James Eaton, 17 May 1870.

10 EA, Timothy Eaton to James Matthewson, Nov. 1869

11 Nasmith, *Timothy Eaton* 67–8

12 The high visibility of those who had succeeded in the wholesale business was responsible for the creation of a somewhat inaccurate myth. The *Monetary Times* in May 1871 demonstrated that of the twenty wholesale houses in business in 1851 only three were still in business in 1871, and only one of the twenty had 'retired with a competency,' *MT* 19 May 1871, 787.

13 *Globe* 9 Dec. 1869

14 EA, Timothy Eaton to James Eaton, 1 Feb. 1870

15 *Globe* 9 Dec. 1869. The opening of the Eaton store obviously attracted custom, for one customer later recalled that she had been told by her mother that she had been down to Eaton's opening and had then gone home to give birth to her. EA, Miss Nan Grant, *Eaton's Magazine* 9 Nov. 1942

16 W.N. Hancock, *Is the Competition between Large and Small Shops Injurious to the Community?* (Dublin: Hodges and Smith 1851) 6–7

17 EA, Timothy Eaton to James Eaton, 19 Feb. 1870

18 See, for example, *Globe* 11 Apr. 1860.

19 BP, 25/21372-3, EA, Timothy Eaton to James Eaton, 13 June 1872

20 EA, Timothy Eaton to James Eaton, 19 Feb. 1870

21 Ibid., 28 Apr. 1870

22 'Studied the People's Wants,' *DGR* Mar. 1909, 27

23 EA, Timothy Eaton, *Notebook* 167

24 EA, Letter from Alex White, 18 Jan. 1919

25 EA, Timothy Eaton, *Notebook* 3–4, 76

26 EA, Timothy Eaton to James Eaton, 28 Apr. 1870

27 Hancock, *Competition between Large and Small Shops* 12

28 EA, Timothy Eaton to James Eaton, 26 May 1872, 6 May 1873

29 Dorothy Davis, *A History of Shopping* (London: Routledge and Kegan Paul 1966) 256; EA, Timothy Eaton to James Eaton, 27 June, 4 Nov. 1874

30 'Studied the People's Wants,' *DGR* Mar. 1909, 27

31 See, for example, *Globe* 13, 29 Dec. 1869, 1, 15, 26 Jan. 1870, 2 Feb. 1870; *Christian Guardian* 9 Feb. 1870.
32 EA, Timothy Eaton to James Eaton, 17 May 1870
33 Nasmith, *Timothy Eaton* 90; EA, Letter from Alex White, 18 Jan. 1919
34 'Studied the People's Wants,' *DGR* Mar. 1909, 27
35 EA, Timothy Eaton, *Notebook* 20, 39, 41, 43
36 *Globe* 21 Apr. 1870
37 EA, Timothy Eaton to James Eaton, 9 Oct. 1870
38 EA, Timothy Eaton, *Notebook* 5 and 10
39 EA, Timothy Eaton to James Eaton, 17 May 1870
40 EA, George Young Eaton to James Eaton, 9 July 1870
41 EA, Timothy Eaton to James Eaton, 31 July 1871, 26 Jan. 1872
42 Ibid., 26 Jan. 1872
43 Ibid., 31 July 1872
44 Ibid., 17 May 1870
45 David Alexander, *Retailing in England during the Industrial Revolution* (London: Athlone Press 1970) 166–7, Table 6-1; Harold V. Barger, *Distribution's Place in the American Economy since 1869* (Princeton: Princeton University Press 1955) 81, table 24; *DGR* Mar. 1903, 50 ff, Jan. 1905, 48
46 EA, Timothy Eaton to James Eaton, 27 June 1874; Timothy Eaton, *Notebook* 26, 76
47 Sidney Pollard, *The Genesis of Modern Management: A Study of the Industrial Revolution in Great Britain* (London: Edward Arnold 1965) 227–9
48 *MT* 9 Dec. 1870, 327
49 Neil McKendrick, 'Josiah Wedgwood and Cost Accounting in the Industrial Revolution,' *Economic History Review* 23 (1970) 46–7, EA, Timothy Eaton to James Eaton, 22 May 1872, 6 May 1873, 28 July 1880
50 EA, Timothy Eaton to James Eaton, 22 May 1877
51 Ibid., 8 June 1975, 22 May 1877. W.H. Eaton, born around 1860, was the eldest son of John Eaton, Timothy's brother who remained in Ireland.
52 EA, Timothy Eaton to James Eaton, 27 June 1874
53 Ibid., 28 Nov. 1871, 27 June 1874. References in subsequent letters (8 June 1875, for example) suggest that this may indeed have been the case and that both Timothy and James Eaton were in contact with a number of British suppliers when operating the St Marys store; see also 4 Nov. 1874.
54 'Studied the People's Wants,' *DGR* Mar. 1909, 27

55 EA, Timothy Eaton, *Notebook* 20, 21, 22, 24, 36, 38
56 EA, Timothy Eaton to James Eaton, 1 July 1874
57 Ibid., 8 June, 10 July 1875
58 Ibid., 4 Nov. 1874
59 Ibid., 22 May 1877; Timothy Eaton, *Notebook* 26, 30
60 EA, Timothy Eaton to James Eaton, 8 June 1875, 22 May, 7 July 1877, 31 May 1878
61 EA, Letter from Alex White, 18 Jan. 1919
62 *MT* 25 Feb.1875, 982, 25 May 1875, 1344, 25 June 1875, 1457, 9 July 1875, 45, 10 Sept. 1875, 300
63 EA, Timothy Eaton, *Notebook* 26, 76, 78; Timothy Eaton to James Eaton, 22 May 1877; Saturday, 19 May 1877, 850 sales – $824.00, Monday, 21 May 1877, 454 sales – $456.00
64 EA, Timothy Eaton, *Notebook* 17, 21, 43
65 EA, Timothy Eaton to James Eaton, 27 June 1874
66 OA, MS 489, *Dun and Bradstreet Reference Books 1869–77; R.G. Dun and Co. Collection* (Baker Library, Harvard University Graduate School of Business Administration) York County, Canada West, vol. 27 (27 Nov. 1874) 254
67 EA, Timothy Eaton to James Eaton, 13 June 1872, 14 July 1873
68 EA, T. Eaton and Co. flyer, Jan. 1878; Timothy Eaton, *Notebook* 26, 76
69 EA, Meeting of Eaton Company shareholders, 22 Feb. 1898, statement by W.G. Dean
70 EA, Timothy Eaton to James Eaton, 17 May 1870, 31 July 1871, 30 July 1873
71 Ibid., 28 Apr. 1880. Herby Eaton moved to Manitoba in 1880 where he attained success as a merchant in his own right.
72 EA, W.H. Eaton to James Eaton, 16 Aug. 1877
73 *City of Toronto Assessment Rolls* 1870–80; from 1866 to 1888 the assessment rolls included only those employees paid more than $300 per annum; EA, Letter from Alex White, 18 Jan. 1919; *Royal Commission on the Relations of Labour and Capital in Canada 1889* Ontario Evidence, 291.
74 EA, Letter from Alex White, 18 Jan. 1919; Timothy Eaton, *Notebook* 167; Sarah Smith Malino, 'Faces across the Counter: A Social History of Female Department Store Employees, 1870–1920,' PH D Diss., Columbia University 1982, 159
75 EA, Letter from Alex White, 18 Jan. 1919; 'Studied the People's Wants,' *DGR* Mar. 1909, 27
76 EA, Timothy Eaton, *Notebook* 331

77 EA, Eaton staff magazine *Flash*, about 1943

78 EA, R.Y. Eaton, about 1940

79 Ralph Barnes Grindrod, 'The Wrongs of Our Youth: An Essay on the Evils of the Late Hour System,' in *Demands for Early Closing Hours; Three Pamphlets* (New York: Arno Press [1843] 1972) 33, 44; see also Maurice Corina, *Fine Silks and Oak Counters: Debenham's 1778–1978* (London: Hutchinson Benham 1978), quoting from a report in *The Observer* 18 Dec. 1826.

80 W.A. Craik, 'The Struggle for Early Closing,' Toronto *Telegram* 24 Nov. 1959; *Globe* 15 Jan., 30 Dec. 1872, 31 July 1873

81 EA, Letter from E. Devine, 31 Oct. 1930, who was employed by Isaac Laidley in 1874

82 Quoted in Craik, 'Struggle for Early Closing'

83 *Toronto Daily Star* 22 Aug. 1928

84 EA, Letter from Herby Eaton, 10 Feb. 1919; see also Toronto *Mail* 1, 7, 8 May, 18 Oct. 1877.

85 Maxine Brady, *Bloomingdale's* (New York: Harcourt Brace Jovanovich 1980) 15–23; Ralph M. Hower, *A History of Macy's of New York, 1858–1919: Chapters in the Evolution of a Department Store* (Cambridge: Harvard University Press 1943) 109

86 EA, Timothy Eaton to James Eaton, 7 July 1877

87 Ibid., 1 Feb. 1870, 26 Jan., 13 June 1877

88 Ibid., 16 May 1874; the records at the Toronto Necropolis also gave evidence of further sadness with the birth of a stillborn baby, 6 June 1872, *City of Toronto Necropolis Records* 1870–4, entries 10853, 12248, 13853.

89 EA, Timothy Eaton to James Eaton, 22 May 1877

90 Ibid., 4 Nov. 1874, 10 July 1875

5 THE MOVE TO 190 YONGE STREET

1 MT 27 May 1881, 1384; *Royal Commission on the Relations of Labour and Capital in Canada 1889*, Ontario Evidence, 8; *Journal of Commerce* 7 Sept. 1888, 452; C.C.Taylor, *Toronto 'Called Back' from 1886 to 1850* (Toronto: William Briggs 1886) 241; Canada, *Census* 1881, 1901

2 MT 12 Nov. 1880, 563, 3 June 1881, 1415, 5 Aug. 1881, 160

3 *City of Toronto Assessment Rolls* 1883; assessment taken 21 Sept. 1882; *Daily News* 8 Apr., 22 Dec. 1882

4 EA, Timothy Eaton to James Eaton, 17 Nov. 1880

5 Ibid.

6 *City of Toronto Assessment Rolls* 1882 and 1883; EA, Timothy Eaton, *Notebook* 47, 49. This was in addition to stock carried at the Yonge Street store, which amounted to $47,428.00 and $62,219.41 respectively.

7 EA, Timothy Eaton, *Notebook* 47, 49

8 *MT* 3 Dec. 1880, 647, 15 July 1881, 69, 15 Aug. 1881, 160, 3 Dec. 1881, 800–1, 3 Feb. 1882, 954, 17 Feb. 1882, 1019

9 *History of Toronto and County of York* (Toronto: C. Blackett Robinson 1885) vol. 1, 413

10 EA, Timothy Eaton, *Notebook* 41, 47, 78; 1882 sales figures are based on only the eight months that were available. To obtain the annual volume the average figure was multiplied by twelve, which gives a possible total for the year.

11 Alfred D. Chandler, *The Visible Hand: The Managerial Revolution in American Business* (Cambridge: Harvard University Press 1977) 223; Ralph M. Hower, *A History of Macy's of New York, 1858–1919: Chapters in the Evolution of a Department Store* (Cambridge: Harvard University Press 1943) 129

12 See *Daily News* 3 June 1884, for example; also 3 Jan., 1, 17 Feb. 1888. The business was finally terminated with the death of James M. Simpson in Nov. 1889.

13 Chandler, *Visible Hand* 225

14 Taylor, *Toronto 'Called Back' from 1886 to 1850* 329; *Globe* 3 Nov., 5, 29 Dec. 1877, 15 Jan., 2 Mar. 1878

15 EA, Secretarial office files no. 84

16 Taylor, *Toronto 'Called Back' from 1886 to 1850* 329

17 See, for example, *Daily News* 9, 27 Jan., 15 Feb., 1, 3, 22, 24 Mar., 29 Apr. 1883; *Telegram*, 16, 27 Feb., 13, 16 Mar., 11 May 1883.

18 *Daily News* 10 July, 18, 22 Aug. 1883

19 EA, Copies of original leases dated Nov. 1883 and 21 Feb. 1884; letters from Alex White, 18 Jan. 1919, and F.W. Murdy, 10 Dec. 1930; *Daily News* 3 Apr. 1884

20 Taylor, *Toronto 'Called Back' from 1886 to 1850* 329; *Daily News* 22 Aug. 1883

21 EA, *Eaton's Catalogue* 1884, inside front cover; 1890, 1; Bruce West, *Toronto* (Toronto: Doubleday Canada 1967) 174

22 *Telegram* 24 Aug. 1883; *Daily News* 18, 20 Sept. 1883. During this period the exhibition was usually held during the latter part of September rather than the last weeks of August, as is now customary.

23 *Daily News* 9 June 1883, 15 Apr. 1887; EA, *Eaton's Catalogue* 1886, 5, 1887–8, 7

24 Hower, *History of Macy's* 165–9

25 EA, Gray Correspondence, 1884–5, Secretarial office file no. 84

26 *Daily News* 28, 29, 30 July 1886

27 Taylor, *Toronto 'Called Back' from 1886 to 1850* 330; *Daily News* 11 Aug., 4 Sept. 1886

28 EA, *Eaton's Catalogue* 1887–8, 3

29 EA, John James Eaton, *Memorandum* 1884–5

30 G.G. Nasmith, *Timothy Eaton* (Toronto: McClelland and Stewart 1923) 151–2; EA, John James Eaton, *Memorandum* 1884–5

31 *MT* 6 July 1883, 20, 13 July 1883, 36, 5 Oct. 1883, 381–2, 25 July 1884, 93, 15 Aug. 1884, 185, 14 Nov. 1884, 617, 9 Jan. 1885, 774; *Daily News* 3, 5 May 1884, 14 Oct. 1884

32 OA, *Partnership Records* County of York, book CP 2, 4219

33 EA, John James Eaton, *Memorandum* 1884–5

34 EA, Timothy Eaton, *Notebook* 46. Outstanding Canadian accounts by contrast amounted to only $4,241.70; correspondence with Molson's Bank, 31 Dec. 1885.

35 Nasmith, *Timothy Eaton* 152–3; EA, R.Y. Eaton to G.G. Nasmith, 30 Oct. 1923; Timothy Eaton *Notebook* 46, 50

36 EA, Stewart and MacDonald correspondence, 18 Dec. 1884 to 31 Dec. 1885

37 G.H. Stanford, *To Serve the Community: The Story of Toronto's Board of Trade* (Toronto: University of Toronto Press 1974) 38–9; Leo, *An Alphabet of Dry Goods Men and the Journey They Took* (Toronto: Rose Publishing 1887) 16–18, 46–8. The publication of this little book appears to have been heavily subsidized by the firm of John Macdonald in the form of advertisements.

38 EA, Agreement between T. Eaton and E.Y. Eaton regarding Wilson and Company, 7 May 1892. An earlier date, Apr. 1889, had been typed in and the later date then added in ink, perhaps after the official incorporation of the T. Eaton Company in 1891. OA, *Partnership Records*, East Toronto, book CP 1, 462, 12 Feb. 1892; EA, Timothy Eaton to E.Y. Eaton, 4 May 1896

39 EA, Timothy Eaton to Hepton Brothers, and Hudson, Sykes and Bousfield, Leeds, 2 Mar. 1891

40 Alan Wilson, *John Northway: A Blue Serge Canadian* (Toronto: Burns and MacEachern 1965) 50

41 EA, Letters from Alex White, 18 Jan. 1919, and R.A. McQuarrie, 28 Aug. 1962

42 EA, Letter from R.A. McQuarrie, 28 Aug. 1962

43 EA, Timothy Eaton to Frank McMahon, 8 Feb. 1893

44 Gene Allen, 'Competition and Consolidation in the Toronto Wholesale Trade, 1860–1880,' unpublished paper, May 1982, 20–1; EA, R.Y. Eaton to G.G. Nasmith, 5 Nov. 1923

45 *MT* 27 May 1881, 1384; Tom Naylor, *The History of Canadian Business, 1867–1914* (Toronto: James Lorimer 1975) vol. 1, 50–1

46 *Telegram* 7 Apr. 1883

47 EA, Secretarial office file no. 127

48 EA, Timothy Eaton, *Notebook* 18, 59

49 EA, Property file, information compiled by T. Eaton Realty Company, 1 Apr. 1929; *Eaton's Catalogue* 1889, inside front cover; 1890, 5

50 EA, *Eaton's Catalogue* 1887–8, 3; Timothy Eaton to Pratt and Watkins, Hamilton, 21 Jan. 1894. Timothy Eaton added that if he had to do it over, he would have used electricity, but did not do so at the time because he wished to wait until electrical elevators 'became more complete in their management.'

51 *Globe* 14,19 Sept. 1889; EA, Timothy Eaton to Royal Electric Company, Montreal 18 Nov. 1891

52 *Royal Commission on the Relations of Labour and Capital* 293; EA, *Contacts* Dec. 1935

53 EA, Letter from Mrs R.F. van Zytveld, 25 July 1962

54 EA, Harry McGee, *Notebook* unpaginated; *Daily News* 11 Feb. 1887; report of a meeting of heads of departments at T. Eaton Company; EA, Timothy Eaton to Mrs W. Smith, 4 Feb. 1890, $125.00

55 See, for example, *Mail* 20 Apr. 1885; *MT* 31 Mar. 1882, 1207.

56 EA, Letter from Mrs. R.F. van Zytveld, 25 July 1962; Thomas E. Tausky, *Sara Jeannette Duncan – Selected Journalism* (Ottawa: Tecumseh Press 1978) 31–2

57 *Royal Commission on the Relations of Labour and Capital* 289, 291, 293

58 Margaret Smith, née Stephenson, was employed as a buyer of fancy goods in the 1880s and travelled overseas to obtain merchandise for the store; see *Daily News* 11 Feb. 1887; see also EA, W. Smith to Miss Doughty, Shoe Department, 7 Aug. 1889; G.H. Pack to General Office, 10 July 1893.

59 *Royal Commission on the Relations of Labour and Capital* 292, 294; EA, *Eaton's Catalogue* 1887, 71; *Daily News* 11 Feb. 1887; Hower, *History of Macy's* 121–2

60 *Globe* 1 Sept. 1884; *Daily News* 6 June 1888. Already in 1871 the Macy

store closed on Saturday afternoons during July and August, Hower, *History of Macy's* 200–1.

61 *Telegram* 15, 16 June, 22 July 1886; *Daily News* 2 June 1886; Sarah Smith Malino, 'Faces across the Counter: A Social History of Female Department Store Employees, 1870–1920,' PH D Diss., Columbia University 1982, 61–2; *Royal Commission on the Relations of Labour and Capital* 349

62 *Telegram* 16, 19 July 1886; *Royal Commission on the Relations of Labour and Capital* 292

63 *Telegram* 20 June 1886, 29 June, 10 Aug. 1888; *Daily News* 6 July 1888

64 *The Ontario Factories Act, 1887* Ontario Sessional Papers (1888), no. 25; *Ontario Shops Regulation Act* 23 Mar. 1888. This act is similar in all its features to an act passed in Great Britain in June 1886. *City of Toronto Council Minutes* 7 May 1888, Appendix 101, minute 2000; Ontario Sessional Papers, no. 39, Reports of the Inspectors of Factories for the year ending 31 Dec. 1888, 12

65 *Globe* 13 June 1887; United Church Archives, Trinity Church Minutes, 12 May to 2 July 1887; Register of church members, 17 Feb. 1889

66 EA, Timothy Eaton, *Notebook* 330

6 'TRIAL IS THE SUREST TEST'

1 *Daily News* 21 Nov. 1884; Paul Rutherford, *A Victorian Authority: The Daily Press in Late-Nineteenth-Century Canada* (Toronto: University of Toronto Press 1982), 123. Rutherford gives the impression that such stores as Eaton's, Simpson's, and the Mammoth House were early advocates of large advertisements. Research revealed that full-page advertisements were seldom inserted by any of the above stores before the late 1890s.

2 EA, Timothy Eaton, *Memorandum* about 1880s. Such principles were widely held by this new breed of retailer; see, for example, Herbert A. Gibbons, *John Wanamaker* (New York: Kenibat Press 1971) vol. 1, 99.

3 Frank S. Presbrey, *The History and Development of Advertising* (New York: Doubleday, Doran 1929) 307, 331–3; Joseph H. Appel, *The Business Biography of John Wanamaker* (New York: Macmillan 1930) 104. Both Robert Simpson and James Eaton subsequently adopted the same style in 1887.

4 *Globe* 26 Sept. 1889

5 EA, Copy of a *Truth* advertisement about 1884–5; *Eaton's Catalogue* 1889–90, 94; *Daily News* 22 June 1887, 27, 30 Jan. 1888

6 Alison Adburgham, *Shopping in Style: London from the Restoration to Edwardian Elegance* (London: Thames and Hudson 1979) 78; Michael B. Miller, *The Bon Marché: Bourgeois Culture and the Department Store, 1869–1920* (Princeton: Princeton University Press 1981) 26

7 James C. Worthy, *Shaping an American Institution: Robert E. Wood and Sears, Roebuck* (Chicago: University of Illinois Press 1984) 26; Stuart Ewen and Elizabeth Ewen, *Channels of Desire: Mass Images and the Shaping of American Consciousness* (New York: McGraw-Hill 1982) 64; Boris Emmet and John E. Jeuck, *Catalogues and Counters: A History of Sears, Roebuck and Company* (Chicago: University of Chicago Press 1950) 20–1; Ralph M. Hower, *A History of Macy's of New York 1858–1919: Chapters in the Evolution of a Department Store* (Cambridge: Harvard University Press 1943) 119; Appel, *Business Biography of John Wanamaker* 101

8 EA, Contacts 1934, letters on occasion of the company's fiftieth anniversary

9 EA, *Eaton's Catalogue* 1884, 1; Timothy Eaton to E.Y. Eaton, 4 May 1896

10 EA, Letters from Mrs R.F. van Zytveld, 25 July 1962, and the Rev. Leon B. Wright, Mahone Bay, NS, 17 Aug. 1968

11 EA, Eaton flyer 1885

12 Ibid., *Eaton's Catalogue* 1886–7, 1; *Daily News* 11 Aug. 1886

13 EA, *Eaton's Catalogue* 1884, inside front cover

14 Ibid., inside back cover

15 See, for example, EA, *Eaton's Catalogue* 1884, 8–9, 32, 1887–8, 69; by contrast the Bon Marché in Paris did not carry work clothes until 1914, and even then these were of the type ordered by employers for grooms, chauffeurs, valets, and maids, Miller, *Bon Marché* 179; *Daily News* 9 Aug. 1886.

16 EA, Letter from Fred H. Brigden, 31 Mar. 1955

17 EA, Letter from Mrs R.F. van Zytveld, 25 July 1962; *Eaton's Catalogue* 1886–7, 2

18 EA, *Eaton's Catalogue* 1887–8, inside front cover, 1890, 52

19 EA, *Contacts* 1934; Report by Kitty Fells, Eaton archivist, 11 Sept. 1956

20 *Globe* 14 Jan. 1890, 5 Jan. 1892

21 EA, *Eaton's Catalogue* 1888–9, 77

22 EA, *Eaton's Catalogue* 1887—8, 10, 30, 1888–9, 68–71 inc.

23 EA, *Eaton's Catalogue* 1886–7, 33, 1887–8, 52, 1888–9, 19

24 Asa Briggs, *Friends of the People: The Centenary History of Lewis's* (London: Batsford 1956) 45–6; Gene Allen, 'Competition and Con-

solidation in the Toronto Wholesale Trade, 1860–1880,' unpublished paper, May 1982, 42; *Daily News* 6 Aug. 1886; EA, Timothy Eaton, *Notebook* 58; Timothy Eaton to Hill Bros, New York, 18 Jan. 1890

25 *Telegram* Oct. and Nov. 1879; EA, *Eaton's Catalogue* 1886–7, 6, 1887–8, 66–70, 1888–9, 28–9

26 *Mail*, 22, 29 Apr. 1873; EA, Timothy Eaton to James Eaton, 27 June 1874; Alison Adburgham, *Shops and Shopping 1800–1914: Where and in What Manner the Well-Dressed Englishwoman Bought Her Clothes* (London: Allen and Unwin 1967) 123–8. Some stores in London, England, for example, sold ready-made skirts but made jackets to match in their workrooms. See also Eileen Collard, *Clothing in English Canada, Circa 1867 to 1907* (Burlington: 1975), 14–15, 21.

27 EA, *Eaton's Catalogue* 1886–7, 34, 39, 1887–8, 50; Alan Wilson, *John Northway: A Blue Serge Canadian* (Toronto: Burns and MacEachern 1956) 67

28 Dorothy Davis, *A History of Shopping* (London: Routledge and Kegan Paul 1966) 292; Hrant Pasdermadjan, *The Department Store: Its Origins, Evolution and Economics* (London: Newman Books 1954) 27, 34, 118–19, 180–1

29 Glenn Porter and Harold C. Livesay, *Merchants and Manufacturers: Studies in the Changing Structure of 19th Century Marketing* (Baltimore: Johns Hopkins Press 1971) 224–8

30 EA, Timothy Eaton, *Notebook* 331, paraphrase of Prov. 2:1, 'A good name is rather to be chosen than great riches'; *Eaton's Catalogue* 1887–8, inside front cover, 1889–90, 5, 1890, 39

31 *Daily News* 14 June 1886; Timothy Eaton's advertisement for that day was on the facing page; EA, *Eaton's Catalogue* 1888–9, 2

32 *Daily News* 6, 22 July 1888, 3 July 1889

33 EA, Timothy Eaton, *Memorandum c.* 1880s; *Telegram* 25 June 1886; EA, *Eaton's Catalogue* 1889–90, 94

34 EA, *Eaton's Catalogue* 1888–9, 2

35 *Telegram* 15 Sept. 1883

36 *Telegram* 18 Mar. 1880; EA, Eaton flyer, 1885; *Eaton's Catalogue* 1886–7, 2, 13, 1887–8, 7

37 EA, *Eaton's Catalogue* 1886–7, 27, 1888–9, 25

38 EA, *Eaton's Catalogue* 1887–8, 94, 1888–9, 77

39 *MT* 17 June 1881, 1481

40 Hower, *History of Macy's* 190; W.N. Hancock, *Is the Competition*

between Large and Small Shops Injurious to the Community? (Dublin: Hodges and Smith 1851) 19–23

41 *Telegram* 8 Jan. 1885; Robert Simpson, not to be outdone, on the following day referred in the same paper to his own 'Special Cheap Sale.'

42 EA, *Eaton's Catalogue* 1887–8, 7; Rosalind Williams, *Dream Worlds: Mass Consumption in Late Nineteenth-Century France* (Berkeley: University of California Press 1982) 12, 99

43 Quoted in Frank Presbrey, *History of Advertising* 310, 315; M. Jeune, 'The Ethics of Shopping,' *Fortnightly Review* NS 57 (1 Jan. 1895) 123–32

44 EA, *Eaton's Catalogue* 1888–9, 19, 1889–90, 32; see also *Globe* 4 Feb. 1892.

7 PRIVATE INCORPORATION AND PUBLIC EXPANSION

1 Jacob Spelt, *Toronto* (Don Mills: Collier-Macmillan Canada 1973) 35; C.C. Taylor, *Toronto 'Called Back' from 1894 to 1847* (Toronto: William Briggs 1894) 291, 330, 335; David G. Coombs, 'The Emergence of a White Collar Work Force in Toronto 1895–1911,' PH D Diss, York University 1978, 12, table III

2 *Telegram* 8 Oct. 1891

3 EA, *Letters Patent* 21 Apr. 1891; *Indenture* 10 Sept. 1891, transferring all company assets from Timothy Eaton and E.Y. Eaton to the T. Eaton Company Limited. Information relating to shares and shareholders is taken from List of Shareholders and Summary of State of Affairs, 1891–1901.

4 EA, *Supplementary Letters Patent* 28 Apr. 1905

5 EA, *Suggestion Book* 18 Sept. 1893, 2, 19 Sept. 1893, 9, 31 July 1896, 47

6 Ralph M. Hower, *A History of Macy's of New York 1858–1919: Chapters in The Evolution of a Department Store* (Cambridge: Harvard University Press 1943) 257–60

7 EA, John James Eaton, *Notebook* unpaginated; Frank McMahon to Timothy Eaton, 1 May 1895

8 Premises at 21, 23, and 25 James Street were acquired leasehold in 1890 and by the spring of 1892 housed a factory operation; 15, 17, and 19 Albert Street were acquired in 1893, 14–20 Queen Street West running through to 9–11 Albert Street in 1896, and 27–9 James Street and 202–10 Yonge Street in 1897; EA, Building and Expansion, Toronto, 1882–1923, plan 12, 1903.

9 EA, *Eaton's Catalogue* Spring-Summer 1896; *Globe* 27 Aug. 1895. These farms were large operations and in 1895 had 105 cows and 35 farm horses, in addition to the 65 delivery horses.

10 EA, Information compiled by T. Eaton Realty Company, 16 July 1958; *Eaton's Catalogue* 1890, 1, Fall-Winter 1893–4, 2, Spring-Summer 1896, 1; *Globe* 30 Dec. 1893; *Mail and Empire* 20, 23 Nov. 1897

11 *DGR* Dec. 1895, 30, Dec. 1897, 10, 54; *CJF* Jan. 1900, 13

12 EA. See, for example, S.H. Janes to Timothy Eaton, 17 Jan. 1897, R.W. Prittie to Timothy Eaton, 20 Feb. 1897, Pearson Bros to Timothy Eaton, 9 July 1897, Staff Captain A. Smeeton to Timothy Eaton, 20 Nov. 1895.

13 EA, City of Toronto Licences, 4 May 1896; Toronto City Council, *Minutes*, Appendix A, 701, Report 1; Committee on Public Works, Report 19, 45, Report 9, 12 Oct. 1898, 6 Apr. 1900, 314, 897

14 EA *Teco Transfer* 8 July 1891; G.G. Nasmith, *Timothy Eaton* (Toronto: McClelland and Stewart 1923) 188–9; see also *Globe* 4 Dec. 1923.

15 EA, Timothy Eaton to J.G. Howes, 5 Mar. 1891

16 EA, Correspondence between Timothy Eaton and Larratt Smith, Jan. to Mar. 1891; Secretarial office file no. 86, North British and Mercantile Insurance Company, 1894–8; OA, *Wadworth Papers*, B.III, 11, M 3086, no. 9217, the London and Canadian Loan Agency Co. Ltd, 9 Feb. 1892

17 EA, Timothy Eaton to J.G. Howes, 5 Mar. 1891

18 *Globe* 20 Sept. 1893, 1 Sept. 1896; *Mail and Empire* 22 Nov. 1897

19 EA, Timothy Eaton to Frank McMahon, 27 Apr. 1892

20 EA, Timothy Eaton to Butterick Publishing Co., New York, 13 Dec. 1889

21 EA, *Teco Transfer*, bills payable against T. Eaton and Co., 8 July 1891; Shareholder's Meeting, 1894, statement by Mr Minty; Timothy Eaton to Frank McMahon, 17 Nov. 1892

22 EA, Secretarial office file no. 127

23 EA, Correspondence between Geo. Merz, R.D. Warburg and Co., Berlin, and Timothy Eaton, 6 Feb. to 13 Mar. 1891. Merz was not the only such liaison; W. Depmeyer, also in Berlin, organized arrangements with forty-five German companies; a commission rate of $2^{1}/_{2}$ per cent was exacted by Depmeyer.

24 EA, Interview, Mr Van Roomen, 1958

25 EA, *Suggestion Book* 40–5, N.R. Miller, B.D. Pearson, J. Whitaker to E.Y. Eaton, Aug. to Sept. 1893; Timothy Eaton to the Rev. D. Macdonald, Tokio, Japan, 9 Apr., 4 May 1891

26 Toronto Board of Trade, *Annual Report 1896* 32–7
27 *Globe* 2 July 1896
28 *CJF* Jan. 1897, 25, Feb. 1897, 47; *MT* 21 May 1897, 1530
29 *MT* 6 Dec. 1895, 719, 3 Jan. 1896, 846; *CJF* Feb. 1896, 40
30 *MT* 29 Mar. 1894, 1264. *DGR* Nov. 1894, 5, reported that the number of buyers from retail houses going to Europe was double what it had been ten years earlier; see also *MT* 28 Aug. 1896, 280.
31 *Globe* 22 Oct. 1890, 15 May 1895; *Daily News* 15 May 1896
32 EA, Geo. Merz to Timothy Eaton, 13 Mar. 1891
33 EA, Timothy Eaton to Geo. Merz, 30 Mar. 1891
34 EA, Shareholders Meeting 1894, statements by Mr Whitaker and J.A.C. Poole; Alfred D. Chandler, *The Visible Hand: The Managerial Revolution in American Business* (Cambridge: Harvard University Press 1977) 6; Pearl Wilson, 'Consumer Buying in Upper Canada, 1791–1840,' *Ontario History* 36 (1944) 37; EA, Shareholders Meeting, 22 Feb. 1898, statements by Mr Moreland and Timothy Eaton
35 EA, Shareholders Meeting 1894, statement by Secretary-Treasurer James Wood
36 Ibid., statement by Timothy Eaton
37 *DGR* Mar. 1896, 43
38 EA, Stock Report, 8 July 1891; Hower, *History of Macy's* 261
39 EA, Timothy Eaton to Frank McMahon, 17 Nov. 1892
40 EA, Interview, Mrs R. Brophy, 2 Oct. 1961
41 EA, J.H. Forster, *Notebook* 1901, unpaginated
42 EA, Dun Wiman and Co. rating, 31 Jan. 1894
43 EA, Timothy Eaton to Frank McMahon, 17 Mar., 17 Nov. 1892; *Globe* 15 May 1895
44 EA, Shareholders Meeting, 22 Feb. 1898. The staff in Macy's Paris office, which had been opened in 1888, were reduced to one in 1893, largely, because the company was not able to obtain experienced personnel, see Hower, *History of Macy's* 163, 243.
45 EA, John James Eaton, *Notebook* unpaginated; Shareholders Meeting 1894, statement by Mr Brown
46 EA, Frank Beecroft to Lady Eaton, Jan. 1957; John James Eaton, *Notebook*
47 EA, Notice to Departments, 22 June 1900
48 EA, *General Ledger, 1893–1895* 387–9
49 EA, Letter from Mark Chisholm, 27 Dec. 1963, recalling an incident that happened in 1896. In this case Timothy Eaton scored a first, because it was some ten years before Sears-Roebuck adopted such a practice,

referring to it as 'Iowaization'; see Stuart Ewen and Elizabeth Ewen, *Channels of Desire: Mass Images and the Shopping of American Consciousness* (New York: McGraw-Hill 1982) 66.

50 EA, *Eaton's Catalogue* Fall-Winter 1893–4, 18

51 Nellie McClung, *The Stream Runs Fast: My Own Story* (Toronto: Thomas Allen and Son 1965), 3

52 EA, Letters from customers on fiftieth and one-hundredth anniversaries of the Eaton Store; Barry Broadfoot, *The Pioneer Years, 1895–1914: Memories of the Settlers Who Opened the West* (Toronto: Doubleday Canada 1976) 162

53 EA, John James Eaton, *Notebook*; T. Eaton Co. Ltd to Miss M. Doherty, Mattawa, 24 Sept. 1895, 2, 15 Mar. 1897, to Mrs Annie Scott, Melville Cross, 11 Aug. 1897, to Miss Anne E. Palmer, 5 July 1903; order no. G84665, 20 Oct. 1898, for $42.62, covering fifty-one items ranging from Worcester sauce to overshoes

54 Canada, *Royal Commission on Price Spreads*, Special Committee on Price Spreads and Mass Buying, Proceedings and Evidence, 1934, vol. 3, 4864

55 United Church Archives, Trinity Church, register of church members, 1889–1902; notebooks listing church officials, 1897, 1900, 1905

56 In 1899 Timothy Eaton was elected to sit on the board of directors of the Toronto-Dominion Bank but there is nothing to indicate that this was anything more than an honorary position, see EA, Toronto-Dominion Bank to Timothy Eaton, 18 Oct. 1899; Timothy Eaton to W.H. Eaton, 2 Jan. 1895.

57 Ross Harkness, *J.E. Atkinson of the Star* (Toronto: University of Toronto Press 1963) 19–21, 23, 52–3, 62–3. In 1905 Timothy Eaton gave Atkinson a further $20,000 to help pay for the construction of a new building and the purchase of new printing presses, in return for which he received seventeen more shares.

58 *CJF* Oct. 1897, 316. The tents had been ordered by the Ontario government, but the company refused to accept payment for them; EA, correspondence with John Anderson, Arthur, Ontario, 21 June, 8 Aug. 1892, Jean Jeny, Elizabeth Street School, Toronto, 11 Dec. 1896, S.H. Blake, President, YMCA, 5 Nov. 1892, $2,000, 26 Sept. 1894, $1,000, and the Rev. W.F. Wilson, 18 Oct. 1894, $700.

59 EA, Timothy Eaton to Commissioner Herbert H. Booth, Salvation Army, 27 Feb. 1894

60 EA, Timothy Eaton to Dwight Moody, 5 Mar. 1894

61 Nasmith, *Timothy Eaton* 252

8 A DEPARTMENT STORE

1 *Journal of Commerce* 2 Nov. 1906
2 Stuart Ewen and Elizabeth Ewen, *Channels of Desire: Mass Images and the Shaping of American Consciousness* (New York: McGraw-Hill 1982) 210–12
3 Ralph M. Hower, *A History of Macy's of New York, 1858–1919: Chapters in the Evolution of a Department Store* (Cambridge: Harvard University Press 1943) 100, 141
4 Hrant Pasdermadjian, *The Department Store: Its Origin, Evolution and Economics* (London: Newman Books 1954) 11
5 Hower, *History of Macy's* 69; see also Paul H. Nystrom, *The Economics of Retailing* (New York: Ronald Press 1915) 199–200.
6 Wayland A. Tonning, 'Department Stores in Down State Illinois, 1889–1943,' *Business History Review* 29 (Winter 1955) 337
7 Brenda K. Newell, 'From Cloth to Clothing: The Emergence of Department Stores in Late 19th Century Toronto,' MA Diss., Trent University 1984, 5
8 EA, *Eaton's Catalogue* 1886–7, 1, Fall-Winter 1892–3, 3, Spring-Summer 1895, 4; Flora McCrea Eaton, *Memory's Wall* (Toronto: Clarke, Irwin 1956) 15; *Globe* 18 May 1895
9 EA, *Suggestion Book* 18 Sept. 1893, 2, 19 Sept. 1893, 9, 31 July 1896, 47
10 EA, Eaton flyer, 1877; *Eaton's Catalogue* 1886–7, 44, Fall-Winter 1892–3, 50–3, Fall-Winter 1893–4, 125–56; *Globe* 25 Jan. 1890, 19 Sept., 4 Oct. 1892
11 EA, *Eaton's Catalogue* 1889–90, 93, Fall-Winter 1892–3, 56, Spring-Summer 1893, 91–2
12 Hower, *History of Macy's* 234–6
13 EA, Correspondence between Joseph Tetley and Co. and Timothy Eaton, 14 Nov. 1889 and 8 Jan. 1890; *Globe* 10 Nov., 28 Dec. 1889
14 EA, Correspondence between Joseph Tetley and Co. and Timothy Eaton, 14 Nov. 1889 and 6 Feb. 1890; *Eaton's Catalogue* 1890, 50, Spring-Summer 1896, 130
15 EA, *Eaton's Catalogue* 1890, 50, Fall-Winter 1892–3, 73, Fall-Winter 1894–5, 78–80, Spring-Summer 1898, 126–8, Spring-Summer 1899, 123; *Telegram* 8 Apr. 1890
16 EA, *Suggestion Book* Aug. 1893, 44–5; Richard S. Lambert, *The Universal Provider: A Study of William Whiteley and the Rise of the London Department Store* (London: Harrap 1938) 76, 236, 456; Robert Simpson and Co., *Canadian Shopper's Handbook* Spring-Summer 1896, 132–43

17 EA, *Eaton's Catalogue* 1889–90, 59–61, Fall-Winter 1892–3, 71–6, Fall-Winter 1895–6, 104–9; *Suggestion Book* 2 Sept. 1893, 40; Charles Lewis to R.Y. Eaton, 2 Nov. 1923; *Telegram* 6 Aug. 1892; *Globe* 20 Jan. 1896; Robert Simpson and Co., *Canadian Shopper's Handbook* Spring-Summer 1896, 121–8

18 EA, *Eaton's Catalogue* 1887–8, 93–4, 1888–9, 72–7, 1890, 40, Fall-Winter 1892–3, 61–4, Fall-Winter 1893–4, 116; *DGR* Oct. 1898, 14

19 EA, *Eatons Catalogue* 1886–7, 7, 1887–8, 24, Fall-Winter 1892–3, 20–1, Spring-Summer 1893, 23, Fall-Winter 1893–4, 50–4. Alex White stated that jewellery had first been introduced into the Eaton store in 1881 and was carried on the same counter as ribbons; letter from Alex White, 18 Jan. 1919.

20 EA, *Eaton's Catalogue* Fall-Winter 1892–3, 93–6, Spring-Summer 1897, 1, Fall-Winter 1893–4, 177; *DGR* May 1896, 7

21 EA, *Eaton's Catalogue* 1888–9, 63, Spring-Summer 1893, 95–7, Spring-Summer 1895, 126; *Globe* 1 Mar., 18 May 1895; Barry Broadfoot, *The Pioneer Years 1895–1914: Memories of Settlers Who Opened the West* (Toronto: Doubleday Canada 1976) 255

22 Hower, *History of Macy's* 98, 104, 220–6, 439n20

23 EA, Timothy Eaton to Frank McMahon, 17 Mar. 1892

24 Margaret Walsh, 'The Democratization of Fashion: The Emergence of the Women's Dress Pattern Industry,' *Journal of American History* 66:2 (1979), 304–6

25 EA, Formal agreements between Butterick Publishing Co., New York, and T. Eaton and Co., 23 May 1890; *Globe* 12 Nov. 1889; *Daily News* 1 Apr. 1887

26 EA, Timothy Eaton to Mrs Fieroe, King Street East, Toronto, 7 Dec. 1889, 13 Jan. 1890

27 *Globe* 12 Nov. 1889; EA, *Eaton's Catalogue* 1890, 52; T. Eaton and Co. to Austin, Werrett and Potts, Simcoe; McLaren Co., St Catharines; Henry Morgan, Montreal, Dec. 1889 to Feb. 1890

28 EA, Timothy Eaton to Frank McMahon, 27 Apr. 1892

29 EA. See, for example, *Delineator*, June 1896, *Metropolitan Fashion Sheet*, Mar. 1891; formal agreements, Butterick Publishing Co., 23 May 1890, 1 May 1894.

30 EA, List of agents, 31 Jan. 1890. By 1900 subscriptions to the *Delineator* totalled more than 77,000; Robert Simpson and Co., *Shopper's Handbook* Fall-Winter 1898–9, 139, Spring-Summer 1899, 29.

31 EA, Timothy Eaton to Frank McMahon, 27 Apr. 1892

32 EA, Shareholders Meeting 1894, statement by Mr Keens

33 EA, *Eaton's Catalogue 1887–8*, 47, 50, 1890, 9, Fall-Winter 1892–3, 12; Secretarial office file no. 38, 8 July 1891; *CJF* Aug. 1896, 225

34 EA, *Eaton's Catalogue* Spring-Summer 1900, 2–5; Maurice Corina, *Fine Silks and Oak Counters: Debenham's 1778–1978* (London: Hutchinson Benham 1978) 50

35 *CJF* Feb. 1896, 51; *DGR* July 1899, 174; Wayne Roberts, *Honest Womanhood: Feminism, Femininity and Class Consciousness among Toronto Working Women, 1896–1914* (Toronto: New Hogtown Press 1976) 38

36 EA, Shareholders Meeting 1894

37 Hower, *History of Macy's* 249, 251

38 EA, Petition to Province of Ontario, July 1897, to form the Paint Oil and Chemical Company; J.W. Dryden, Minister of Agriculture, Province of Ontario, to Timothy Eaton, 27 Jan. 1897

39 Merle Curti, 'The Changing Concept of "Human Nature" in the Literature of American Advertising,' *Business History Review* 41 (1967) 338

40 EA, Timothy Eaton to A.E. Rose, 30 June 1891; Shareholders Meeting 1893, statement by A.E. Rose

41 *Globe* 3, 4 Jan. 1893, 3 Jan. 1894; EA, Eaton flyers, Feb. 1896, Aug. 1897

42 *MT* 20 Nov. 1891, 600; EA, R.Y. Eaton to G.G. Nasmith, 1 Nov. 1923

43 *Globe* 12 Mar. 1892

44 EA, *Eaton's Catalogue* Fall-Winter 1893–4, 1, 2, Spring-Summer 1896, 7

45 J.W.M. Bliss, 'A Living Profit: Studies in the Social History of Canadian Business 1883–1911,' PH D Diss., University of Toronto 1972, 263

46 EA, *Eaton's Catalogue* Spring-Summer 1894, 3, Fall-Winter 1894–5, 2, Spring-Summer 1895, 1

9 A DEPARTMENT STORE: THE HUMAN ELEMENT

1 G.G. Nasmith, *Timothy Eaton* (Toronto: McClelland and Stewart 1923) 273–7

2 Edwin Rose, 'The Man behind the Store – Mr. Timothy Eaton,' *DGR* July 1904, 163

3 *Toronto Daily Star* 22 Aug. 1928

4 EA, Interviews with Eaton employees, Fred Mannell, Frederick W. Storey, J.J. Vaughan, Georgina Marshall, 1959–60

5 *Saturday Night* 3 Dec. 1887, 5; *DGR* Mar. 1897, 36; *CJF* Mar. 1899, 83; *Mail and Empire* 15 Dec. 1897; Michael Bliss, *A Canadian Mil-*

lionaire: The Life and Business Times of Sir Joseph Flavelle, Bart., 1858–1939 (Toronto: Macmillan of Canada 1978), 62

6 Robert Wellington Eaton, son of Timothy's oldest brother, Robert, joined in Feb. 1891, John Craig Eaton in 1892, shortly after his sixteenth birthday; Edward Young Eaton, John James Eaton, and J.A.C. Poole, Timothy's son and nephews, were already on the managerial staff.

7 EA, Timothy Eaton to Edward Young Eaton, 25 Apr. 1896

8 EA, Shareholders Meeting 1894, statements by B.D. Pearson, J.B. Hayes, J.A.C. Poole, W.J. Archibald; see also R.A. McQuarrie to John D. Eaton, 28 Aug. 1962.

9 EA, Timothy Eaton to Frank McMahon, 27 Apr. 1892

10 *Telegram* 31 Mar. 1922

11 EA, Shareholders meeting 1894, statements by John James Eaton, J.B. Hayes, H. Gibson, S.H. Laughlin, W.H. Emery

12 Susan Porter Benson, 'The Customers Ain't God: The Work Culture of Department Store Saleswomen, 1890–1940,' in Michael H. Frisch and Daniel H. Walkowitz, eds, *Working Class History: Essays in Labor, Community and American Society* (Urbana: University of Illinois Press 1983) 190

13 EA, Shareholders Meeting 1894. Whole sections of this opening statement by Timothy Eaton have been lifted in their entirety from brochures and lectures written by John Macdonald in 1876 and 1889 and published in full in Hugh Johnston, *A Merchant Prince: Life of Hon. Senator John Macdonald* (Toronto: William Briggs 1893) see 122, 130–1, 135–6.

14 EA, Meeting held in T. Eaton Company offices, 22 Apr. 1897

15 EA, Memorandum relating to Mr Penney, freight department, 31 Jan. 1900; Timothy Eaton to Frank McMahon, 17 Nov. 1892

16 EA, A. Swan Brown of Syndicate Trading Co., New York, to Timothy Eaton, 3 Dec. 1899. Syndicate Trading Company represented eleven department stores in the United States.

17 EA, Interviews with employees, H.L. Stewart, J.J. Vaughan, 1959

18 *City of Toronto Assessment Rolls* 1899 lists sixteen executives and managers with taxable income for municipal purposes; after 1892 only income over $700 was taxable; *Saturday Night* 11 July 1898.

19 EA, John James Eaton, *Notebook* unpaginated

20 Ibid.

21 *DGR* June 1897, 6; see also Elizabeth Beardsley Butler, *Saleswomen in Mercantile Stores, Baltimore, 1909* (New York: Survey Associates Inc. 1913) 105; Jean Thomson Scott, 'The Conditions of Female Labour in

Ontario,' *Toronto University Studies in Political Science* 111 (1892) 25–6.

22 Ibid., 17; *Toronto Daily Star*, 14 Feb. 1902; Susan Porter Benson, *Counter Culture: Saleswomen, Managers and Customers in American Department Stores, 1890–1940* (Urbana: University of Illinois Press 1986)

23 Wayne Roberts, *Honest Womanhood: Feminism, Femininity and Class Consciousness among Toronto Working Women, 1896–1914* (Toronto: New Hogtown Press 1976) 8–9, 27; see also Graham Lowe, 'The Administrative Revolution in the Canadian Office: An Overview,' in Tom Traves, ed., *Essays in Canadian Business History* (Toronto: McClelland and Stewart 1984) 117, 119; *Royal Commission on the Relations of Labour and Capital in Canada 1899* 350; EA, Secretarial office file no. 50.

24 At Macy's in 1870 approximately 88 per cent of the staff was female, but by 1913 this percentage had dropped to 52 per cent. In England, where selling was still regarded as a profession requiring an apprenticeship of four to five years, the reverse was the case, and up until 1914 men continued to outnumber the female work-force in large British retail outlets.

25 EA, John James Eaton, *Notebook* unpaginated; Secretarial office file no. 38

26 J.W.M. Bliss, 'A Living Profit: Studies in the Social History of Canadian Business 1883–1911,' PH D Diss., University of Toronto 1972, 145; EA, Shareholders Meeting 1894; statements by John James Eaton, A.E. Emery, B.D. Pearson, W.H. Laughlin; *Suggestion Book* 42–3, Aug. 1893

27 EA, Shareholders meeting 1894; statements by Timothy Eaton, W.H. Laughlin; *Globe* 22 Oct. 1890

28 EA, Shareholders meeting 1894, statement by B.D. Pearson; Secretarial office file no. 13, Jan. 1902; *DGR* Jan. 1896, 6, Feb. 1896, 73

29 EA, Chief Constable H.J. Grasset to Messrs T. Eaton & Company, 7 Dec. 1897; Secretarial office file no. 13, Jan. 1902; *Scrapbook – Eaton Company History 1899–1900* 2, handwritten notes Dec. 1899 to Feb. 1900

30 Sarah Smith Malino, 'Faces across the Counter: A Social History of Female Department Store Employees, 1870–1920,' PH D Diss., Columbia University 1982, 77–89; Susan Porter Benson, 'The Cinderella of Occupations: Managing the Work of Department Store Saleswomen, 1900–1940,' *Business History Review* (Spring 1981) 10–12

31 EA, Notices to Departments, 1 Jan. 1899, 14, 16 Mar., 1 June 1900; *Eaton's Catalogue* Spring-Summer 1894, 2

32 EA, Marshall Field and Co., *Book of Rules* 1899; Malino, 'Faces across the Counter,' 124–7; see also *DGR* Aug. 1892, 8, Feb. 1896, 12, June 1900, 10, Nov. 1900, 2, Oct. 1902, 12.

33 EA, *Rules and Regulations and General Information* T. Eaton Co. Ltd, *c.* 1905

34 Malino, 'Faces across the Counter,' 75; EA, J.L. Hudson Co., Detroit, *Book of Information.* The Eaton Company obtained rule books issued by several large American department stores; the one issued by Marshall Field in Chicago was noticeably well-thumbed and contained many pencilled notations.

35 *Ontario Shops Regulation Act* 1888

36 Ontario, Sessional Papers no. 8, *12th Annual Report of the Inspector of Factories 1899* (1900) 25; *Royal Commission on the Relations of Labour and Capital* 93-4

37 Ibid., 349–50; Scott, 'Conditions of Female Labour,' 17; Ontario, *12th Annual Report of the Inspector of Factories 1899* 29; *CJF* Dec. 1899, 367–8; *DGR* July 1899, 65

38 *DGR* Aug. 1896, 10, Sept. 1896, 10, see also June 1899, 46

39 Annie Maclean, 'Two Weeks in a Department Store,' *American Journal of Sociology* 4:6 (May 1899) 735

40 EA, Timothy Eaton to Staff Inspector Archabold, 8 Mar. 1890

41 EA, Dr J.H. Cotton to Timothy Eaton, 18 Mar. 1890

42 EA, Dr E. Herbert Adams to E.Y. Eaton, 15 Apr. 1896

43 EA, Timothy Eaton to Staff Inspector Archabold, 8 Mar. 1890

44 *Women Workers of Canada* Report of the Proceedings of the First Annual Meeting and Conference of the National Council of Women of Canada (Ottawa: 1894) 63

45 *Globe* 11 Jan. 1890, 17 Dec. 1891, 22 Dec. 1893, 1 May, 15 July 1896; *Mail and Empire* 18 May 1895, 23, 24 Dec. 1897; *DGR* July 1892, 4, Aug. 1895, 7

46 *DGR* Aug. 1892, 3

47 EA, J.W. Dryden, Department of Agriculture, Ontario, to Timothy Eaton, 19 Feb. 1897

48 EA, Interviews with Eaton employees, F.W. Storey, 1959; Isaac H. Sanderson, Secretary, Toronto Trades and Labour Council, to Timothy Eaton, 7 Apr. 1897; Geo. W. Dower, Secretary-Treasurer, Trades and Labour Congress of Canada, to Timothy Eaton, 25 Oct. 1897

49 Canada, Sessional Papers no. 2, Alexander Whyte Wright, *Report upon the Sweating System in Canada* 29:61 (1896) 7

50 Greg Kealey, *Working-Class Toronto at the Turn of the Century* (Toronto: New Hogtown Press 1973) 4; Canada, *Census* 1901; *Toronto Daily Star*, 2, 3 Jan. 1894; see also *Mail and Empire* 9 Oct. 1897; Canada, Sessional Papers no. 2 *Supplementary Report Upon the Sweating System in Canada* 29: 61a (1896) 41.

51 Ibid., 37

52 EA, 'Canada's Greatest Store,' Eaton promotional booklet 1899

53 Wayne Roberts, *Honest Womanhood* 29; *Toronto Daily Star*, 25 Oct. 1910

54 Eugene Forsey, *Trade Unions in Canada, 1812–1902* (Toronto: University of Toronto Press 1982) 267; EA, John James Eaton, *Notebook* unpaginated; *Report upon the Sweating System in Canada* 24

55 EA, John James Eaton, *Notebook*

56 EA, Employee Reminiscences, Miss N. McClure, 1959

57 EA, R.Y. Eaton to Executive officers, 21 Dec. 1934

10 HOSTILITY AND REACTION

1 *CJF* Dec. 1894, 380; *DGR* Feb. 1892, 5, 6, 13, Mar. 1892, 11, Feb. 1893, 59, Mar. 1893, 4, May 1893, 1, June 1893, 2, Aug. 1894, 29, Mar. 1895, 74, Apr. 1895, 7, Feb. 1898, 28

2 Ibid., Mar. 1892, 11, Apr. 1895, 4

3 Toronto Board of Trade, *Annual Report 1896* 32–7; *MT* 17 May 1893, 1379, 26 May 1893, 1409–10; *DGR* June 1893, 2

4 *Globe* 8 Jan. 1892, 4, 20 Jan. 1896; *Mail and Empire* 22 Nov. 1897; *DGR* Dec. 1892, 19, Mar. 1893, 17; *CJF* Jan. 1897, 20; *MT* 4 June 1897, 1591; *History of Toronto and County of York: A Handbook of the City* (Toronto: W.E. Caiger 1885), 454, 457; C. Pelham Mulvany, *Toronto: Past and Present* (Toronto: 1884) 307

5 Alison Adburgham, *Shops and Shopping, 1800–1914: Where and in What Manner the Well-Dressed Englishwomen Bought Her Clothes* (London: Allen and Unwin 1967) 240; EA, G. Powell to Timothy Eaton, 2 Dec. 1896; Herbert A. Gibbons, *John Wanamaker* (New York: Kenibat Press 1971) vol. 1, 175–8; W.N. Hancock, *Is the Competition between Large and Small Shops Injurious to the Community?* (Dublin: Hodges and Smith 1851) 17–19, 29

6 See, for example, OA, Pamphlet, 'Departmental Stores. The Modern

Curse to Labor and Capital. They Ruin Cities, Towns, Villages and the Farming Community' (Toronto: 1896); *MT* 26 May 1893, 1409–10, 6 July 1894, 17, 2 Nov. 1894, 567, 31 May 1895, 1549–50, 6 Dec. 1895, 722–3, 5 Feb. 1897, 1043, 5 Mar. 1897, 1174, 26 Mar. 1897, 1280–1; *CJF* July 1895, 223, Dec. 1896, 372; *DGR* Oct. 1892, 2, Sept. 1896, 5. One merchant, a Mrs Bilton, was so incensed at what she considered Timothy Eaton's propensity for pushing people out of business that instructions in her will forbade the sale of her property on Yonge Street in perpetuity to any department store. This caused something of a problem when properties were being assembled for the present Eaton Centre; see *Globe* 19 Oct. 1973.

7 *DGR* July 1893, 6, Aug. 1894, 5–6, Mar. 1895, 25; *Canada Farmer's Sun* 28 Nov. 1893

8 *World* 9 Feb. 1895; John Benson, 'Hawking and Peddling in Canada, 1867–1915,' unpublished paper given at Canadian Historical Association Conference, Montreal, 1985, 11; EA, Timothy Eaton to Chief Constable H.J. Grasset, 9 Apr. 1895

9 *DGR* Oct. 1892, 2, Dec.1892, 1, Mar. 1893, 4; *MT* 26 May 1893, 1409–10; E. McKeown, 182 Yonge Street failed 1892, McLean and Mitchell, 240 Yonge Street failed 1893, H.A. Stone, 212 Yonge Street failed 1895, J.N. McKendry, 202–8 Yonge Street failed 1896, see *MT* 26 Feb. 1892, 1023, 11 Mar. 1892, 1091; *DGR* Feb. 1893, 31, Feb. 1895, 26, July 1896, 48, 50; *CJF* July 1896, 213, Feb. 1897, 53

10 *DGR* Dec. 1892, 1, July 1893, 18; *MT* 19 May 1893, 1379, 31 May 1895, 1550, 6 Dec. 1895, 722–3

11 *DGR* Feb. 1892, 6, Nov. 1892, 1, May 1893, 1; *MT* 11 Nov. 1892, 552

12 J.W.M. Bliss, 'A Living Profit: Studies in the Social History of Canadian Business 1883–1911,' PH D Diss., University of Toronto 1972, 304

13 *Globe* 3 May 1892

14 J.C. Johnston, 'Existing Evils of the Drug Trade and Their Remedy,' paper read at Ontario Druggists' Convention, Aug. 1892, printed in *CPJ* Sept. 1892, 1; see also Harold W. Stephenson and Carlton McNaught, *The Story of Advertising in Canada* (Toronto: Ryerson Press 1940) 234–5.

15 See, for example, *CPJ* Jan. 1891, 84, Mar. 1891, 123, May 1891, 148, Dec. 1891, 74, Jan. 1892, 83, 86, May 1892, 149, 157–8, Feb. 1896, 92, Mar. 1896, 107, Oct. 1896, 90, 116; EA, Maynwright, Meyer and Co., London, England, to T. Eaton Company Limited, 10 June 1896.

16 See, for example, *MT* 4 Mar. 1892, 1061; *CPJ* Sept. 1892, 17, Oct. 1892, 36–7, 42–3, Nov. 1892, 50–1, Jan. 1893, 82, Aug. 1893, 16, Dec.

1893, 88–9, Nov. 1894, 61, Apr. 1895, 127, 141–2, Sept. 1895, 25–6, Mar. 1896, 109–10, May 1896, 145–6, July 1896, 175–6.

17 *CJF* Aug. 1894, 236. The Thompson family also had two other stores, the Mammoth House at 136–40 King Street East, and the Army and Navy Clothing Company at 133–5 King Street East, Toronto.

18 EA, Handwritten credit rating, untitled and unsigned, 6 Sept. 1895; *DGR* Mar. 1895, 70, Sept. 1895, 33; *Daily News* 3, 4, 21 May 1895

19 *Daily News* 3, 31 May 1895

20 *Globe* 10 May 1895

21 *Globe* 2 Oct. 1895

22 Samson, Kennedy and Gemmel's entire stock was purchased by John Eaton in January 1896, and not by Timothy Eaton as stated by Christopher Armstrong and H.V. Nelles in *The Revenge of the Methodist Bicycle Company* (Toronto: Peter Martin Associates 1977) 140; see *Daily News* 16 May 1895; *Globe* 4, 17 Jan. 1896, 29 Feb. 1896; *DGR* Feb. 1896, 10, Feb. 1898, 38.

23 *Globe* 15 Jan. 1896

24 *City of Toronto Directory* 1895 and 1896, 668 and 664, respectively; *Globe* 2 May 1896

25 EA, Timothy Eaton to E.Y. Eaton, 15 May 1896

26 *CJF* Mar. 1896, 84; *DGR* Apr. 1896, 10; *Globe* 25 Apr. 1896, 11 July, 3 Sept. 1896; *Daily News* 5 May 1896

27 EA, Credit rating, 6 Sept. 1895; *MT* 21 May 1897, 1531, 28 May 1897, 1563; *DGR* Aug. 1897, 54; *CJF* Oct. 1897, 307

28 *CJF* Jan. 1898, 21; EA, John W. Eaton to King's County Furniture Company, Brooklyn, New York, 19 July 1897

29 Toronto City Council, *Minutes* no. 8, 21 Jan. 1895, 3; *Globe* 2 Mar. 1895; *World* 2 Mar. 1895

30 *World* 4 Mar. 1895; *Globe* 4, 15 Mar. 1895

31 *World* 16, 26 Feb., 6 Mar. 1895

32 *MT* 8 Mar. 1895, 1162; *DGR* Apr. 1895, 4, Aug. 1895, 18, Aug. 1897, 46

33 *Globe* 29 Nov. 1893, 4, 8 Feb. 1895

34 *CPJ* Sept. 1892, 17

35 Quoted in *CPJ* Mar. 1896, 107

36 Ross Harkness, *J.E. Atkinson of the Star* (Toronto: University of Toronto Press 1963) 54

37 EA, John Macdonald and Co., to Timothy Eaton, 3 Apr. 1895

38 EA, T.G. Dexter, H.S. Howland and Sons to Timothy Eaton, 22 Mar. 1897

39 EA, Newspaper clipping, *Daily News* c. 1895

40 EA, Timothy Eaton to H.S. Howland and Sons, 23 Mar. 1897

41 *Globe* 4 Feb. 1895

42 EA, Scott and Bourne Manufacturing Chemists to Timothy Eaton, 18 Oct. 1897; Tosh and Ashton, London, England, to Timothy Eaton, 13 Jan. 1893; *CJF* Oct. 1898, 307

43 EA, Timothy Eaton to Tosh and Ashton, 31 Jan. 1893

44 Toronto City Council, *Minutes* no. 896, 16 Dec. 1895; EA, Newspaper clipping, *Once a Week* 16 May 1896

45 *DGR* Jan. 1892, 1, Nov. 1892, 2–3, Dec. 1892, 19, Feb. 1893, 29; Toronto Board of Trade, *Annual Report 1898* 13, 28–9; see also G.H. Stanford, *To Serve the Community: The Story of Toronto's Board of Trade* (Toronto: University of Toronto Press 1974) 10, 58–9.

46 Toronto City Council, *Minutes* no. 577, 28 Apr. 1890, no. 738, 9 June 1890, no. 1084, 29 Sept. 1890, no. 1271, 24 Nov. 1890, no. 200, 15 Mar. 1891

47 Ibid., no. 24, 16 Jan. 1888, no. 23, 20 Jan. 1890, no. 164, 3 Feb. 1890; *DGR* Jan. 1891, 6, Jan. 1892, 1, Apr. 1892, 1, Nov. 1892, 2–3; James Mavor, 'Finance and Taxation: Recent Municipal Finance and Taxation,' in Adam Shortt and Arthur G. Doughty, *Canada and Its Provinces* (Toronto: Glasgow, Brook and Co. 1914) vol. 17, 268–70; Ontario, Sessional Papers, no. 73, *Report of the Commission on Municipal Taxation 1893* 71

48 A clause in the 1892 Assessment Act continued to exempt 'so much of the personal property of any person as is equal to the just debts owed by him on account of such property except such debts as are secured by mortgage or real estate or purchase money thereof.' See *The Consolidated Municipal Act 1892 and the Consolidated Assessment Act 1892* (Toronto: Warwick and Sons 1892) 312, no. 21.

49 Toronto Board of Trade, *Annual Report 1897* 18, *Annual Report 1898* 28–9; *City of Toronto Assessment Rolls 1869–95*

50 Toronto City Council, *Minutes* nos 11, 99, 167, 7 Feb. 1896; *RMJ* 20 July 1893, 11; *MT* 5 Mar. 1897, 1174, 21 Apr. 1897, 1312; *DGR* 1897, 1312; *DGR* Apr. 1897, 26–8, Aug. 1897, 60. Legislation was proposed in Illinois, Minnesota, Iowa, Kansas, Ohio, and Missouri. Feelings were sufficiently embittered in Chicago in 1897 that the mayor of that city was elected on an anti-department-store platform.

51 *CJF* Apr. 1897, 107; *DGR* Apr. 1899, 27; Toronto Board of Trade, *President's Report 1897* 18

52 Toronto City Council, *Minutes* no. 896, 16 Dec. 1895. Comments in the minutes and in the press stated that this was raised to $400,000, but

the assessment rolls indicate otherwise; *Globe* 7 Dec. 1897; *World* 11 Dec. 1897.

53 *DGR* Jan. 1899, 58; *City of Toronto Assessment Rolls* 1898–1900

54 Criticism was also aimed at individuals with annual incomes in excess of $2,000. The subsequent investigation revealed some 463 individuals in Toronto; it included the three principal partners of the Robert Simpson Company, but not Timothy Eaton, see Toronto City Council, *Minutes* 1900, App. C, 577 ff; *DGR* Dec. 1900, 34

55 EA, W.A. Littlejohn, City Clerk, to T. Eaton Co. Ltd, 5 Sept. 1900, Secretarial office file no. 89; *Globe* 11 May 1901; *Telegram* 20 Dec. 1901; Ontario, Sessional Papers, *Report of the Ontario Assessment Commission* (1901) 103

56 *RMJ* May 1904, 81; *DGR* June 1904, 11. The trade journals had carried considerable detail regarding proposed legislation directed at restricting department stores both in Europe and the United States; see, for example, *DGR* Apr. 1897, 28, Apr. 1899, 26, Sept. 1900, 35, May 1901, 13, July 1901, 66.

11 TIMOTHY EATON: THE FINAL YEARS

1 EA, Secretarial office file no. 93

2 EA, *Eaton's Catalogue* Spring-Summer 1900, 173, Fall-Winter 1902, 272, and back cover

3 EA, Interviews with Eaton employees, Frank W. Slater, 1959; *Eaton's Catalogue* Spring-Summer 1900, 174, 259, Fall-Winter 1905–6, 3, 252–61, 281–6, Fall-Winter 1906–7, 160, Fall-Winter 1908–9, 310–14, Fall-Winter 1909–10, 181; *DGR* Dec. 1905, 107

4 *Toronto Daily Star* 16 Nov. 1901; EA, *Eaton's Catalogue* Spring-Summer 1902, inside front cover

5 EA, Address by R.Y. Eaton to Eaton Executive Office, 4 Jan. 1934; Interviews with Eaton employees, J.J. Vaughan, 28 Jan. 1959; Secretarial office file no. 8; Ralph M. Hower, *A History of Macy's of New York 1858–1919: Chapters in the Evolution of a Department Store* (Cambridge: Harvard University Press 1943) 341–4

6 EA, Address by R.Y. Eaton to Eaton executive office, 4 Jan. 1935

7 EA, Interviews with Eaton employees, J.J. Vaughan, 28 Jan. 1959; *Toronto Daily Star* 24, 28, 29 Nov., 1, 4 Dec. 1905; *DGR* Aug. 1908, 19–21

8 EA, Notice to Departments, 1 Nov. 1902

9 *DGR* December 1906, 31, Jan. 1907, 170, Feb. 1907, 66

10 *DGR* Aug. 1908, 20

11 EA, Rev. Wm Elliott to T. Eaton Co. Ltd, 6 Nov. 1907
12 Hower, *History of Macy's* 329–30
13 EA, Catalogue Analysis and Stats, *c.* 1900; Notices to Departments, 8 Mar. 1907, 10 Feb. 1909, 4 Jan. 1910
14 EA, Notices to Departments, Letter from R.Y. Eaton, 1910; letter to all mail order customers, Mar. 1907; *Eaton's Catalogue* Fall-Winter 1905–6, 3; *DGR* Nov. 1905, 77, Jan. 1906, 37
15 EA, Notices to Departments, 14 Mar., 6 June, 30 July 1907
16 G.G. Nasmith, *Timothy Eaton* (Toronto: McClelland and Stewart 1923) 278–9
17 EA, John Craig Eaton, *Diary* 1899, 2–5 May notations; *Globe* 4 July 1904; *DGR* July 1905, 212
18 Winnipeg *Telegram* 27 July 1904; *Winnipeg Free Press* 14, 17 July 1905
19 EA, Interviews with Eaton employees, J.J. Vaughan, 1958; *DGR* May 1905, 32, Oct. 1905, 47; Flora McCrea Eaton, *Memory's Wall* (Toronto: Clarke, Irwin 1956) 68
20 EA, Interviews with Eaton employees, J.J. Vaughan, 1958; *Eaton's Catalogue* Fall-Winter 1905–6, Winnipeg, on front cover, Fall-Winter 1906–7, Winnipeg, 2, 20, Spring-Summer 1907, Winnipeg, 88–92, Fall-Winter 1908–9, Winnipeg, 110–11
21 Ruben Bellan, *Winnipeg First Century: An Economic History* (Winnipeg: Queenston Publishing 1978) 114; EA, Unsigned handwritten memo, *c.* 1915
22 Canada, *Royal Commission on Price Spreads, 1934* Special Committee on Price Spreads and Mass Buying, Proceedings and Evidence, vol. 3, 2741, 2745, 3056, 2069–70, 4864–5
23 EA, Indentures between Timothy Eaton, E.Y. Eaton, and J.C. Eaton, and T. Eaton Co. Ltd, 1897, see also Secretarial office file no. 40
24 EA, Letter from Fred Brigden, 1955; Sally F. Zerker, *The Rise and Fall of the Toronto Typographical Union 1832–1972: A Case Study of Foreign Domination* (Toronto: University of Toronto Press 1982) 147–9
25 *Globe* 21 Apr. 1909; *Toronto Daily Star* 21 Apr. 1909; *DGR* May 1909, 25 Aug. 1909, 34, 153–4, Sept. 1909, 20
26 EA, Factory statement, July 1904 to Jan. 1905; the T. Eaton Drug Company was formally incorporated in 1906 with a capitalization of $25,000, not in 1896 as G.G. Nasmith stated; *DGR* Nov. 1903, 84, Dec. 1903, 132, Mar. 1907, 90.
27 EA, Mayor H.L. Fowke, Oshawa, 24 June 1902; Mayor T.H.G. Denne, Peterborough, 9 June 1902; Mayor Haines, Brampton, 12 May 1902;

John T. Hall, Assessment Commissioner, Hamilton, 21 Feb. 1903, all to T. Eaton Co. Ltd

28 EA, Employee statistics compiled in 1973

29 EA, Notices to Departments, 26 Mar. 1909, 28 Mar. 1910

30 *Saturday Night* 5 Dec. 1903; *Toronto Daily Star* 1 Dec. 1903; EA, Notices to Departments, Apr. 1907, 25 Apr. 1910, May 1913

31 EA, *Summary of State of Affairs of T. Eaton Co. Ltd* 1900–2 inclusive

32 EA, Frank D. Beecroft to Lady Eaton, Jan. 1957; Interviews with Eaton employees, J.J. Vaughan, 1958; *Summary of State of Affairs at T. Eaton Co. Ltd* 1891–8 inclusive; Timothy Eaton to E.Y. Eaton, 5 May 1896

33 Edwin Rose, 'The Man Behind the Store – Mr. Timothy Eaton,' *DGR* July 1904, 163

34 *World* 1 Feb. 1907; *Globe* 1 Feb. 1907; Interview, Mrs Brophy, *c.* 1959; Nasmith, *Timothy Eaton* 289–311

35 EA, Meeting of Company Shareholders, Feb. 1898

36 Montreal *Daily Herald* 1 Feb. 1907; *Daily News* 31 Jan. 1907

37 *DGR* Oct. 1908, 22; *Globe* 29 Sept. 1908

38 EA, Interviews with Eaton employees, J.J. Vaughan, 1959; John Craig Eaton also stipulated in his own will that the son most fitted for the task should become president, and that the board of directors were to decide this when his sons were old enough.

CONCLUSION

1 Edwin Rose, 'The Man behind the Store – Mr. Timothy Eaton,' *DGR* July 1904, 163. Hugh Robb also stated that he left Timothy Eaton's employ because there 'was too much Irish between us,' see *DGR* Mar. 1909, 27.

2 EA, Timothy Eaton, *Notebook* 330

3 Edwin Rose, 'Man behind the Store,' 163; John Macdonald, *Diary* 4 Mar. 1883; I am indebted to Michael Bliss for allowing me access to his notes from the Macdonald Papers, and thus to this quotation.

4 David Alexander, *Retailing in England during the Industrial Revolution* (London: Athlone Press 1970) 136

5 EA, Letter from Alex White, 18 Jan. 1919; *DGR* Mar. 1909, 27

6 EA, Timothy Eaton to James Eaton, 6 May 1873, and to Butterick Company, New York, 13 Dec. 1889

7 *Globe* 31 Dec. 1898

8 David Monod, 'Bay days: The Managerial Revolution and the Hudson's Bay Company Department Stores, 1912–1939,' *Canadian Historical Papers* (1986) 178–9

9 Gene Allen, 'Competition and Consolidation in the Toronto Wholesale Trade, 1860–1880,' unpublished paper, May 1982

10 Albert O. Hirschman, *The Strategy of Economic Development* (New Haven: 1958) 187–19, quoted in Sidney Pollard, *The Genesis of Modern Management: A Study of the Industrial Revolution in Great Britain* (London: Edward Arnold 1965) 257

11 EA, Stock Report, 1904–5

12 EA, Notice to Departments, 14 Mar. 1900; Ross Harkness, *J.E. Atkinson of the Star* (Toronto: University of Toronto Press 1963) 54

13 Neil McKendrick, 'Home Demand and Economic Growth: A New View of the Role of Women in the Industrial Revolution,' in Neil McKendrick, ed., *Historical Perspectives: Studies in English Thought and Society* (London: Europa Publications 1974) 208, 210

14 *Christian Guardian* 11 Nov. 1896

15 *Report of the Ontario Assessment Commission, Being the Interim or First Report and Record of Proceedings, 1901* 85

16 G. Binnie Clark, *A Summer on the Canadian Prairie* (London: Edward Arnold 1910) 73; I am indebted to W. Cherwinsky for drawing my attention to this quotation at the CHA Conference in Winnipeg, 1986.

17 *MT* 1 Jan. 1892, 785, Nov. 1893, 567; *DGR* Feb. 1893, 10

18 EA, Newspaper clipping, *The Vanguard* 17 Sept. 1968

19 See, for example, *DGR* Aug. 1895, 18, July 1897, 49, July 1900, 20, Jan. 1903, 52, Aug. 1904, 31, Jan. 1907, 41–5, 52, Mar. 1907, 17–19, July 1907, 44–9, 70, 73–7, Feb. 1908, 32–3, Aug. 1910, 20–2, 29, Oct. 1910, 19–22, Nov. 1910, 26–7, 16 Jan. 1911, 48; *CJF* Sept. 1897, 258.

20 Michael B. Miller, *The Bon Marché: Bourgeois Culture and the Department Store, 1869–1920* (Princeton: Princeton University Press 1981) 33

A Note on Sources

By far the most valuable source for this study of Timothy Eaton's business life has been the material stored at the company's archives. This collection (which has now been donated to the Ontario Archives) comprised an immense holding of business papers, secretarial files, corporate documents, notebooks, and family papers that was of inestimable value in the effort to understand the development of the store and to illuminate the private and public Timothy Eaton. The almost complete set of Eaton catalogues from 1884 to 1910 provided an excellent silent testimony to the expansion of both store and merchandise. However, like most Canadian business sources, the material in the Eaton Papers confirmed what is already known about nineteenth- and even twentieth-century businessmen's interests in conserving business and commercial records for posterity. As with most other sales-oriented companies, the constant need to save both space and financial resources is usually of more significance than the desire to maintain a complete record of the past. The collection therefore contains several huge gaps. For example, no letters from Timothy Eaton exist for nearly the whole of the 1880s. Once he acquired the services of a typist, at the urging of his son Edward, that gap is partially filled. However, even here the record is sadly incomplete, although sufficient material remains to allow the historian to go beyond the realm of speculation to some degree of certainty. Similar gaps where sales figures are concerned are surprising in a company oriented to sales volume.

The papers also contain a very useful treasury of reminiscences given by family members, store employees, and customers. These have been collected over the past seventy years for a variety of publications relating to the Eaton dynasty and, more especially, to Timothy Eaton and his store. Where possible such personal recollections have been cross-checked with other references, and where differences occur the most feasible have been selected for inclusion. Given the enormous variety and richness of this material, it was somewhat surprising to discover the limited use made of these in earlier studies of Timothy Eaton.

This vast source was supplemented by material from the Ontario Archives, where numerous microfilmed copies of old deed and abstract books and rural newspapers shared in bringing to light the important and somewhat shadowy years of Timothy Eaton and his family in Perth County. Research undertaken at the Bank of Montreal archives, which contained an original branch ledger from the 1860s, was of great use in furthering knowledge of these early pre-Toronto years.

Douglas McCalla's *The Upper Canada Trade* directed my attention to the Buchanan Papers at the National Archives in Ottawa. Although this collection did not contain a full record of Timothy Eaton's early commercial life in Kirkton and St Marys, it did allow for a fairly accurate appraisal of his commercial endeavours in these centres. Both Douglas McCalla and Gene Allen were kind enough to grant me access to their unpublished studies on the Toronto wholesale trade in the last half of the nineteenth century. These were of immeasurable assistance for the insights they provided into the retail industry at this time.

The nature of the retail business and its constant need to attract the attention of the general public, made necessary a fairly extensive study of contemporary newspapers, primarily for advertising material. The St Marys *Argus*, while not a complete record of the years 1860 to 1869, provided local colour and allowed a glimpse into retailing in a rural centre in the 1850s and 1860s.

For Toronto the record was one of almost impossible abundance. After 1870 Timothy Eaton advertised widely. The *Globe, Mail* (later *Mail and Empire*), *Telegram, World, Daily News*, and *Toronto Daily Star* all published during all or part of the period from 1860 to 1910. Restrictions of time allowed for only a limited selection, since the whole period had to be subjected to some form of continuous investigation.

Several trade journals were useful for the background material they provided on a variety of levels. The *Dry Goods Review* and the *Canadian Journal of Fabrics*, the former first published in 1891 and the latter in 1883, were directed primarily to the wholesale trade but proved excellent guides to both the retail and wholesale trade of that era. The earlier years were more than adequately covered by the *Monetary Times*. The *Canadian Pharmaceutical Journal* and the *Retail Merchants Journal* were necessary primary sources for the chapter dealing with hostility. Supplementing these was material taken from the minutes of the Toronto City Council and the Toronto Board of Trade.

Several relevant official commissions, the Royal Commission on the Relations of Labour and Capital, the Sweated Commission of 1896, and the Ontario Assessment Commission of 1900, allowed for a greater appreciation of the problems facing the nineteenth-century business and labour community.

In the almost complete absence of published Canadian material, several British and American secondary sources provided important pointers and directional guides. Foremost among these was Ralph Hower's *A History of Macy's*, which was endlessly useful. This excellent study of the retail trade in the United States covered the entire commercial evolution of Rowland Macy and the Macy store in New York from Macy's early beginnings in Haverhill to the large New York department store. Since it covers almost the same period as that of Timothy Eaton's career, it served both as a sounding board and as an instrument of comparison.

David Alexander's *Retailing in England during the Industrial Revolution* accomplished the same purpose from a more general standpoint for the British retail industry. Finally, Alison Adburgham's excellent study, *Shops and Shopping*, whose subsidiary title, *Where and In What Manner the Well-Dressed Englishwomen Bought Her Clothes*, only hints at the material covered in its pages, was invaluable regarding much of the actual dry goods merchandise available for sale in this period.

Index

DATE DUE